COMMUNITY PSYCHOLOGY AND SOCIAL SYSTEMS

A Conceptual Framework and Intervention Guide

Stanley A. Murrell, Ph. D.
Department of Psychology
University of Louisville

Behavioral Publications   New York

1973

HM
291
.M864

Library of Congress Catalog Number 73-8504
Standard Book Number 87705-108-9
Copyright © 1973 by Behavioral Publications

BEHAVIORAL PUBLICATIONS,
2852 Broadway—Morningside Heights,
New York, New York 10025

Printed in the United States of America

Library of Congress Cataloging in Publication Data

Murrell, Stanley A
    Community psychology and social systems.

    Bibliography: p.
    1. Social psychology. 2. Social systems.
3. Social interaction. I. Title. [DNLM: 1. Interpersonal relations. 2. Psychology, Social. 3. Socia
conditions. HM251 M982c 1973]
HM291.M864   301.1   73-8504
ISBN 0-87705-108-9

To my mother Adeline Murrell
and to the memory of my
father Clyde Murrell.

We live at a period when the defect of governments is to make Man for Society rather than Society for Man. There is a perpetual struggle going on between the Individual and the Social system which insists on using him, while he is endeavoring to use it to his own profit; whereas, in former days, man, really more free, was also more loyal to the public weal.

Honore de Balzac
The Vicar of Tours

TABLE OF CONTENTS

List of Figures

PREFACE

This book was written from the belief that we must find new ways of thinking about man and that man must learn new ways of behaving toward his fellows. It was written from the conviction that community psychology, young and uncoordinated as it now is, can contribute importantly to these new ways.

This book was intended as a tool. Its purpose is to provide students of community psychology with a practical working conceptual framework for assessing man—social-system relationships and for introducing helpful changes in social systems. Hopefully, this framework will also be useful to currently practicing community scientists, but it was written specifically for students. Being written by a psychologist, with the immeasurable help of psychology graduate students, this book inevitably carries the language and background of psychology. However, while a background in psychology would no doubt be useful, I would not consider it essential for grasping and using the framework herein. Hopefully, the framework may also be of use to students in such related areas as community development, urban planning, management, social work, sociology, and education. Community psychology by its very nature cannot be monopolized by psychology.

Kurt Lewin once said that there is nothing so practical as a good theory. While I have not aspired so high as to propose a "theory," the practical necessity for a workable conceptual framework has been the impetus for these efforts. This framework should be general enough to be applied to a variety of widely different social systems; it should be flexible enough that it can be adapted for different-sized intervention tasks and amounts of resources; and yet it should still be sufficiently definite to be useful as a guide.

Many people helped me in many ways. I did not always take their advice and suggestions. Since this book is for students, it was invaluable to have had their reactions and thoughtful criticisms of various versions over the last three years. Particularly helpful were James Block, Roger Bednarsky, Patricia McCarthy, Roseanne Reed, Charles Schanie, and Donald Woodward. Sheila Schuster re-read a final draft and gave me very helpful and frank comments. My friends and colleagues, Raymond Kemper, Robert Silver, and Donald C. Klein took time from very heavy schedules to read the manuscript and provide useful reactions. Joy Kitterman, a friend who has been on the firing line of social system change for several years, read the manuscript and helped me a great deal with her observations and comments. I thank Mary Tucker for her careful and diligent typing of the manuscript.

Finally, I am glad to express my gratitude to my wife Pat, and my children Jeffrey, Jill, and Allison for providing me a supportive, restorative, and facilitative social system.

S. A. Murrell, Ph.D.

1. ASSUMPTIONS OF COMMUNITY PSYCHOLOGY

The typical first reaction to the term "community psychology" is to ask, "what is it?" This is difficult to answer for several reasons. First, because community psychology is still very much in the process of formation, it is still changing. In the nearly four years that this book was in preparation there were a number of shifts of emphasis, perhaps the major one being the more clear separation of community psychology from community mental health (Iscoe & Spielberger, 1970). A major thrust now is toward the goodness-of-fit between the individual and his environment and this obviously involves many other social problems in addition to mental health. The reader should be aware at the outset that this book is not about mental health. As community psychology's closest "parent," however, there will be a brief review of community mental health in this chapter. Second, community psychology has not had a clear comprehensive conceptual framework (Newbrough, 1964). This book attempts to be a step in that direction. Third, community psychology has not had distinctive methods, distinctive home bases of operations, nor distinctive and separate training programs (with a few exceptions). It is something like a homeless, inexperienced, but determined toddler trying to reach rather lofty goals.

It is easier to answer the closely related questions "what do community psychologists believe in?" and "what are they trying to accomplish?" To this end I will offer some orienting assumptions which seem to be fairly generally accepted at this time. I will also indicate some of the diversity among com-

1

munity psychologists in what they try to accomplish. Finally, I will attempt to answer the first question by offering my own definition of community psychology, without claims for its universal acceptance, to tell the reader what I think the field is and should be and to give him a general orientation for the remainder of the book.

PARENTS OF COMMUNITY PSYCHOLOGY: COMMUNITY MENTAL HEALTH AND THE WAR ON POVERTY

Community Mental Health

There is a fine historical perspective on the community mental health field by Cowen and Zax (1967) from which this discussion will frequently borrow.

The community mental health movement is a product of many forces, among which are: (1) a ground-swell of discontent; (2) money incentives from the federal government; and (3) changing values and new awarenesses in our society.

Areas of Discontent.   One area of discontent stemming from perceived inadequacies of services by a minority of mental health professionals was the recognition that the demand, and the need, for mental health services would always outstrip available resources. There are simply not enough professionals to serve those who ask for service, much less reach out to those needing but not seeking help. The Midtown Manhattan project found 80% of their sample showing some indication of emotional disturbance (Langer & Michael, 1963). Cowen, et al. (1963, 1966) in their early detection studies of young children found up to *one-third* of these children showing signs of moderate to severe psychopathology.

A closely related area of discontent has been the disenchantment with the effectiveness of psychotherapeutic methods. There has been a failure to conclusively demonstrate the effectiveness of psychotherapy even with highly motivated, affluent, well-educated people. Even more marked has been the general ineffectiveness of psychotherapy with disorders such as alcoholism, drug abuse, juvenile delinquency, and so-called "character" disorders, and its inappropriateness for persons of the lower socioeconomic class (Reiff, 1967). This state of affairs has made psychotherapy (and its derivatives) a dubious weapon for any *population-focused* attack upon mental illness.

To say that psychotherapy is not effective with many people is not to say that it should be scrapped. Applying psychotherapy to persons with inadequate education, substandard housing, continued financial crises, chronic health problems, and uncertain unemployment may be similar to attacking a tank with a flyswatter, but that does not make it ineffective for swatting flies. As a single method it is simply insufficient. Any service program that restricts its armamentarium to psychotherapy exclusively assures its own defeat.

If psychotherapy is ineffective with large segments of the population, and if psychotherapy is the only tool to be used by the mental health professions, then it is clear that there are inequities in the delivery of mental health services. If a person cannot "make it" with psychotherapy, often the only mental health service remaining available to him is incarceration in a state hospital.

This discontent by professionals from clinical psychology, psychiatry, and social work with traditional therapy methods was joined by discontent with traditional theories of psychopathology. Predominant psychoanalytic theory came under fire increasingly, particularly because of its intrapsychic (inside the mind) emphasis, or rather, because of its inattention to the strong current causative forces in the individual's environment. The gradual departure from this intrapsychic theory can be traced in the halting movement from long-term individual psychotherapy toward group therapy, then to family therapy, then to consultation, and then to prevention programs aimed at the individual's environment.

Government Incentives.   Hand-in-hand with increased discontent from a minority within the mental health professions, forces from government were also contributing, with more immediate effect, to an increased momentum for the community mental health movement. In 1955 Congress passed the Mental Health Study Act which established a Joint Commission on Mental Illness and Mental Health for the purpose of studying the nation's mental health resources and for recommending ways to combat mental illness. The Joint Commission in its final report (1961) emphasized the magnitude of the mental illness problem, and the shortages of mental health professionals. It also described limitations in then current practices. The community was given particular importance as a potential therapeutic resource for resolving some of the problems. In 1963 Congress passed the Community Mental Health Act which was to implement, in part, the Commission's report by allocating federal funds for the construction of comprehensive community mental health centers. Before they could qualify for these federal funds, however, the centers already had to be providing five services: inpatient care, outpatient care, partial hospitalization (e.g., day hospitals), emergency care, and consultation and education in the community.

With the potential reward of generous federal money for fine buildings, mental health clinics all over the country began scrambling to qualify. The only required service that was significantly new was that of consultation and education. With these incentives, mental health professionals began moving out into their communities, ostensibly to establish community-based programs, but often, in reality, primarily to qualify for federal money.

Societal Changes.   The federal government was soon to offer still greater incentives to mental health professionals to go into their communities through the money and programs available in antipoverty programs. Mental health professionals were enticed into this movement as consultants and advisors, and sometimes directly as administrators. Along with the antipoverty program, social protest movements became increasingly visible and audible. As the black poor received a taste of hope, and some appearance of power, they began to talk and demand. They presented their case against the institutions in their communities: the schools, welfare agencies, local government agencies, etc. They received a better hearing than ever before. And, together with many other white Americans, the mental health professionals reexamined their social institutions and found them wanting in areas directly related to mental illness concerns.

Patients Versus Systems.   It is at about this point that community mental health began to divide into two wings holding rather divergent conceptual views. The first wing might be described as operating from a "community of therapists" orientation. Their chief aim was to teach more and more people in the community, such "caretakers" as ministers, policemen, probation officers, teachers, etc., to behave more therapeutically toward mentally-ill persons in the community. They were taught, via the mental health professional-consultant, to recognize symptoms, to make appropriate referrals, and to respond generally as a therapist should (e.g., Spielberger, 1967; Altrocchi, Spielberger, & Eisdorfer, 1970). This wing focused primarily on the individual patient.

The second wing had a population focus and located causes of mental illness, at least in part, in the inappropriate and destructive responses of social systems to the people in them. To change mentally ill behavior, they believed, these social institutions themselves must first change. Also, this wing decreased the emphasis on mental disability and increased the emphasis on the responsibility of social systems for the psychosocial growth and development of individuals (Adelson, 1972; Glidewell, 1971a). It is from this wing that community psychology most directly has developed.

Birthplace

If community psychology was not an illegitimate offspring of community mental health, it was clearly an unplanned one. On May 4-8, 1965, the Conference on the Education of Psychologists for Community Mental Health was held in Swampscott, Massachusetts for about thirty psychologists. The explicit reason for the conference was to focus on training in community mental health, yet as the discussions continued broader concerns surfaced. Many of the participants had had experiences in antipoverty programs, the Peace Corps, and other social action programs, and the mandate of the conference was expanded to confront a new field, tentatively labeled "Community Psychology" (Bennett, et al., 1966). The term itself apparently had come into use as early as 1958 at George Peabody College (Newbrough, 1970).

While the Swampscott conference provides a clearly identifiable birthplace for community psychology, it must be recognized that forces beyond community mental health and psychology had definitely contributed to its conception. More than any other specialty in the history of psychology, community psychology is a response to governmental activities and social reform movements. It has been particularly committed to the principle of participation by consumers in social system decisions (Adelson, 1972).

The Antipoverty Program

The psychotherapist attempts to change the individual patient; the community mental health worker tries to train community caretakers to change their responses to the individual patient. The community psychologist tries to change social systems. The early emphasis of placing blame on social systems derived from experiences highlighted by the antipoverty program.

In 1960, Richard Cloward and Lloyd Ohlin published a theory of juvenile delinquency (Cloward & Ohlin, 1960) which identified the *blocking of opportunities* for economic advancement and for attainment of middle-class possessions by *social institutions* as a basic reason for the formation of delinquent subcultures and behavior patterns. This basic postulate soon permeated many antipoverty programs beyond the area of juvenile delinquency. Cloward and Ohlin suggested that when legitimate means for economic and social status attainment are restricted by inadequate education and racial discrimination, the adolescents then use available but illegitimate means for advancement. In the criminal subculture the adolescents are required to perform delinquent acts to follow the norms of the subculture. In areas where even illegitimate means are not available, the youngsters are limited to retreatist or escapist behaviors, such as drug use. In either case, the causes of delinquency were placed in a context of inequality of economic and educational opportunity, not in terms of individual or family pathology.

Cloward and Ohlin were working to apply their theory with the Henry Street Settlement House on the Lower East Side of Manhattan. In the summer of 1962, the Mobilization for Youth project was begun there as a demonstration and research project funded through the Ford Foundation, the National Institute of Mental Health, and the City of New York. It was to become one of the most controversial projects of the antipoverty program. It gradually introduced the idea that users of services should have a voice in the delivery of those services. Weissman (1969) reports the transition of Mobilization for Youth staff from individual counselors to community organizers in order to force welfare offices and schools to be more responsive to their clients. Herein began the controversy. The people who ran these institutions would not admit to inadequacy in their services, they were certainly not willing to give away any control of the services, they bridled at having their professional competence called into question, and in particular they could not accept this from people they perceived as irresponsible and unsuccessful.

From similar confrontations in other programs all over the country, combined with student protest movements, emerged the core problem for community psychology: how to effect changes in social institutions so that they are more facilitative of individual needs.

ORIENTING ASSUMPTIONS

After the review of its brief history above we now return to the community psychology of today. What do community psychologists now believe? What are the basic assumptions underlying their work? The following are offered as being generally accepted by most community psychologists today.

Social Systems Affect Individual Behavior

The major assumption of community psychology is that social system factors play a crucial part in determining the behaviors of individuals who participate in these social systems. This assumption has been suggested as the basic postulate of community psychology by Robert Reiff (1968), the first president of the A.P.A. division of community psychology. From this view, deviant or "pathological" behavior is a function of the social system in which it occurs. The individual's behavior cannot be studied separately from the social context in which it occurs. The individual does not behave in isolation from his social environment.

This view contrasts with the emphasis given to intrapsychic factors in determining behavior by psychoanalytic theories of personality. The psychoanalytic view finds the causes of behavior in defenses against, or expressions of, anxiety generated by experiences in the individual's childhood, and then carried inside the person. The social system view emphasizes that the individual's behavior is to a large degree a function of the current environmental forces impinging upon the individual from the social systems in which he now exists. The social system view also goes beyond simply an interpersonal emphasis and insists upon specific effects of the *system* of relationships.

The term *social system* requires further elaboration. The term refers to a consistent network of interacting relationships between persons, with the persons considered as units of the system, above and beyond their individual characteristics. One looks at a group of people not in terms of their individual personalities, but as units having certain positions and tasks within a network. One looks at the relationships *between* these units, rather than at each unit as an independent entity.

The participation in the social system by the individual has two aspects for Parsons (1951), who has referred to statuses and roles. These are not personal attributes of the actor, but are his properties as a unit in the social system. For example, an adult male in a family occupies the father-*role* and has father-*status,* neither of which is a personal attribute. A status has positional properties, i.e., it designates the actor's place in the relationship structure of the social system. A role to Parsons has "processual" properties, i.e., it designates what the actor *does* in his relations and orientations to other actors, and derives in part from expectations developed by the specific system.

As part of a social system, an individual member exists in an interdependent relationship with other members: his behavior affects the others, they affect him. Straus (1962) has described the social system as a structure in which a change in any one part requires changes in other parts.

An *adaptive* social system is also regarded as maintaining a *dynamic stability* (Berrien, 1968) of patterns of interrelationships. There is a consistency in accepted behavioral styles, a continuity of norms and expectations which remain the same on a day-to-day basis. However, in order for a social system to be adaptive and effective it must also be able to *change* its structure. A system may need to change in order to better accommodate the abilities and needs of its members. For example, in a family as the children grow older rules for their behavior must change. A system may need to change in order to fit effectively into its environment; for example, a university department may need to change its structure as the university receives more students and develops new goals, such as graduate programs.

An example of the influence on the behavior of members by the *inability* of the social system to change is given in Haley's (1963) conceptualization of families containing members with psychologcal problems. Haley describes the power struggles of these families by a homeostatic model. The family system is seen as a set of governors, with each member acting as a governor and trying to control the behavior of other members. Whenever any member begins to behave in ways deviant from family expectations, the other members begin to place limits on his behavior. With the reciprocal placement of these limits, a system of circumscribed behavior is maintained. These mutually responsive behaviors serve to define the "rules" of the family system, and to coerce the behavior of members.

On another level, Haley sees each member of the family striving to be the "metagovernor," i.e., the one who sets the limits of permitted behavior. Members are involved in struggles to possess the supreme governing influence. As any member tries for control, other members react to keep him from gaining ascendency. The more members try to change the system, the more they activate the governors which maintain the system. Thus, the more discontented members are, the more they try to change the system, the tighter it becomes. This, as Haley puts it, is the "tragedy" of the malfunctioning family.

Seymour Sarason (1967) in an insightful paper has emphasized the importance to any science of behavior of recognizing social system effects:

> "... as psychological theorists move in the direction of stating comprehensive formulations about the determinants of human

behavior they will become increasingly concerned with the nature of social organizations, the ways in which they change, and consequences of these changes. This development will not be a matter of choice but rather of necessity in that in reality the relationship between the individual and 'organized setting' is not a matter of choice" (p. 227).

". . . any theory which purports to explain behavior and which does not come to grips with man-system relationships is a naive, incomplete, and mischief-producing theory" (p. 230).

Thus, the transactions between man and his social systems must be understood not only to improve the individual's lot, but also to improve our knowledge of man.

As Sarason asserts, it is not necessary to debate whether or not the environment affects behavior. There is ample evidence that for accurate prediction of individual behavior there must be information about the environment as well as the individual, for example: Endler and Hunt (1966); Moos (1968); Pervin (1968); Rausch, Dittman, and Taylor (1959); and Raush, Farbman, and Llewellyn (1960). Barker (1968) has reported that for some aspects of child behavior better predictions could be made from knowledge of the environment than from knowledge of the stable traits of the individual. Clearly, certain settings determine very homogeneous behavior, e.g., classrooms, highways. Skinner (1971) has recently reiterated his position that the environment totally determines behavior (given certain genetic constraints). The debatable question, then, is the *degree,* the *extent,* of the environment's effect on behavior compared with intraindividual factors.

A final explicit qualifying word for this assumption is necessary before proceeding. While the premise is that social systems do affect individual behavior, this should not imply a one-way affect. The relationship between the social system and the individual is interactional; the individual can have a powerful impact on the social system as well as being powerfully influenced by the social system. Also, the individual may reside in a number of different social systems at the same time, the social systems affect each other, and their influences on the individual also interact. The individual is not a passive recipient of social system influences, and the influences of one social system do not suddenly lift when he enters a different social system.

Community Psychology as a Psychology of Social Conscience

This is a less explicit assumption, but it is a strong if not unanimous concern. Many psychologists in the community psychology movement have strong commitments to directly fighting social problems. This is perhaps most clear in the writings of Reiff (1966, 1968). There is a conviction that our social problems reflect inadequacies and injustices in social systems and organizations. Major societal bureaucracies such as public schools, courts, police departments, and welfare departments are viewed as obstructing and denying individual needs and potentials, or at least being unable to properly support and enhance the lives of people they involve (Lipton, 1968). While community psychologists may disagree as to the exact nature of change to promote, they typically agree that changes in our current social organizations are critically needed.

A student once asked me whether community psychology would support status-quo society, or the established social institutions, against deviant or unconventional individual behavior. Such support would be clearly the opposite of community psychology's intent. In 1967, at a workshop on training for community psychology at the A.P.A. Convention, the question was raised regarding the usefulness of community psychology in aiding local governments to combat riots. An immediate and forceful rejoinder was that this definitely was not the proper function for community psychology. Rather, the place for the community psychologist would be to work to change social organizations, in order that conditions for individuals could be improved. If "it came to a showdown," its prevalent orientation would place community psychology on the "side" of the individual against existing institutions.

In line with this orientation, there is also the strong interest in working for opportunities for individuals to participate in the policies and decisions of institutions. As Reiff (1968) indicates, the idea of citizen participation is a central theme of current social reform movements. Its acceptance into community psychology is partly a function of the individual involvement by community psychologists in social reform efforts, but it also has foundation in the work of social psychologists in industry suggesting that increased participation and influence in an organization leads to greater personal satisfaction and improved performance for the worker (e.g., Likert, 1961). The view that individual participation is "good" stems both from its implications for social justice and from its value for the psychological condition of the individual. Adelson (1972) has emphasized this in his conception of community psychology:

> "With a 'growth model' we move to concern with individuals who through group and community processes join together in achieving their own objectives as they help themselves and are not the objects of help from professionals, and as they are concerned with reconstructing social systems to provide conditions more congenial for their own growth." (p. 13).

To speak of social concerns or social conscience as a part of psychology may well cause discomfort to those psychologists who feel such concerns are incompatible with a field of science. Indeed, the history of psychology tends to reveal an aloofness toward social problems that may well reflect the preference of most psychologists to remain professionally neutral toward such issues as racial and religious discrimination, political corruption, educational system inadequacies, etc. However, the content, social problems as an area of study, is surely as legitimate a problem as visual perception or verbal learning. To me, it seems that psychology *can* raise legitimate objections with regard to the *method* of investigation or of system change.

Community *psychology* is obligated to use those methods which are proper for a *psychological* specialty. This should still allow for innovation in methods, and surely for developing and using methods not heretofore used in psychology, but such methods should abide by the "spirit" of psychological methods. (Clinical psychologists, particularly, should be well aware of problems occurring as the result of adopting methods from outside a psychological framework, e.g., psycho*therapy*.) In my view the appropriate methods for community psychologists, in their *professional* role, should be psychological rather than political. I also recognize that for many social institutions change will not occur in the absence of political pressures. Community psychology, however, should not be expected to be able to change any system, any place, any time. Its legitimate constraints are to remain within the limits of a behavioral science.

Community Psychology as a New Applied Psychology

One of the purposes of community psychology is to develop methods of *intervention* in social systems. It exists primarily to effect change, not primarily at this point at least, to contribute to a fund of knowledge. It thus takes its place with clinical psychology, educational psychology, counseling psychology, and industrial psychology as a specialty primarily of an applied nature (Newbrough, 1970). This will not mean that research and evaluation will be secondary concerns, as too often seems to be the case in clinical psychology. Nor should community psychology become a collection of practitioners who neglect conceptualization and evaluation.

Community psychology could be described as an applied arm of social psychology, although clinical psychology has a more legitimate claim to parentage, and social psychology might wish to disclaim a connection. Many of the first community psychologists are "converted clinicians"; witness the list of participants at the Swampscott Conference in 1965. This background of training and experience is a significant contribution to the applied nature of community psychology. However, community psychology has clearly rejected the "psychiatric model" as a conceptual orientation, whereas the practice of clinical psychology is, like it or not, enmeshed in psychiatric methods, concepts, and terminology. It is, therefore, conceptually incompatible to view community psychology as a subspecialty of clinical psychology, although it may be possible administratively to provide community psychology training in existing clinical training programs.

At the Swampscott Conference it was generally agreed that the community psychologist should base his actions on knowledge from psychology and other social sciences, and that in the process of his actions should be committed to the generation of concepts and to the development of knowledge of the relationships between individuals and social systems. He should, in other words, be more than a practitioner. One description of the appropriate role for the community psychologist was termed the "participant-conceptualizer":

> "The role of the community psychologist may therefore be seen as that of a "participant-conceptualizer." As such he is clearly involved in, and may be a mover of, community processes, but he is also a professional attempting to conceptualize those processes within the framework of psychological-sociological knowledge" (Bennett, et al., 1966, pp. 7-8).

The community psychologist is an applied psychologist in the sense that he attempts to translate social science knowledge into social change (and in so doing provides additional information). He should not, however, be concerned with his social change activities to the exclusion of contributing to social science knowledge. This means that the community psychologist should make evaluation research an integral part of his social change activities.

Social Systems as Targets for Change

Clinical psychology, psychiatry, and even the casework arm of social work have all directed their change efforts at the individual. This has also carried the implicit assumption that any "improper" behavior is the exclusive responsibility of the individual, with the environment essentially held blameless. Community psychology holds that such difficulties are results of the transactions between the individual and his environment. Interventions are directed at social systems toward the end of a better accommodation between the system and its population.

To begin with, this assumption requires that the analysis of any psychological problem include a broader range than individual behavior. Robert Sears (1951) has complained that:

> ". . . psychologists think monodically. That is, they choose the behavior of one person as their scientific subject matter. For them, the universe is composed of individuals. . . the universal laws sought by the psychologist almost always relate to a single body" (pp. 478-479).

From the social system perspective, the universe is composed of individuals *organized into system groupings*. For instance, if one observes a family in interaction and attends only to the behavior of individuals, one sees the trees and neglects the forest. If one attends to the system *qua* system, one looks for the range of permitted behavior, at the expectations and norms, at the patterns of relationships; one observes who talks to whom, who supports, and who attacks, whom. One endeavors to understand the function of individual behaviors for the system. In short, one seeks to understand family member behavior in its relationship to the family unit's requirements and constraints.

Intervening at the social system level need not be confined to modifying existing systems, it can also include designing *new* experimental social systems. George Fairweather's work (1967, 1969) is a good example. In a comparatively rigorous approach,

Fairweather has designed alternative social systems, e.g., a residential and job support system for discharged mental hospital patients, and then drawn comparisons with old systems having the same functions. The whole new area of social planning (Kahn, 1969) has considerable promise for enhancing the psychosocial responsiveness of social systems, particularly if on a community-wide basis, such as in New Towns (e.g., Murrell, 1971b).

The reader may well desire a discussion in more concrete terms of just what an intervention at a social system level might entail. Let us take, for example, a public high school which has requested consultation from a psychologist to help with "discipline problems." After doing an extensive series of observations, administering questionaires, and conducting interviews, the psychologist identifies these two problems in the system: First, there is a lack of clarity about what types of deviant behavior by students merit which degrees of disciplinary action. This has led to inconsistent disciplinary actions. Second, the set of norms established informally by the faculty regarding the proper relationship between faculty member and student has created intense conflicts. These informal norms require a formal, distant, and suspicious relationship by faculty toward students. From his analysis, the psychologist concludes that the students are *reacting* to these norms with aggressive, untrustworthy behaviors and are perceiving the inconsistency of disciplinary actions as further reflecting hostile unfairness on the part of the faculty.

The psychologist then sets out to develop an intervention program which will attempt to (1) clarify disciplinary policies, (2) change the faculty behavior toward students, and (3) give students greater participation in the disciplinary process. He then meets with the administration and presents these recommendations:

> 1. The establishment of committees to suggest policies for disciplinary actions to be made up of representatives from the

administration, faculty, and student body. The committees are to be advisory with the administration writing the final policies. Then these policy statements are to be distributed to all faculty and students. The psychologist views this action as a way to clarify the policies and at the same time increase interaction and communication between the different levels of the system. He must, of course, present this recommendation in such a way that it does not threaten or label the administration as the "bad guy."

2. In order to change the behavior of the faculty the psychologist decides that a system of differential rewards will be necessary. He feels that an educational approach such as giving talks or having seminars would be insufficient to change the norms. He recommends that the administration choose a "teacher of the month" on the basis of the *least* number of disciplinary actions. The new orientation would place value on *prevention* of deviant behavior rather than on the punishment of such behaviors. These criteria would be made explicit to the faculty. Also, the psychologist recommends that the administration adopt the procedure whereby the student council, if it receives a certain number of complaints about a teacher from students, may request that an administrator monitor that teacher's classes to determine whether or not the teacher is, in fact, being unfair or over-punitive to students. This recommendation gives students recourse and allows them greater influence in the institution, but at the same time allows the administration to maintain its authority position (which the psychologist at this point has no power to change even if he felt it was desirable).

The psychologist would develop evaluation procedures to determine to what degree his recommended programs did have the desired effect. Such procedures might well serve as a basis for introducing modifications of the programs or pointing out needs for additional programs.

If the analysis of the problem was accurate in this example, then change efforts directed at the individual level would have been unsuccessful. If the deviant students had been identified and worked with and even if their behavior had changed, or if these students were ejected from the system, eventually other students would also reflect the *system* problems in their behavior. The roles that these students had held would soon be filled by others unless the system were changed in such a way that these roles were modified or no longer necessary.

A complication needs to be noted at this point. A number of different social systems may be affecting an indidividual at the same time, but some systems will have more impact than others. Thus, if for John Jones social system A has a primary influence and system B has only a minor influence on his behavior, then changes in system B will not necessarily affect his behavior. Change efforts at the social system level, then, would be expected to have a *broad* rather than intense effect. It would touch all individuals in the system, but the degree of these effects on any one individual would vary according to the strength of his relationship to that particular system.

The Proper Setting is the Natural Environment

This assumption holds that the basic phenomena of community psychology exist in the natural environment. The community psychologist may draw on data from the laboratory, in the absence of any other, but his concern is with studying behavior *in situ* and he accepts the complexity and uncontrolled nature of this data. This requires training in field-research methods. Newbrough (1970) has suggested that community psychology training at the predoctoral level needs to especially emphasize the field-research methods which have heretofore been so lacking in our training programs.

The term "community" in community psychology in practice has typically not referred to the study of communities as such, as definite entities. Rather, it has referred to the practice of studying the relationship between the individual and his social institutions *in* the community. The proper *setting* for this work is out there in the natural environment of the community rather than in the laboratory or clinic office.

This natural environment emphasis has been suggested in the advocacy of ecological models by community psychologists.

James Kelly (e.g., 1966, 1968) has provided an ecological model for community psychology, and this emphasis has been recommended by Newbrough (1964, 1970), Lehmann (1971), and others. An ecological system is a complex interlocking network of supplies, consumers, and conditions which together help or hinder the adaptation of species within it. Lehmann suggests that community psychologists should study the community as an ecological system and observes that community psychology should serve as a counterpoint to bioecology, studying the human rather than the biological community. Lehmann points out that psychology up to now has neglected man's more complex habitats although there have been voices calling for its examination, e.g., Murray (1938), Lewin (1951), Barker (1963), and Willems and Raush (1969), and also recommends that naturalistic study, in line with Barker's work, is particularly appropriate as a methodology for community psychology. Lehmann further emphasizes that community psychology must develop a conceptual framework that appreciates this complexity of the interrelationships between the person and his social environment. This book will make an effort in that direction.

DIVERSITY IN COMMUNITY PSYCHOLOGY

The assumptions presented above reflect the prevalent perspectives of those in the field of community psychology. They are not, of course, shared equally by all community psychologists, as is understandable considering the variation in background, experiences, values, and skills of the psychologists who have launched this movement. In a useful essay, Sylvia Scribner (1968) has described the diversity of community psychology as manifested in four different "types" of community psychologists.

Social movement psychologists are those who work for social change in a *political* way. They support and work with political action groups, contributing their professional knowledge and skills. They are ". . . professionals concerned with basic social change who are not identified by their locus of work (community or laboratory), by their specific function (activist or conceptual), or by a common theoretical frame of reference *within their* discipline (p. 5)." Their contributions may be offered on a voluntary basis, outside their professional position. They reflect a strong "social conscience."

The *social action* psychologist is also concerned with social problems but participates as a professional within his psychological discipline. He is not committed to political movements as methods for social change. He works on a variety of problems, with populations that heretofore have received little attention from psychologists, and in the process develops new techniques in action programs for human betterment.

The *new clinical psychologist* is one who has become disenchanted with psychotherapy and the psychiatric model in general, and who is increasingly interested in new techniques involving environmental intervention. "Nonetheless, the clinical psychologist remains primarily oriented to a target individual and committed to evaluating intervention techniques on this basis (p. 6)."

The *social-engineer psychologist* is one who concentrates on the diagnosis of systems and their effects, and on the design of programs for introducing change in systems. He may participate in plans for new public housing, or he may be an advisor to government on social behavior. His principal focus is on the system or institution, ". . . the system is his object and he is only indirectly concerned with the people whose behavior, experience or ideology is to be modified (p. 6)." His commitments to humanistic values are less certain than those of the social movement or social action psychologist.

In Scribner's view, the social-engineer psychologist could be expected to contribute knowledge and theory in the ecological and systems analysis area. The social action psychologist would make a particular contribution to the development of techniques for intervention programs. The social movement psychologist could analyze and evaluate theories of how social and political organizations develop, function, and dissipate. The new clinical psychologist will be increasingly aware of environmental effects on his patients (Murrell, 1971a), and can utilize this awareness in his work with community agents regarding a particular patient. (The new clinical psychologist might also be called a "community mental health psychologist.") Also, since social system interventions will often be extensive rather than intensive, and not equally effective for all individuals, the new clinical psychologist may be necessary to work with the "residue" individual and his relationships to *all* of his social systems.

With respect to our list of assumptions: all of these "types" of community psychologists would fit into an "applied" mold in the activist sense of working for change. All would likely accept the proposition that social systems are strong determiners of individual behavior. All could focus their work in natural environments, with the new clinical psychologist doing so less exclusively. The emphasis on change efforts being directed at the social system level would probably be accepted by all, but perhaps practiced least by the new clinical psychologist. The social conscience orientation would be accepted readily by social movement and social action psychologists, but would apply to a lesser degree to the new clinical psychologist and the social-engineer psychologist. The "conceptualizer" component of the "participant-conceptualizer" role would be adopted most readily by the social-engineer psychologist and social action psychologist, but would have less relevance for the social movement psychologist and the new clinical psychologist.

A DEFINITION FOR COMMUNITY PSYCHOLOGY

In my view, community psychology is still very much in the process of development. I offer a definition of the community psychology of today realizing that aspects of this definition will be less appropriate for the community psychology of tomorrow.

In this sense I offer the definition as a preliminary one, with refinements surely to follow.

I would define community psychology as the area within the science of psychology that *studies* the transactions between social system networks, populations, and individuals; that *develops* and *evaluates* intervention methods which improve person-environment "fits"; that *designs* and *evaluates* new social systems; and from such knowledge and change seeks to *enhance* the psychosocial opportunities of the individual.

Orientation to the Book

In practice, I favor the following approach. The prospective intervener either is asked to come into a social system or he goes to the target system and makes a general proposal for the intervention. After gaining access (which is becoming easier as more and more systems are asking for evaluations and this kind of help) the would-be intervener gathers informaion about the system and its impact upon the individuals within it. This information-gathering will be referred to hereafter as the preliminary analysis. On the basis of his preliminary analysis, the intervener then outlines a general intervention plan, which he then develops in detail in *collaboration* with key system personnel who would also participate in its implementation (the superior, patronizing attitudes of some professionals are usually counter-productive to effective interventions). During and following the intervention its effects are evaluated. On the basis of the evaluation, modifications are made in the intervention program.

With our present limited state of knowledge about man-system relationships and of methods for measurement, the preliminary analysis must be rather crude and imprecise. It cannot be nearly as precise, for example, as the analysis procedure recently developed by Volkswagen for computerized monitoring and assessment of the functioning of its automobiles. The "preliminary analysis" is made possible because *sensors* in *key areas* are built-in during construction. When the owner later brings his car in for a checkup (to see if he needs an intervention), his car is literally plugged into a computer and 20 minutes later out comes a print-out that describes the strengths and weaknesses of the mechanism. Our preliminary analysis of social system "mechanisms" is a long way from this kind of precision (cars are, after all less complex than social systems), but we may recall the phrase "sensors in key areas" to describe the aims of a preliminary analysis. We do not know now just exactly which are the key areas and we do not have very sensitive or precise measures of key areas. This book will, nonetheless, attempt, on the basis of evidence that is available, a list of *key areas* for the preliminary analysis. This will include individual variables, group variables, and population variables. It will include within-system variables and between-system variables. It will consider social systems and networks of social systems. It will examine variables of behavior settings and of organizations. It will attempt to be something of a "guidebook," suggesting points of interest that the prospective intervener should look at before he intervenes. Throughout, it attempts to highlight implications for interventions. Finally, it will describe in detail five actual interventions of varying levels of complexity.

The intent, then, is to provide a framework for preliminary analyses and guidelines for interventions. The intent is not to develop a theory, in the sense that a theory predicts and explains relationships between variables. Hypothetical concepts will be introduced to help provide conceptual clarity for the framework, and at points hypotheses about relationships will be offered as illustrations for intervention targets. But a formal comprehensive theory, in my view, is not possible without considerably more knowledge about the behaviors of persons in their natural environment.

2. PERSONALITY
IN SOCIAL SYSTEMS

It is not easy to "get into" the idea that as individuals we are as we are partly because of the forces in our social systems. Our culture constantly emphasizes the individual dominating his environment. Our television heroes conquer all through direct (often violent) independent action. Assassins change the world through direct independent acts, no matter what their other limitations had been. We boast of our frontier forebears who "conquered" the wilderness (as we today continue to do in a destructive way). We have "conquered" space by going to the moon. But for each "conquest" the environment exacts a price.

This cultural emphasis on the individual is good to the degree that we value each and every person. But it is a delusion if we absolve the environment from responsibility for its debilitating effects and do not credit it for its positive contributions. The idealization of independent individual action is fictional if it ignores individual-system *interaction*.

Since for many this conception may take some getting used to, this chapter is offered to help ease the transition. It will examine the individual personality, since community psychology is essentially dedicated to the welfare of the individual. But it will insist on placing personality in a social system context. It will stress personality as the result of an interplay between individual and social system.

The four positions to be presented here all emphasize this interplay. Katz and Kahn introduce the concept of role expectations which emanate from social systems and constrain individuals. Sarbin further refines this concept by describing the important distinction between ascribed and achieved statuses. Secord and Backman amplify on the goodness-of-fit idea with their congruency model of personality. Carson contributes to the individualization of these ideas, or why different "strokes" are important for different "folks," and adds an information-processing component.

KATZ AND KAHN: ROLE TAKING

Katz and Kahn (1966) view personality as a social interaction product which is modified throughout the individual's life. They offer a model of role-taking which attempts to integrate organization factors, interpersonal factors, and personality factors. Their model makes liberal use of the findings and concepts from the study (now something of a classic) of the school superintendent role by Gross, Mason, and McEachern (1958).

Definitions of Terms

An individual in an organization occupies a location, called an *office,* which is defined in terms of its relationships with others in the system, and with the system itself. For each office there are prescribed activities or behaviors, which have been assigned by the organization or social system. A *role* is a set of recurrent activities which is assigned to the particular office. Roles are more a function of the social system than of the particular occupant's personality characteristics. Each office is engaged in interdependent relationships with any number of other offices. The network of interdependent relationships is called a *role set.* The individuals who are members of a role set develop aggregate evaluative behavioral prescriptions and proscriptions— they develop *role expectations* for each office within the role set. These role expectations are typically related to the history of the social system and to its formal achievement task. After Rommetveit (1954), role set members are called *role senders* and their communicated expectations are the *sent role;* that is, role expectations for an office are sent by other members of a role set to the occupant of that office. This sent role is then interpreted by the occupant according to his particular psychological makeup. The product of his interpretation is the *received role,* which can range from being very similar to very dissimilar to the sent role.

Acknowledging the complexity of the natural environment, Katz and Kahn allow that there may be multiple activities in one role, multiple roles for one office, and multiple offices for a single individual.

Role behavior is the output of the following role *episode:* evaluations are developed, usually over an extended period of time, which form role expectations; these evaluations are routinely and continuously communicated to the occupant along with messages urging the person to conform to the expectations (sent role), the sent role is interpreted (received role), and the occupant then behaves on the basis of the received role.

As an example consider a school. Being a nonadult in a school qualifies one only for the office of "pupil." Within the pupil role, the appropriate behaviors are repeatedly pointed out to the child, primarily by his teacher (role sender), e.g., "We don't run in the halls. . . We raise our hand when we wish to say something," etc. These behavioral and programmatic *regularities* are nicely described by Sarason (1971) and represent very resistant obstacles to change. The role expectations are frequently sent and generally are held to apply to all pupils about equally. The particular children, however, may interpret these roles differently. One may perceive that his teacher is "picking on him" unfairly, another may interpret the admonitions casually as just part of the "malarkey" you have to put up with in school. The expectation is that all children should *sit* for long periods of time, that they be *quiet* for long periods of time, and that they do their own work. The role expectations apply equally to the child with high physical energy and a propensity for verbal expression as well as to the low-energy, quiet child.

Over a career of many years in such settings these expectations can be expected to differentially interact with individual personalities. The verbal, high-energy child would experience more frustration and receive more blame than the low-energy, quiet child. The low academic achiever will receive many inputs to his self-concept that he is inadequate. The messy, the awkward, the timid, the boisterous also have psychologically uncomfortable fits between their individual predispositions and classroom role expectations.

Role Conflicts

Katz and Kahn point out a number of potential binds for the individual occupant, called *role conflicts.* One is the *intrasender* conflict in which one sender sends several role expectations which are incompatible with one another. This is similar to the general idea of the "double-bind" concept developed by the Bateson group (Bateson, et. al., 1956) to describe the mutually exclusive messages sent in schizophrenic families. For example, a mother who has not seen her schizophrenic child for a month greets him saying, "Oh, I've missed you so," while simultaneously physically restraining the child from hugging her. Another is the *intersender* conflict in which the occupant is sent conflicting expectations from different senders. For example, one supervisor tells the psychology graduate student not to report IQ scores to parents; a second supervisor encourages him to do so. Another is *interrole* conflict, in which one person is simultaneously in two different roles, the expectations of which are in conflict. This is very similar to the concept of conflicting *intersystem accommodation* which will be discussed at length at a later point, an example being that a child's parents encourage independent expression in his "son" role while his teacher encourages conforming suppression in his "pupil" role. The fourth conflict is that of *person-role* as discussed in the above classroom example, in which the received role is incongruent with the individual occupant's values, need priorities, or capacities. For example, a graduate student may interpret the performance standards of a doctoral program as requiring an unquestioning subservient role, and this conflicts with his needs for expression of independent ideas and to rebel against authority—for this student there is a bad "fit" between his needs and the program's role expectations.

While there are a number of potential conflicts in any role, the role itself is not necessarily detrimental to an individual's psychological functioning. A role can serve the advantageous function of providing guides to accepted behavior. Compatibility of person, role behavior, received role, and sent role would combine to offer the occupant a very comfortable and satisfying office.

Implications

What are the implications of the Katz and Kahn role-taking model for a definition of social system impact upon individuals?

1. Role expectations can act as guides and as constraints for the individual. They can limit his choices, but they can also protect his choices. For example, if Johnny obtains great creative satisfactions from doing free-form drawings with wild explosions of color, and if his teacher strongly emphasizes conformity to a more literal, representational approach, then the role expectations in that classroom are handicaps to Johnny. They may, in fact, be "stifling his creativity." Also, if a school principal adopts the role expectations developed over a number of years in a school system that allow for no discussion of changes in school policies by parents or teachers, this expectation serves as a constraint (and probably as an over-all system weakness). On the other hand, in newly formed social systems where the role expectations have not yet developed, the individual's choices are limited because he does not know what is

acceptable. Where role expectations are clear, the individual knows those choices that are open to him. His choices are, in a sense, "guaranteed" by the role expectations.

2. The effect of the social system upon the individual is highly determined by the "fit" between social system role expectations and the values, aspirations, beliefs, and capabilities of the individual. An incompatible fit will lead to psychological dissatisfaction; a compatible fit will provide psychological comfort.

SARBIN: SOCIAL IDENTITY

Sarbin (1970) does not make explicit claims for the cause or change of *personality* characteristics by social system forces, but does insist that social system forces have significant effects upon the individual's social identity.

Four Ecologies

Sarbin suggests four differents "ecologies" which he rather vaguely describes as areas in man's world of occurrences in which he must find his place or identity. One such ecology is that of *self-maintenance*, in which the central problem is to survive as a biosocial organism. A second is *social ecology*, or set of role systems in which the problem is to define one's social identity which is a function of one's role performances and their match with the expectations of relevant other persons. A third is the *normative ecology*, the system of societal norms in which the problem is to ascertain how well one is meeting society's standards. The fourth is the *transcendental ecology* in which the problem is to define the relationship between one's self and the larger meanings of life—God, mankind, the human condition, etc.

The problems of these four areas are related by Sarbin to the perspectives of various psychological theory orientations. The problems of the self-maintenance ecology are regarded as the chief target of behavior theory. The problems of the normative ecology are regarded as appropriate targets for psychodynamic theory. The problems of meaning, or the transcendental ecology, are regarded as fitting targets for the humanist-existential theories (such as those of Maslow, Bugental, etc.). The problems of the social ecology are those of social identity and are regarded by Sarbin as falling within the baliwick of community psychology.

Sarbin defines social identity as: "a cognitive outcome that follows from actor's conduct *and* 'the evaluations declared by relevant others on such conduct (1970, p. 101)." This outcome is the result of relationships between the actor and others in his social systems—thus, one's social identity is made up of a variety of different roles occurring in different relationships in different settings. Sarbin suggests a three-dimensional model to assess the person's social identity; it utilizes status, value, and involvement.

Status

Sarbin's "status" refers to a set of expectations applied to a certain position in a social system. (Sarbin's "status" appears to be very similar to the "sent role" of Katz and Kahn.) Statuses may be *ascribed,* i.e., those which are defined on the basis of biosocial attributes (e.g., woman, husband, child). Or, statuses may be *achieved,* which are defined on the basis of attainment and choice (e.g., mayor, corporation vice president, Rhodes scholar). Sarbin suggests a status continuum, the underlying concept being degree of choice. At the ascribed end there is little choice involved and there are only very limited guaranteed minimal rights (the rights provided simply for being a person). As statuses fall more toward the achieved end of the continuum, the occupant is accorded increasing amounts of power and/or esteem.

Value

The value dimension as conceived by Sarbin is orthogonal to the status dimension and runs from negative to positive with a

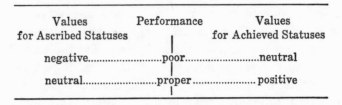

Figure 1   Values for achieved and ascribed performances

central neutral point. Value here corresponds to the esteem given by others. Sarbin describes value as applied to the achievement statuses as being neutral with respect to poor performance or nonperformance and positive with respect to proper performance. For ascribed statuses the values run from neutral for proper performance to negative for poor or non-performance. See Figure 1.

The dilemma of the woman in today's society can be represented by these two different statuses. The roles of mother and wife are generally perceived by society as ascribed statuses. Being a good wife and mother is only proper and receives only neutral value; one does not receive much esteem or power from it. On the other hand, being a poor wife or mother is viewed as being extremely negative—one would be perceived as mentally or morally very inadequate for poor performance in these roles.

Sarbin holds that the individual who performs poorly in ascribed statuses has violated propriety norms and is given the social identity of a "nonperson." In popular terms, he is labeled an animal, a beast, a low-grade human; or in more sophisticated language as lower class, underprivileged, mentally ill, delinquent, hippie, homosexual, etc. For example, the homosexual is not meeting the expectations for the ascribed status of male adult; the chronically unemployed male is not meeting the expectations of the statuses of husband or father. The extreme negative psychological effect of the social identity of "nonperson" should be clearly imaginable.

Involvement

The third dimension describes the person's degree of participation of self in the behaviors of the role. This involves the relative amount of time spent in the role behaviors compared to other roles and the degree of "organismic energy" devoted to the behaviors. Ascribed statuses require higher involvement more of the time (e.g., in "mother" or "elderly person") than achieved statuses (e.g., in "chess champion" or "PTA president"). Obviously, the involvement in ascribed statuses is not necessarily voluntary. It would appear that this dimension could be subsumed under the status dimension, as its underlying concept is mainly degree of choice.

Sarbin suggests that social identities can be upgraded by: (1) *promotion,* which refers to providing increased numbers of statuses in social systems with greater choice and achievement potential; and (2) *commendation,* or applying positive values to proper performance even in ascribed statuses. By implication, Sarbin charges social systems with responsibility for degrading or upgrading social identities.

Implications

What are the implications of Sarbin's approach to social identity for defining a social system's impact upon an individual?

1. The social identity is a *cognitive* outcome. That is, it is the individual's idea of the relationship between his conduct and the social system's evaluation of that conduct. The social identity is, then, an internal psychological state; and, presumably, enduring so long as that relationship between conduct and evaluation continues. It sounds, then, as if a social identity is a personality characteristic.

2. As in Katz and Kahn's role taking, there is the conception that the *compatibility* between conduct and the social system's evaluation of it is a prime determinant of the psychological

impact of the social system upon the individual. The social identity of "nonperson" would appear to define the extreme of such incompatibility, and perhaps the extreme of negative impact that a social system can have.

3. A social system can likely upgrade social identities, or improve individual need satisfactions, if the social system extends positive evaluations to a wider variety of conduct (and capability). In the terms of Katz and Kahn, a social system should use a wide variety of offices having a wider range of role expectations. There are also indications, which we shall pursue later, that such a widening should have positive effects upon the total system's functioning.

SECORD AND BACKMAN:
AN INTERPERSONAL THEORY OF PERSONALITY

Secord and Backman (1961, 1965) explicitly describe social system effects upon personality. They also refer specifically to the compatibility between the individual and his social environment as being critical to his personality.

Congruency

The basic postulate of Secord and Backman's approach is that personality stability and change are a function of the person's immediate two-person interpersonal system. This system includes three components: (1) some aspect of the individual's self-concept, e.g., "I am an intelligent person"; (2) his interpretation of his behavior relevant to that aspect of his self-concept, e.g., "I answered that question intelligently"; and (3) his perception of another person's feelings and behavior toward him with respect to that aspect of his self-concept, e.g., "the teacher treats me as if he thinks I am intelligent." When the behaviors of the other person (O) and the focal individual (S) are such that they correspond with the relevant aspect of S's self-concept, the system is in a state of congruency. Congruency contributes to both personality stability and personality change.

Congruency is a desired and rewarding state. It derives from a postulated|*need for predictability* of events in social interaction. The more congruent the interpersonal system, the better the predictability for S. Incongruency leads to a loss of predictability and, therefore, to discomfort. Presumably, perfect congruency would be a positive affective state and any degree of incongruency would constitute a negative affective state.

Personality Stability. Stability of S's behavior is believed to be a function of both constitutional and social system factors. The constitutional factors include such things as energy level, facial features, etc., and characteristics of temperament which may have a biochemical basis. The social system factors (those in addition to congruency considerations) apply to the positions S occupies in institutional and subinstitutional structures. Institutional structures, or, broadly speaking, societal norms, appear to serve the same functions as Sarbin's "statuses" or Katz and Kahn's "sent roles." The position in an institutional structure has built-in expectations for behavior independent of the specific characteristics of the occupant and these expectations serve to maintain the same set of behaviors over time (e.g., male behavior, in-church-on-Sunday behavior, etc.). Subinstitutional structures refer to features of particular interpersonal relationships which include affect, power, and status. For example, S may have a warm, bantering relationship with one friend, and a more guarded, competitive relationship with another friend, and these particular relationships persist over time. Subinstitutional characteristics will be explored in greater detail below via Carson's conception.

Institutional and subinstitutional factors also contribute to the stability of O's behavior. The institutional status or position of S constrains the behavior of O toward him, e.g., children receive behaviors that are consistently different than those received by adults, O's respond to males differently than to females, etc. The subinstitutional characteristics of particular interpersonal relationships, being relatively persistent, maintain the behavior of O equally as well as that of S.

Congruency Processes. It is the congruency of the interpersonal system which receives the most attention in Secord and Backman's work. It very explicitly involves the goodness-of-fit between the three components of the interpersonal system and the nature of the interaction between S and O. The more congruent the system, the more stable the S behavior. The following are some of the ways that S attempts to maintain or achieve congruency:

1. Cognitive restructuring. If faced with an incongruency, S may misperceive or distort O's behavior or his own. In effect, he modifies the potentially incongruent information by *thinking* differently about it.

2. Selective evaluation. More precisely this process is a *re*-evaluation of an information source, e.g., self, self's behavior, or O's behavior. If this source contributes incongruent information it is re-evaluated more negatively; if it provides congruent information the source is re-evaluated more positively. If a teacher credits low creative ability to a student whose self-concept ascribes to him large amounts of this attribute, the student will re-evaluate the teacher negatively. (Secord and Backman acknowledge other complexities, namely the "positivity effect," but what we have already explained is sufficient for our purposes.)

3. Selective interaction. By this process, S chooses to engage in interpersonal relationships on the basis that O behave toward S in a way that is congruent with his self-concept. If S's self-concept is, for example, one of weakness and dependence, he would likely choose to interact with Os who would advise, protect, support, perhaps even exploit him, since this behavior

would fit or be complementary to his self-concept.

4. Evocation of congruent rrsponses. This process is a set of behavioral techniques which elicit or pull behaviors from O which are congruent with S's self-concept. For example, a patient who sees himself as inadequate may continuously solicit reassurance and advice from his therapist. His therapist will then be inclined to respond to him with support, advice, etc.; in this way he treats the patient as if he were indeed inadequate.

5. Congruency by comparison. This process is not directed at achieving congruency per se, but at reducing the impact of incongruency through attributing the same behavior or result to others. A girl with a highly moralistic self-concept but who nevertheless has sexual intercourse with her fiance may reduce the impact of this incongruency by comparing herself to "Susie Brown" who is reputedly promiscuous. By comparison, she can claim to be more moral than Susie.

Secord and Backman (1965) describe research which generally documents the use of the above processes.

Incongruency as a Force for Personality Change. For Secord and Backman, incongruency is of central importance in producing personality change. If the interpersonal environment changes so that the others behave uniformly toward the individual in new ways, then the individual "would rapidly modify his own behavior and internal structure to produce a new set of congruent matrices. As a result, he would be a radically changed person (1961, p. 28)." The stability of personality depends upon congruency among the three components of the interpersonal matrix. The introduction of incongruency into this matrix would require S to: (1) change his behavior or at least his perception of his behavior, or (2) he would have to change his perception of O, or (3) he would have to modify part of his self-concept. Or, (4) he would need to change his behavior. Or, some combination of these. If incongruency occurs, S cannot just stand there—he has to do something!

The critical reader may protest that Secord and Backman are talking about *behavior* change, not personality change. I cannot answer for them, but would say that I see behavior as a part of personality and that if the behavior change is an enduring one, then for me that would constitute a change in part of the personality. The critical reader may also well ask "how does one get a self-concept in the first place?" I am not certain how Secord and Backman would answer this, but I will provide my conception of the relationship between the social environment and the development in the next chapter.

Centricality

Secord and Backman (1965) rather briefly allude to an *intersystem* aspect of personality stability. Recognizing that S is in a number of *different* dyadic interpersonal systems *at the same time*, they suggest that any particular personality attribute (aspect of the self-concept) is stable to the degree that it fits in a congruent relationship in *all* of the systems. For example, a child functions in interpersonal relationships with his mother, his teacher, and his peer friends simultaneously. If all respond to him as a smart, attractive, trustworthy person, and if this fits his self-concept, congruency is enhanced. Stability is a function of not only the *number* of congruent systems, however, but also their relative importance. For the young child, his parents will probably have higher salience than any number of peers. Also, attributes vary in importance depending on their criticalness for the current self-concept. An adolescent boy may value masculinity much higher than kindness because it is more crucial for his self-concept at his age. The term centricality is applied to summarize these three forces which strengthen the stability of the attribute: (1) the number of different congruent systems, (2) the value of Os in those different systems, and (3) the value of the attribute in question for the self-concept. If Johnny, his mother, his teacher, and 15 of his peers think he is a "good leader," then the centricality of his leadership in interpersonal systems would be very high. In other words, the centricality of an attribute is reflected in the degree to which salient congruent interpersonal systems coincide. The higher the centricality the greater the stability. If, nonetheless, a high centrical attribute *is* changed, this will have a wide "ripple" effect upon his other interpersonal systems and upon S's personality in general.

Institutional Forces for Personality Change

Two institutional forces will be discussed: status passage and what I call role latitude.

Status Passage.   Here Secord and Backman refer to the progression of changing expectancies for a person, depending on his office or role in the institutional structure. As a child grows older, for instance, the expectations of others toward him progressively change: from being at home to being in kindergarten, from sixth grade to junior high, from junior high to high school, etc. Passage through occupational positions also pulls expectations for different kinds of behaviors, e.g., bank teller to bank president. As the individual passes from one position to the next, he is confronted with a concerted change in the behaviors of others toward him. These are strong pressures for him to change in response.

Role Latitude (as I call it).   This is discussed by Secord and Backman as referring to the degree of freedom that a position in an institutional structure allows to the individual to carry out his role activities. This defines his "niche breadth" in the structure. The wider the latitude the less impact institutional role expectations have on the individual and the less force they have in changing his personality. This latitude is frequently a function of the clarity of role expectations: the more clear the expectations the less the latitude. One can engage in a wider variety of activities as a community psychologist than as a clinical psychologist because very few people know what a community psychologist *should* be doing!

Implications

What are the implications of Secord and Backman's theory for defining social system impact upon the individual?

1. The theory further emphasizes, as did Katz and Kahn and Sarbin, with its focus on congruity, the importance of compatibility between the person's self-concept and the social system's perception of and expectations for him. The process of selective interaction further implies that the individual *actively* seeks congruent systems and avoids incongruent systems.

2. The theory further emphasizes the importance of the position required for the individual by the social system. A position with wide role latitude reduces social system impact, and probably increases the opportunity of high need satisfaction for a wider variety of persons in that position.

3. The emphasis that a change in the interpersonal system will require changes of some kind in the individual would suggest that social systems *can* upgrade social identities by concerted changes in responses and expectations toward the person. The success of many behavior modification programs in classrooms bears testimony for this point.

4. The concept of centricality, particularly, points out that it is not enough to look at the impact of any one social system upon an individual. He is a member of several systems and their expectations of him may differ cosnsiderably between systems. This requires that the impact of the *network* of social systems upon the individual be examined.

5. Secord and Backman's description of the congruency processes emphasizes the importance of the individual's

cognitive functioning in mediating the impact of the social system upon him.

CARSON: INTERPERSONAL
INTERACTION PROCESSES

Robert C. Carson (1969) has presented a brilliant integration of exchange theory, social learning theory, and information-processing theory and produced a fresh look at social behaviors in a dyadic interpersonal system. My only significant disappointment with Carson's theory is the restriction to two-person systems.

Carson suggests that interpersonal behaviors are determined by a number of forces. Among these forces are: (1) the rewards and costs of a particular relationship, (2) the person's stable and enduring interpersonal style, (3) the regulation of role behavior by social norms, and (4) cognitive plans and goals.

Interpersonal Payoff Matrix

This concept says that a person has both potential rewards and potential costs in his relationship with another person. Each person engages in those behaviors which maximize the probability that the other will react toward him with behaviors which are rewarding to himself. Each has a set of preferred interpersonal behaviors and preferred responses from others. Each wishes to maximize the opportunity for his preferences and minimize either the reduction of his own favored behaviors or the production of nonpreferred responses from the other. Any interpersonal behavior has some degree of potential cost and some degree of potential benefit, and these potentials are different in different relationships. The payoff in a particular relationship (as between John Smith and Mary Moore) depends on the specific preferences (generalized interpersonal styles) of the two individuals.

Generalized Interpersonal Style

This refers to a set of largely habitual interpersonal behaviors which predominate in a person's relations with many other persons. These behaviors persist across different dyadic relationships. Thus, John Smith's style may consist largely of friendly, dominant behaviors which he enacts not only with Mary Moore, but also with Jerry Jones, Fred Johnson, and Priscilla Goodbody.

Why do these behaviors become habitual and, therefore, a style? Carson proposes that a style is adopted because it consistently evokes certain preferred responses from the other. These consistent responses from the other are preferred in that they serve to maintain and enhance the person's experience of security. Carson assumes that it is in the very nature of interpersonal behaviors that one particular style will fairly consistently pull the same kind of complementary response. On the basis of considerable empirical data he adopts Leary's (1957) classification of interpersonal behaviors on two central dimensions: *control* (dominance—submission) and *affiliation* (love—hate). If John engages in hateful behavior, he will receive hateful behavior in return; if he engages in submissive behavior he may receive dominating behavior in response. Carson suggests a natural fit or complementarity between style and responses. This fit is on the basis of reciprocity with respect to the control dimension, on the basis of correspondence with respect to the affiliation dimension. Thus, generally speaking, dominance pulls submission, hostility pulls hostility, friendliness pulls friendliness, and submission pulls dominance (see Figure 2). To some degree, complementarity is in itself mutually reinforcing. The prime reinforcement value of the style, however, is that it evokes or prompts behavior from the other which maintains security. This security may depend upon congruency between self-concept and behavior from the other (this is similar to Secord and Backman's position, i.e., security may be a function of predictability). At any rate, because of a

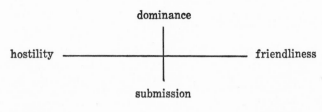

Figure 2   Complementarity of interpersonal behavior

person's experiences, certain interpersonal responses to him are more rewarding than others. He will persist in enacting those behaviors which evoke the desired responses.

Carson only briefly deals with personality development or the early acquisition of interpersonal style. He offers that it is highly likely that children learn to respond to their parents in complementary ways by dint of having little opportunity for escaping their parents' evocations. Presumably in most cases complementary responses by children were more frequently rewarded than were anti-complementary responses. The parent-child complementary behaviors (e.g., parent being friendly—dominant, the child being friendly—submissive) then became habitualized and were incorporated into the person's interpersonal style. This suggests that parental behaviors toward the child—when security enhancing—become prototypes for later preferred reeponses from others.

Becker's (1964) review of the consequences of parental behavior generally gives confirmation to the idea of typical complementarity of child response. Parents who were defined as being restrictive and hostile (Carson's hostile—dominant) were more likely to have children who were self-aggressive, socially withdrawn, had signs of internal "neurotic" problems, were shy and quarrelsome with peers—that is, the children showed behaviors which would generally fit Carson's "hostile—submissive" category and were complementary to those of their parents. Parents who were generally categorized as being permissive and hostile (Carson's hostile—submissive) were likely to have children who were highly aggressive, non-compliant, and most likely to become juvenile delinquents—behaviors which generally fall into the hostile—dominant quadrant, and again would be complementary to hostile—submissive parental behavior. Parents who were warm and restrictive (Carson's friendly—dominant) tended to have children who were submissive, compliant, dependent, unfriendly, uncreative, and rule enforcers with peers—behaviors which would generally fall into the hostile—submissive quadrant, which is not complementary since the friendly parental behavior should pull friendly behavior from the child. Parents who were warm and permissive (Carson's friendly—submissive) tended to have children who were creative, socially assertive, independent, friendly and outgoing, and somewhat lacking in persistence—behaviors which generally would fall in the friendly—dominant quadrant and again would be in a complementary relationship to their parents' behavior.

The beginning, ending, and maintenance of dyadic relationships are founded upon the foregoing processes. If John Smith has a general interpersonal style of friendly—dominant behaviors, he anticipates a rewarding relationship with Mary Moore to the degree that he receives friendly—submissive responses from her, and the relationship will be maintained to the degree that these responses continue. Should Mary respond with the maximally anticomplementary response of hostile—dominant behaviors, the relationship would soon be terminated if John has any choice in the matter.

Through this selective interaction process, John attempts to homogenize his social environment. To the degree that he has choice of relationships, he will be able to maintain the interpersonal responses which are complementary and desirable

to him. His personality would thus remain stable to the degree
that he is successful in homogenizing his social relationships.

Social Norms

A third force which influences the behaviors within an interpersonal relationship consists of social norms which regulate
role behaviors. This force is independent of the particular
reinforcement histories or styles of the two persons; it is an
impersonal power source which prescribes acceptable sets of
behaviors for the role in question. Being in the role of "child"
permits the person a variety of behaviors not tolerated in the
"adult" role. The role also prescribes how the other is to
respond. Social norms prevent many forms of physical exploitation of persons in child roles.

Social norms may facilitate or conflict with generalized interpersonal styles. If the prescribed role behaviors coincide with
the person's interpersonal style, the person is in a sense
enlisting impersonal normative power in the support of his own
security maintenance. In contrast, if role and style requirements
conflict, the person bears the brunt of the impersonal normative
power to change. A role may, then, be either personally
rewarding or personally costly. The central idea here, again, is
that the "goodness-of-fit" between system requirements and
individual need satisfaction influences individual behavior.

Social norms account for a large part of the variability in
relationship behaviors by prescribing situation-specific appropriate behaviors. That is, relationship behaviors are different
in different situations. The relationship behaviors between a
man and wife in bed, where role expectations are rather indefinite, can then be very different from those at church where
role expectations are much more definite.

Image and Plans

Carson uses the information-processing model described by
Miller, Galanter, and Pribram (1960) which assumes man to be a

purposeful, decision-making organism whose behavior is importantly influenced by general plans and feedback mechanisms. The concept of "image" refers to a cognitive map which includes all of the person's experience and all his information about his world. It also includes his values. The image is not fixed but changes with additional experience and information (it is an open system concept). Images define the desired end state of plans. Or, in other words, images contain goals.

Plans are essentially programs designed to achieve goals defined by the image. The basic Plan unit is called a TOTE (Test—Operate—Test—Exit). A Plan may include any number of TOTE units depending on its complexity. For example, suppose the simple desired end state (contained in the image) is to saw off the end of a board to make the end perfectly square (curiously, this model seems to elicit carpentry examples). As the carpenter saws he must continually match his saw blade with the sawline. One TOTE unit would be: Test (observe and compare saw blade with saw-line)—Operate (saw)—Test (compare again)—Exit (terminate sawing if discrepency is too great). This TOTE unit is nested within a larger TOTE unit: Test (compare saw-line with square)—Operate (saw)—Test (compare sawed-off end with square)—either Exit (if sawed-off end is square) or Operate again (if sawed-off end is not square, draw a new line, saw again, etc.).

Applied to interpersonal behavior, of central importance is the Image of Self, or the accumulated information and values which have contributed to a concept of self. One's behaviors and the responses of others to one's behaviors are matched up against this Image of Self. Behaviors and responses from others which are compatible with the Image of Self are maintained, those that do not fit are somehow modified, or eliminated. Or, in some cases the Image of Self itself will be modified.

The point here is that Carson is including a subjective cognitive component in his theory. Its exact relationship to the general interpersonal style is somewhat unclear, but it seems logical that the reinforcement history of various interpersonal encounters over one's lifetime, along with the gradual accumulation of a value system, becomes "known" to the individual in a cognitive form. He has an idea of what kind of person he is and should be. This idea then serves him as a guide and as a standard against which to choose and to evaluate his behavior.

Personality Change

Carson discusses personality change for the most part within the context of psychotherapy. Personality change would result from responses by the therapist which were anticomplementary. These therapist behaviors should be very different from those typically "pulled" by the patient's general interpersonal style. Eventually these anticomplementary reactions by the therapist would require different behaviors from the patient, i.e., changes in interpersonal style, and changes in the Image of Self. This experience of atypical interpersonal responses would contribute new information to the Image, and ideally lead to a modified Image of Self. (The therapist must manage to send back anticomplementary responses and at the same time keep the patient from leaving therapy. The "costs" of changing for the patient must be at least balanced by other benefits from therapy.)

Disordered Personality

Carson's position defines personality disorder in terms of behavior which deviates from social norms in ways that lead others to decry the behavior as abnormal. Such behavior violates *reified social norms,* by which Carson apparently means nearly universal criteria as to the correct nature of reality and the correct rules of decency. Examples of such rule breaking would be: running naked in the street; displaying one's genitals in a public place; committing incest; bizarre murders; talking about unreal things as if they were real, etc.

Other characteristics of disordered behavior include: (1) the violation of social norms must be labeled and explained by others as being the result of abnormality; (2) the behavior must be *rigidly* inappropriate, that is, it continues to be displayed in appropriate situations such as talking strangely in all situations (in the absence of other sources such as alcohol); (3) the behavior must be *extreme* in intensity or amplitude—one is not only sad, one cries and wails for long periods of time.

Carson places the cause of personality disorder in the interpersonal pay-off matrix. One engages in disordered behavior because its benefits are much higher than its costs for that person. Such benefits might include attention, gratification of dependency needs, or avoidance of responsibility and demands, etc. It may be that the "crazy" behavior somehow is congruent with one's Image of Self. Basically, Carson's view here is consonant with that underlying behavior modification techniques: one exhibits those behaviors which are reinforced— "crazy" behavior has been rewarded. Carson cites the research by Braginsky and Braginsky (1967) as evidence that disordered behavior serves a function for the person. Thirty "chronic schizophrenics" were randomly selected and then randomly assigned to three different experimental situations: in one the patients were to be interviewed to see if they "might be ready for discharge from the hospital"; in the second situation patients were interviewed only to see if they should be on open or locked wards (all were on open wards at the time)—there was no indication that hospital discharge was a possibility; the third situation was presented to the patients as being an interview to see how the patient was doing, i.e., implicitly to consider hospital discharge. The researchers casually told each patient these reasons prior to the interview by a panel of psychiatrists. The researchers predicted that the patients would present themselves as seriously mentally ill in the two discharge situations in order that they might remain in the hospital, but as much "healthier" in the open or locked ward situation in order to maintain their open ward privileges. These predictions were confirmed. Carson cites additional research (Artiss, 1959; Braginsky, Grosse, & Ring, 1966; Braginsky, Holzberg, Finison, & Ring, 1967; Braginsky, Holzberg, Ridley, & Braginsky, 1968; and Fontana & Klein, 1968) which indicates that the "mental patient" has considerable control over his symptomatic behavior.

It should be clear that for Carson, the designation of "disordered personality" is not referring to or the result of some internal state, or a mental sickness. Such behavior is the result of the individual's "non-fit" with societal role expectations. Therefore, it is actually imprecise to speak of the individual as being disordered. In actuality, it is a maladaptive relationship *between* the individual and societal expectations.

Carson recognizes *disordered social systems,* or those systems where two or more persons develop relationships that are governed by norms which violate reified societal norms. A family system may teach a child to engage in behaviors reinforced within the family, but these behaviors violate societal norms and as a consequence the child soon becomes labeled as abnormal. His behavior is adaptive within the family, maladaptive outside it.

Implications

What are the implications of Carson's thinking for defining the social system impact upon an individual?

1. More specifically than Katz and Kahn, Sarbin, or Secord and Backman, Carson portrays the ways that particular persons in social systems affect the individual's behavior. That is, in the interpersonal pay-off matrix, we cannot talk simply of roles or offices or statuses, but must speak of specific persons with very

specific reinforcement histories and predispositions to certain interpersonal responses. Carson peoples social systems with personalities that must be reckoned with.

2. To change an individual's personality, others in his social system must alter their customary ways of behaving toward him. Social systems, then, should be able to change individuals, for better or worse.

3. Carson implies that the individual actively seeks to elicit security-enhancing responses from his social environment. He is not passively reacting, he is striving to improve his chances for receiving desired responses. He attempts to act on his environment, not simply to be acted upon.

Carson's description of the complementarity-anticomplementarity of interpersonal behaviors is attractive. I remain somewhat sceptical because it is so difficult to confine actual personality styles of unique individuals within only the two dimensions of control and affiliation. These two dimensions do seem particularly relevant to consider, however, as social system contributions to the individual's interpersonal needs.

5. Carson further emphasizes points made by the other three positions: (a) the importance of the "fit" between the individual and social expectations; (b) the importance of differences in social system expectations for the individual (e.g., the disordered family versus society), or the importance of a *network viewpoint;* (c) the importance of *cognitive* operations in the mediation of social system effects upon the individual.

3. INDIVIDUAL—SOCIAL-SYSTEM NETWORK TRANSACTIONS

The conceptual framework of this chapter will aim somewhat beyond (in the sense of complexity) the two-person relationship as emphasized by Carson and by Secord and Backman, and somewhat short of (in the sense of broadness) the norms, roles, and statuses emphasized by Sarbin and by Katz and Kahn.

This will be an open system conception. It assumes that personality is a function of active transactions between the individual and his environment. This viewpoint does not accept personality as being integumented, as being a process which is only internal for the individual. As such, this framework clearly joins the ranks of the situational or environmentalistic theories. By such an orientation, and by such associations, this position risks a danger most clearly stated by Allport (1960), that of demeaning the value and uniqueness of the individual.

For me, this issue most clearly boils down to the time-worn, unresolved debate of individual free-will versus environmental determinism. I will not presume to decide this old issue here; this treatment will not assist the purists nor satisfy the polemicists. My only ambition is to preserve *proactivity* (man acts upon his environment, he is not exclusively a reactor) for the individual in the face of powerful and continual environmental pressures.

I do see the individual as being primarily a prisoner of his past. Primarily but not exclusively. I cannot accept some notion of an innate organ of free choice developing independent of environmental influences. I can conceive of an individual developing a facility for organizing, for seeing new relationships, for evaluating his previous experiences; and that this process is the result of an interaction between genetic characteristics and his experiences. Each individual's experiences are obviously unique to him; his particular integration of experiences is also unique to him. Using his organizing and evaluating facility, the individual selects from alternatives. This choice is not "free" in the sense of being independent of experience and environment. But it is not exclusively reactive, as a previously programmed robot might react every time to a prescribed stimulus. There is not a simple ubiquitous connection between previous environmental stimulation and current response; there *is* the complex monitoring and mediating process that includes highly symbolic values and goals which determines the final response. While the individual remains a prisoner of his past, he is not simplistic, passive, or exclusively reactive. He acts upon his environment. *He is a proactive captive.*

CONCEPTS

Overview of Concepts

This framework adopts a *complex-man* position. It considers there to be no universal top priority need, nor a universal ordering of needs. I would not believe, for instance, that self-actualization is the ultimate or the highest priority need for all men, nor that affiliation is of more basic importance to all men than achievement. From this view, a social system is required to respond to a wide variety of need priorities in its members.

Rather than speaking of needs internal to the individual, I prefer to consider man as basically a problem-solver. He is in constant negotiation with his environment over the solving of *problem-areas*. For different individuals, different problem-areas are of paramount concern, some have been virtually solved while others are constantly requiring new efforts. For some, none of the problem-areas is ever even near solution. The four problem-areas upon which we will concentrate are: survival, affiliation, control, and achievement. These four are not thought to cover all possible problem-areas, they are expected to be frequent importance for the social-system— individual relationship. They will serve an illustrative function for this framework.

The cognitive components for this framework include the *Idealized Problem Solution* and the *Realized Problem Solution*. The Idealized Problem Solution is similar to the "Image" of Miller, Galanter, and Pribram (1960). It is the current collection of information and values that an individual has with respect to each problem-area and it is modifiable with added experiences (e.g., Rokeach, 1971). The Idealized Problem Solution is a goal, it refers to the individual's current idea of the best solution for each problem-area. For example, for one person marriage may be seen as the ideal solution to the affiliation problem-area, to another person the ideal solution might be to have a series of intense but short-lived relationships. The Realized Problem Solution is the current successfulness of the solution as perceived by the individual. The greater the discrepancy between the Idealized and the Realized Problem Solutions, the greater the intrapersonal discomfort. When the two are nearly matched, that problem-area is virtually solved, at least for a time, and then the person will turn to concentrate on another problem-area in which there is a greater discrepancy. As there is constant flux in the environment, solutions to problem-areas are not typically permanent but will require continual modification and "shoring up" in response to the environmental changes.

The particular "place" or "niche" for the individual in a social system I will call a *system assignment*. This term is very similar in meaning to "role" but is considered to be specific to the particular social system and to the particular individual and would not be the same even in similar social systems. For example, a superintendent's "role" would have generality beyond any one particular school system. However, the *system assignment* of "superintendent" for John Jones in the Oakview Public Schools would have many unique features not found in other school systems nor for other individuals. A system assignment is delineated largely by the social system. One's system assignment can abet or it can handicap one in the solving of problem-areas, or it can be a neutral influence.

Goodness-of-fit will refer to the match between an individual's system assignment in a particular system and his high priority Idealized Problem Solutions. First, assume that Bob Wilson's highest priority prolem-area is achievement. Second, assume that his unique preferred solution is to receive a high degree of respect from others and to have authority over many others. Third, assume that his occupational system. assignment at General Motors, as he enacts it, requires only a modest amount of respect from others and gives him authority over only two people. For Bob Wilson, the goodness-of-fit in this system assignment is a moderately "bad" fit. Obviously, "bad" fits for high priority problem-areas create more psychological discomfort than those in low priority areas.

The individual—social-system relationship is further complicated by the fact that an individual is psychologically "in" a number of different social systems and system assignments at the same time. His psychological state is further affected by the match between the expectations of his several *different* system assignments. If one system assignment requires aggressive behavior but the other system prohibits aggressive behavior, he is in a conflicted match. This is similar to the interrole conflict described by Katz and Kahn. The nature of the match among system assignments will be referred to as *intersystem accommodation* (Murrell, 1971a). A *competing* intersystem accommodation refers to system assignments which are mutually opposing. A good match, or an *infusing* intersystem accommodation, refers to system assignments which coincide in their requirements for the individual. It is very difficult to "improve" the lot of an individual in one system while he remains confronted with severe obstacles to problem-solutions in another system (for example, mental hospitals versus families; or classrooms versus families). However, the psychological impact of the congruence between system assignments depends on the goodness-of-fit with the person's high priority preferred problem-area solutions. An infusing accommodation for "bad" fit assignments compounds the person's psychological discomfort.

The impact of a *network* of social systems upon an individual is, then, the result of the interlocking between these different components:

1. The requirements of the social system assignment interlock with the requirements of the individual's cognitive components (his Idealized Problem Solution for each problem area and his preferred strategies for solution). This "goodness-of-fit" is *good* to the degree that the system assignment allows the state of the Realized Problem Solution to advance closer to the Idealized Problem Solution; it is *bad* to the degree it increases the discrepancy.

2. The requirements for an individual of his system assignment in system A interlock with the requirements of his assignment in system B; and this intersystem accommodation interlocks with the individual's preferred problem-area solutions and strategies.

3. The optimal psychosocial condition for the individual is to have an infusing intersystem accommodation among social systems that contribute good fits between his system assignments and his preferred solutions in his high priority problem-areas.

The "Complex-Man" Assumption

Schein (1965) has described a "complex-man" assumption in contrast to other assumptions about "primacy" motives of individuals in organizations. One primacy view is that the individual is motivated primarily by *economic rewards*. This is basically an exchange theory; the individual "sells" his contributions to the organization for monetary return. This view is overly simplistic, failing to recognize other needs and also failing to recognize the symbolic attributes of money—i.e., an individual may value money not only for the material possessions it makes possible, but also because of the status it reflects, and in some cases because of the power it may provide or the autonomy it may protect.

Another primacy assumption emphasizes the importance of *social needs*. Beginning with the Hawthorne studies (e.g., Roethlisberger & Dickson, 1949) demonstrating that individuals would in fact work less and make less money in favor of social pressures and needs to belong, the view that a man's work group was particularly influential on his behavior became widespread and stimulated much research. Schein suggests, however, that these studies revealed that the economic motive is not very general, but also that the social motive is not universal.

A third primacy assumption stresses that the individual's highest priority is his need for *self-actualization*. This term refers to needs for psychological growth, for autonomy, for having the experience of maximally using one's self in a very involved way. This conception was developed from obervations by such psychologists as Maslow, Argyris, and McGregor and asserted that much of the work in industrial organizations, particularly that on the line, had little meaning or challenge—it allowed for no expression of self. However, there is evidence that indicates that while such higher order needs as self-actualization may be important at higher echelons of organizations, such needs are not necessarily primary at all levels or for all workers (e.g., Hulin & Blood, 1968; Vroom, 1960).

Schein concludes that each of these three assumptions suggests oversimplified and generalized conceptions of man; he suggests that choosing any one of the three would be to choose an incomplete model. He prefers a "complex-man" model which emphasizes a multiplicity of needs, and accepts wide variation among individuals as to the primacy of their different needs. Others, for example Seiler (1967) and Lawrence and Lorsch (1969), similarly conceive of individual motivation in terms of a complex system of biological needs, psychological motives, values, and perceptions.

Lawrence and Lorsch (1969) add another motive which they call a "desire to use problem-solving abilities." They recognize the pitfalls of suggesting another general and primary motive, however, and proceed to place their model into a systems framework which recognizes the interacting relationship between the individual and the organization. First, they suggest that the individual's system of motives, values, and perceptions develops as a product of the interaction between the biological factors of his system and the various experiences and problems he has confronted and resolved from infancy up to and continuing in his adult life. Thus, while all individuals endeavor to solve problems facing them, their experiences and biological characteristics are different, thereby leading each individual system to develop different patterns of needs, values, and perceptions, and different priorities.

Usage of the problem-area concept avoids the connotations of universal needs and universal hierarchies of needs. It asserts that each individual is continually confronted with problems that arise from conflicts between environmental factors and his own internal factors. The relative importance of these problems to an individual, the solution he most prefers, the strategies he is most likely to employ, are determined by the combination of his particular current circumstances and unique previous experiences.

While I assume no universal hierarchy of problem-areas—one individual may be most concerned about control, another may be most concerned about achievement—I do assume a hierarchy for each individual. And I assume that these different problem-areas have greater importance at different stages of the individual's physical and psychological development. I assume that his experiences at these stages do play an important role in the structuring of problem-areas, but also that the effects of these early experiences are not irremediable.

The Problem-Area Concept

The problem-area notion is embedded in the context of man as a problem-solver. There are areas in which the person is trying to accomplish some end, to reach some goal; he is trying to attain some Idealized Solution. But the person cannot accomplish this end independently; the environment plays an essential part. The environment can help or hinder the accomplishment, it can provide opportunities that facilitate attaining the desired end, it can pose obstacles that block the desired end. The word "problem" in problem-area refers to the general problem of accomplishing the desired end. Problem-*area* refers to the area of accomplishment that is of concern to the person. It is the area of negotiation with the environment for the accomplishment of the Idealized Solution for that area of concern.

These areas will be labeled with terms often associated with the concept of "need," e.g., survival, affiliation, control, achievment, etc. I prefer to use "problem-area" since need has the connotation of being exclusively an individual internal state. "Problem-area" should convey that these are areas of concern about which the individual must negotiate with the environment.

Problem-areas as areas of concern connote no universal desired solution. Each individual has his own preferred solution. Also, there is no assumed universal hierarchy of areas of concern. Each individual has his own priority of problem-areas, each has his own preferred solutions, and each has his own preferred strategies or methods for attaining his solutions.

In short, each individual has his own unique preferred methods of *problem-management*. Bill Sloane may have as his preferred affiliation solution that of being alone with infrequent contacts with others. His preferred strategy would be to avoid situations involving "small talk" or unproductive (to him) spending of time in social interchange. Frank Jones may have as his preferred affiliation solution that of always being with someone, of always having someone to talk to. His strategy is to seek out gatherings which provide opportunities for social interchange, to be outgoing and friendly to everyone, and to always be available for others to talk with about anything. Thus, a problem-area may be of high priority for two given persons by their respective Idealized Solutions and preferred strategies may be diametrically opposite.

The order of priority of problem-areas, the preferred Idealized Solutions, the preferred strategies, all can change over time. They change as a function of individual performance and the differntial responses of the environment to that performance. Bill Sloane may change when he meets "the right girl." Frank Jones may change when people begin to perceive him as a boring windbag and avoid him rather openly and rudely.

The person's priorities and preferences for his problem-management serve to structure his processing of information given off by the environment. His problem-management preferences "program" his scanning and searching for opportunities and obstacles in the environment. He seeks ways of reducing the distance between his Realized Solution and Idealized Soution, he is vigilant against threats that would widen this distance. All the time he is receiving continous feedback from his environment which is then compared with his present problem-management "program." This feedback will, when there is a significant discrepancy, demand some change by the individual or environment: the individual may change to another environment; he may change the order of his priorities; he may alter his Idealized Solution; he may change his preferred strategies; he may effect a change in the environment so that it responds to him in a more fitting way.

The four areas of survival, affiliation, control, and achievment which have been used here are *examples* of problem-areas. There are many other problem-areas of greater concern to various individuals and populations. For the sake of clarity, I will continue to use these four as examples of problem-areas, but this should not be taken to mean that they are the only problem-areas or that they are the most important problem-areas for all of mankind!

System Assignment

A person's system assignment defines the range of behaviors allowed, expected, and reinforced by the system. The person's assignment includes his interactions with other component persons, and his task-related behavior. His relative degree of power within the system is prescribed by his assignment. The person's assignment also defines the appropriate reactions to him by the system and by other component persons.

A system assignment is not static. It is continually undergoing redefinition. This results from the combination of the individual's particular Idealized Problem Solutions (goals) and strategy preferences; from system variables such as task requirements; from changes in the system and its interrelationships with other systems; as well as from other factors such as his age, time in the system, and newly added (or terminated) component persons.

For the individual, his assignment provides him with guidelines for behavior. In response to his behavior, the system may ignore, reward, restrain, or punish him as determined by its task and power variables. Thus, while the person's behavior is limited by his assignment, he is also informed as to what the system's response to his behaviors will be.

The individual's behaviors are not entirely prescribed by the system, however. Each person will "carry out" his assignment in a unique fashion depending on his preferred methods for his problem-management. One person may play it very conservative, staying well within the range of allowed and expected behaviors; another person may continually press against restraints, striving to modify the system's definition of his assignment. From his current interactions in other social systems, from his past interactions in social systems, and his past experience generally in problem-management efforts, the person has developed a particular set of priorites in his behavior repertoire and a particular set of values which he places on responses by others to him. One individual may place high value on esteem and respect, another person may desire equality and good fellowship, another person may desire power and autonomy, another may seek increasing certainty and structure, etc. In summary, the individual's behavior in his system assignment is a function of social system variables and his set of problem-area priorities and preferences. (This is basically a restatement of Lewin's (1951) formula: $B=f(P,E)$, or behavior is a function of intraindividual factors and environmental factors.)

For illustration, let us examine the fit between his system assignment in first grade and Jerry Jones's set of Idealized Problem Solutions. Jerry's solutions are modest. Achievement: to do well enough in everything so that he does not call attention to himself. Affiliation: to be quietly accepted, he wants to avoid being bullied or picked on or treated aggressively. Control: he desires no control over others, he prefers to take little responsibility or initiative, he desires direction from others. In Carson's classification he would be described as submissive and nonhostile (he is neither overtly friendly nor overtly hostile). Jerry is not a behavior problem in class. His intellectual resources are low relative to his classmates, he is not quick or clever. He tends to avoid doing his work if left on his own, but will respond agreeably when given clear directions.

By a happy combination of his teacher's intelligence and

sensitivity and the composition of his class, whose members are atypically tolerant, Jerry's fit in his classroom system assignment is a good one. His assignment has come to carry these special expectations: Jerry can do passing work if given sufficient direction and casual attention and encouragement; he should not be expected to handle a great deal of responsibility at one time, but could be given small amounts of gradually increasing responsibility if given careful instructions; he can be relied upon to meet the general classroom prohibitions against fighting or being verbally hostile, he will not give any trouble to others; he should not be singled out even for public praise, he should not be abused, he should not be teased or made fun of.

For Jerry, given his particular problem-managment "program," the fit into this system assignment is a good one.

The goodness-of-fit between the individual's problem-management preferences and his assignment in the social system determine the intensity of the "negotiations" between the person and the social system. However, to indicate that there are continual negotiations between the person and the system does not mean that these are always ongoing combative struggles. The fit may be quite good and the intensity of negotiations quite low; however, because of time and change in both the individual and the system, negotiations must be continuous in order to maintain even the best of fits.

Negotiations are not always effective. The gap between the person's problem-area priorities and preferences and the system's requirements may be so large that there are essentially no grounds for negotiations. When negotiations are ineffective, the person may elect to leave the system, or the system may elect to reject the person from the system. This occurs when alternatives within the system are limited and when other allegiances take precedence over the person's membership. The system may be unable to find a different system assignment more suitable to the person, the person may be unwilling or unable to compromise or to meet system demands. If alternatives are not available, the system may decide that the set of tasks of the system, or the maintenance of the system, are in jeopardy if the person remains in the system. For example, a graduate student may be dropped from his program because of his use of hard drugs, a child may be expelled from school because of defiant disruptive behavior, a man may be fired because he was insufficiently subordinate to customers. Or, if there are no other alternatives within the system for the person, he may elect to leave the system if he feels that there is another system which would offer more opportunities for his problem-managment preferences. A divorce may occur if one of the parties can no longer accept the relationship or when another relationship promises greater satisfactions.

Intersystem Accommodation

The match between different social systems in their expectations and demands upon the same individual has been discussed under the concept of intersystem accommodation. Every individual is in several social systems simultaneously. One cannot walk out of a social system, since it is not bounded physically; one remains psychologically "in" several different social systems at the same time.

The individual may be thought of as being a "linking pin" between different systems. His degree of comfort and effectiveness in that position may be enhanced, or reduced, by the nature of the accommodation between the different system assignments. If, for example, the classroom demands strict conformity, quietness, neatness, and a restriction of expression of opinion, and rewards these behaviors; yet the child's family encourages and rewards loud and unconventional expression, independence of opinion, and messes—that child is in a bind. The nature of this kind of intersystem accommodation is one of *competition*. The respective system assignments are mutually opposing. If a classroom expects and rewards good reading ability, high verbal comprehension, and strong motivation for abstract reinforcements (grades); and if the child's family is one in which reading is a frequent and high status activity, where vocabulary level of the parents is high, and where they reward the grades with large amounts of interpersonal attention and praise—that child is in good shape. This is an example of an *infusing* intersystem accommodation. The respective system assignments are mutually strengthening. Thus, the linking pin position, as it were, being a pressure point between different systems, could be unbearable due to being pulled in opposing directions, or it could be highly rewarding due to infusing reinforcements. See Figure 3.

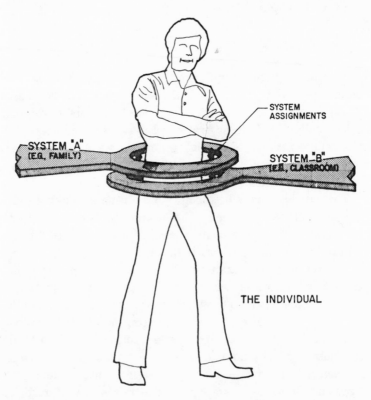

Figure 3   Intersystem accommodation. Artist: Robert Eurie

If the classroom makes no demands and has no expectations regarding religious beliefs, and if the child's family maintains strong and conventional religious beliefs and engages in conventional religious behaviors, there is no effect on the child. The intersystem accommodation with respect to religious behavior in this case is one of *compatibility*, the forces from the two different systems do not engage one another.

A concept that is related to, but different than, intersystem accommodation is that of *partial inclusion* which was developed by F.H. Allport (1933). This refers to the phenomenon that an individual is only partially involved in any one organization. An individual's role in an organization involves only a "slice" or "segment" of the individual—other parts of him are involved in other organizations. Katz and Kahn (1966), in discussing this concept, suggest that organizations may require that the individual put aside other "segments" of his self to meet organization demands. They then suggest that individuals are plagued by boundary problems in social organizations—that is, the individual may be using his wrong slice in the wrong organization. They state that the individual may be uncertain as to which system he is "in" psychologically at any one time.

This concept of partial inclusion implicitly recognizes that an individual is psychologically influenced by his membership in different systems, and that there may be conflicts between demands of different organizations—to this degree it is compatible with intersystem accommodation. The concepts differ in that partial inclusion suggests that an individual can be psychologically "in" only one system at a time, whereas intersystem accommodation assumes that an individual *cannot* choose to be *psychologically* in only one system at a time. Also, partial inclusion seems to suggest that an individual can be neatly divided up and parcelled out to different systems, which denies the unitary integration of individual personality. If this *were* the case, there would be no problems of different systems placing conflicting demands on an individual, since his separate "slices" could be independent.

Another related concept is that of *group status congruence* which has been described as the degree to which the person's status in one group is consistent with his status in a different group (Berrien, 1968). This concept refers to a group characteristic. If, for example, leadership roles in a group are given to seniors over freshmen (or to males over females, or to whites over blacks, or older over younger), this group has status congruence (with respect to ascribed status). If freshmen held leadership roles over seniors, the group would have status incongruence. Trow and Herschdorfer (1965) found status congruent groups to be superior to incongruent groups in production, satisfaction, and organizational stability. This concept reflects the core assumption of intersystem accommodation, namely: individuals are significantly affected by the match between the differing systems to which they belong. It also suggests that the nature of individual intersystem accommodations can affect the entire system, and can affect the accomplishment of the formal achievement task.

Summary of Concepts

1. The complex-man assumption: Men are motivated according to their specific individual experiences, expectancies, and values which have developed over a lifetime of encountering and attempting to master problems. This assumption eschews the principle of a universal hierarchy of needs, or that any one need has the same significance for all men.

2. The problem-area concept: For each individual there are a number of areas of particular psychosocial concern to him in which he is trying to accomplish some end. This end, goal, or Idealized Problem Solution is not necessarily particularly ambitious. In order to attain this end the individual must engage his environment. The environment can help or hinder his attainment of his desired end. The individual develops an order

of priority for these areas of concern, these problem-areas; he develops his own unique preferred solutions; he develops his own preferred strategies for obtaining these solutions. In short, he develops a preferred problem-management program. For any particular system, the individual's psychological comfort or satisfaction depends on the opportunities and obstacles offered by the system. His psychological comfort is a function of the goodness-of-fit between his system assignment requirements and his preferred problem-management program. As examples of problem-areas, I will refer henceforth to survival, affiliation, control, and achievement.

3. The concept of system assignment: The specific individual in a particular social system has a tailored "social niche" constructed from the social system's values, expectations, and tasks. It is constructed out of the system's history with other individuals in similar niches, but also from its particular history, expectations, perceptions, and evaluations of this very particular individual. This system assignment defines acceptable and nonacceptable behavior, it imposes constraints and prescriptions upon the individual, and it also guides him. The "goodness-of-fit" between individual and system assignment reflects the social system's success in providing opportunities for individual problem-management.

4. The concept of intersystem accommodation: This refers to the compatibility among different social systems in their system assignments for the same individual. This refers to the effects of the social systems *network* upon the individual. It refers to a "goodness-of-fit" *among systems.* An infusing (or mutually strengthening) intersystem accommodation, in which the individual—system-assignment fit is desirable to the individual (corresponds with his preferred problem management program), would maximize intrapersonal comfort and effective psychosocial functioning. Competing intersystem accommodations put the individual in a bind, lower intrapersonal comfort, and reduce the effectiveness of his psychosocial

functioning. An infusing intersystem accommodation among systems also has the effect of *freezing* the individual; it holds him tightly in nearly nonmodifiable system assignments. If the goodness-of-fit between the individual's problem management preferences and the system assignments of these infused systems is bad, the individual would be trapped in a position of high intrapersonal discomfort and ineffective psychosocial functioning. Individuals who are black, poor, and poorly educated would be examples of people who can find no systems which can offer better system assignments, all systems fixing them in the same kinds of system assignments.

A clarification may be needed here. The term "social system" has been used by many different writers, in many different ways, referring to many different types and sizes of systems ranging from dyads to nations. I define a social system as one which has *one* clearly defined formal achievement task and which is a component of a social network. A "social network," such as a community, has no one clearly defined formal achievement task and contains, in the geographical sense, many different interrelated social systems.

Individual Problem-Management (IPM) Contributions

At this point I would like to refine our terms somewhat and refer to the social system's *contribution* to individual problem-management. The particular contribution might serve to make such management more difficult or it might facilitate it. An innovative teacher in a strictly traditional school system may well be thwarted in managing her achievement problem-area, while an innovative teacher in an experimental educational setting might be able to give full vent to her achievement solution preferences and strategies, and thereby find it psychologically very rewarding. Henceforth, I will refer to this social sytem contribution as its Individual Problem-

Management contribution, or its IPM contribution. This will be contrasted later with the social system's formal achievement contribution.

SOCIAL SYSTEM INPUTS TO EARLY INDIVIDUAL PROBLEM-MANAGEMENT

It is not the purpose of this general conceptual framework to attempt a theory of personality development. It may help, however, to add flesh to the bones of these abstract concepts by describing what I assume to be fairly typical social system inputs to the individual's functioning during his early years.

Arrival

Some personality theories have assumed that personality determinants of infancy and early childhood are rooted in the mother-child relationship. The impression is sometimes left that the mother is the exclusive influence. This would be a closed, single system assumption—it suggests that mother and child are responding to one another as if in a vacuum. To counter this view I will emphasize the obvious—that the infant upon arrival is an involuntary member of a complex network of social systems.

First of all, at his birth the infant is given the system assignment of a "patient." In his first few days, responses to him are importantly influenced by *hospital* procedures.

Next, he joins the complex system of his immediate family. He is not just an infant, he is given a special place in the family constellation according to his sex and ordinal position (first born male, fourth born male with three brothers, third born male with two sisters, etc.) which by current evidence may itself be important in forming his personality characteristics (e.g., Sampson, 1965).

His mother relates to him not only as her son, but as his

father's son as well. Her responses to him are influenced by her relationship to his father and by the infant's place in their history (is baby the product of their collaborative design, or of her negligence, or his impulsiveness, etc.) Moreover, the responses to him by both parents are influenced by their membership in other systems. Mother may have a job or be in school. Her parental style may be importantly influenced by her current relationship with her mother. Father may be anxious or joyful about the baby depending in part on the status of his career or occupational security. Suffice it to say that the infant's early experiences are contributed to by a wide variety of social system influences of which the mother's responses are only a part (notwithstanding the more important part in most cases).

At birth the infant has a number of ascribed statuses: patient, infant, son, brother, grandson, tax deduction. His system assignments are only grossly defined, expectations for him are minimal. His behaviors are few and simple, his affect states are few but definite, he cannot yet make very fine discriminations. During his first year the following processes would typically evolve: his system assignment becomes increasingly specific in behavior constraints and encouragements; indefinite gross notions of Idealized Problem Solutions for survival and affiliation problem-areas begin to form; initial problem-management strategies in the areas of survival, affiliation, and control are tried; he is increasingly better able to make discriminations and associations.

The Initial Years

For the child's first year or so I will lean heavily upon the concepts used by social learning theorists (e.g., Bandura, Sears, etc.). Since he is without the aid of verbal mediators during much of this time, the infant's learning can be largely understood as simple associations between external stimuli and internal states. Comfort (being dry, well-fed, well-burped) comes to be associated with the presence of a certain pattern of auditory, tactual, and visual stimuli (a human being). This association becomes better (adult human being) and better (mother) differentiated, until the presence of mother has frequently coincided with his experience of comfort. Then, her presence by itself becomes a source of comfort and well-being.

The first problem-area which the infant faces is that of survival. In his experience, this problem is probably a dichotomy: a Very Good Feeling or a Very Bad Feeling. Because the human infant must depend on other human beings for survival, his survival problems very early also become affiliation problems. Affiliation problems would typically be basically derived from survival problems. Early management strategies for survival would become linked to strategies for affiliation problems. Idealized Problem Solutions for affiliation areas would be constructed from materials that had formed solutions for survival areas. For example, a common adult affiliation solution includes frequent sexual transactions with another person. Sexual components typically include warmth, tactile stimulation, and oral contacts which would also be involved in the early survival solutions. Interpersonal components such as intimacy, consideration, and trust, which may be part of a later affiliation solution, would also be consistent with early survival solutions.

During this first year or so the genetic characteristics of the child begin to interact with the perceptions and evaluations by others in the environment, e.g., "with her size she'll be a lady wrestler, . . . with his long fingers he'll surely be a piano player, . . . he's such a *good* baby, never fusses and sleeps all the time, . . . she looks just like her dad!"

Gradually and implicitly the child's system assignment becomes more specialized and unique. Increasingly, responses to him become much more than responses to a role (baby); he comes to have an individualized social identity in his family system and this special identity increasingly influences responses to his attempts at problem-management.

The control problem-area may develop for the most part out of the survival and affiliation areas. Originally, control solutions might develop out of survival and affiliation *strategies* rather than being directed at a particular control solution-goal. Some degree of affecting the environment would be necessary to achieve survival and affiliation solutions. The control problem-area and its solutions gradually come to have a meaning beyond their survival and affiliation strategy implications. Control comes to this higher importance as the child acquires verbal skills and comes to have greater motoric mastery of his environment. As the child acquires greater mastery, he also receives an increase in expectations from his family system. Greater independence is tempered with greater responsibility and more demands.

Toddlerhood

During the next four years or so a rather gross learning process occurs. Some problem-management attempts are actively reinforced, others actively punished by the family system. The child imitates the attempts by others, but also discovers that because of his particular system assignment that what "works" for his dad or older brother does not necessarily work for him. In a vague way he learns the values of the system. The family further refines his system assignment so that responses to him become increasingly refined and consistent. He learns which solutions are complimentary to family system responses to him (Carson, 1969).

Social norms and conditions contribute to his learning and to his preferred solutions. Survival for the young child in many American families is virtually solved so that this problem-area may require only occasional monitoring. Social norms typically facilitate affiliation solutions for the young child. Cuddling, hugging, kissing are all typically socially acceptable responses to young children, and it is considred improper parenting to leave a young child alone. Societal norms prescribe very limited control over others by the young child which may reduce the successfulness of assertive, dominating control-solutions.

While the most crucial years for the achievement problem-area solutions for most people are probably those between six and ten (Sontag & Kagan, 1963), there is also evidence of a relationship between parental behaviors during the preschool years and later achievement-related behavior (e.g., Crandall, Katkovsky, & Preston, 1960; Kagan & Moss, 1959; Winterbottom, 1958). Apparently values related to achievement begin to be transmitted at an early age from family system to child.

The preferred Idealized Problem Solutions to the different problem-areas develop interdependently. A strategy used to manage problems in the control area may be discarded because it conflicts with affiliation solutions (a refusal to obey a command may be met with physical punishment and implied threat to affiliative comfort). Strategies for the different problem-areas must be fairly compatible with one another to be retained in the individual's strategy repertoire. Gradually, these retained strategies may come to form what Carson calls a general interpersonal style.

During the toddlerhood period the child develops a hierarchy of importance to him of the different problem-areas, based largely upon the values of his family system and its differential reactions to his management efforts in the different problem-areas. For one child physical comfort may be primary, for another affiliation, for still another the control solutions may have the greatest significance. For each problem-area, the child develops a rudimentary preferred solution and a repertoire of strategies used to attain that solution. These strategies are rather crude, having been developed during a period when the child's abstracting and discriminating abilities are still rather limited.

For illustration, I offer the following example without making any claims for the generality of specific causal connections.

Billy Johnson has his survival problems quickly and efficiently solved by his family system. He is well-fed, clean, warm, and closely attended. His exploratory behavior is rather limited by his family in the interests of preserving his safety. He is not permitted to take risks. Physical contact with Billy is limited to the practical requirements of excellent physical care, and is not prolonged for the sake of enjoyment. Billy thus associates his well-being with the presence of a human being, but not with large amounts of tactile stimulation with that human being. As he grows older, his models (parents and siblings) demonstrate verbal friendliness and attentiveness but little physical affection. His self-initiated trial-and-error physical contacts are met with mild annoyance: "Oh, Billy, you're too big for that sort of thing," or "Don't crawl on me Billy, you'll mess up my skirt." (During the course of doing a psychological evaluation I once heard a father express concern abut his six-year-old son being a homosexual since he wanted to kiss his father's cheek before going to bed, as he did with his mother). Billy's early attempts at environmental mastery are met with verbal responses to the effect that he is too young and that he is *unable* to get along in his environment without help and that it is risky to try things on his own. His efforts at autonomy and disobedience are typically met with his being removed from the presence of these human beings and strong verbal disapproval. His requests for help and assistance, on the other hand, are usually met with attentiveness and verbal approval, and are frequently anticipated. Dependency behavior becomes linked to the very important human presence of his family members and becomes a preferred problem-managment strategy for survival and affiliation problem-areas. For these outcomes the family system received some social norm support for its effective solution of Billy's survival problems (Billy is "well looked after" as witnessed by his health, cleanliness, and good manners), but would have received no support, even opposition, from social norms for its limitation of physical affection.

By the time Billy was old enough to enter kindergarten his preferred Idealized Problem Solutions might well have been as follows:

Survival. Billy preferred complete physical safety and comfort. This problem was virtually solved and, therefore, was low in his hierarchy of importance.

Affiliation. Billy preferred being in the presence of his parents or siblings; he feared being alone. He sought friendly verbal approval but was discomfited by occasional physical affection. With his peers his preferred behaviors (problem-management strategies) were submissiveness, cautiousness, and helpfulness. He preferred being led to being a leader. His preferred solution with his peers was to be liked, to have many friends, to have his friends take the initiative and responsibility, and to avoid aggressive or physical behaviors.

Control. Billy preferred that he be taken care of, told what to do and when, and to have very clear structure so that he always knew what he should do. He wished to avoid having to take responsibility. His strategies were to repeatedly ask for help and direction, to refuse to try new activities and to complain in advance that he knew he could not do it. As a last resort, he would feign illness or injury to avoid being forced to try something new. As long as he was in his family system, Billy was able to attain his preferred solutions fairly readily. It was more of a difficulty with his peers who were rather unsympathetic to his claims of helplessness, or who sometimes grew weary of his dependency and withdrew their friendship. As he grew older, this problem-area grew higher on his hierarchy since he had increasing difficulty in attaining his preferred control solutions without costs to the affiliation area.

Achievement. The solution for this area was the least well developed for Billy and lowest in his hierarchy of importance. In his family system there had been little encouragement and some discouragement of achievement-strivings by Billy or by other members. Billy also had no outstanding natural abilities which might have strengthened his achievement interests. Generally, in keeping with his style of dependency, Billy's preferred solution was to avoid situations where achievement was called for. He wished to avoid the negative family behaviors likely to occur in response to achievement-striving on his part. Until he started school there had been very few social system demands upon him for achievement behaviors.

Before entering kindergarten, the discrepancy between Billy's Idealized Problem Solutions and his Realized Problem Solutions was small and his intrapersonal comfort was high. He had generally been successful in meeting the demands of the family social system. His resources had been adequate. He had managed a good fit.

The School Years

This period introduces the child to the following new transactions with his social network:

1. The impact of additional social systems—the classroom and the peer group—membership in which creates increasingly important intersystem accommodation issues for the individual.

2. The gradual modification of role expectancies which attend age and maturation changes (status passage).

Intersystem Accommodation. Prior to his entrance into school the influence of the family upon the child has typically been primary. The family's values and expectations and its system assignment for the child have had little competition (the increasing numbers of day care centers may soon change this). Upon entering the classroom social system, the child is exposed to new and different demands. His new system assignment includes classroom values and expectations, some of which may be very unlike those of his family.

The relative power of classroom systems upon individuals has only recently been recognized. Particularly for minority and disadvantaged children, the classroom system has been found to have a significant effect on achievement, for example. Note the following from the Coleman Report:

> "Finally, it appears that a pupil's achievement is strongly related to the educational backgrounds and aspirations of the other students in the school. Only crude measures of these variables were used (principally the proportion of pupils with encyclopedias in the home and the proportion planning to go to college). *Analysis indicated, however, that children from a given family background, when put in schools of different social composition, will achieve at quite different levels* (italics mine). This effect is again less for white pupils than for any minority group other than Orientals. Thus, if a white pupil from a home that is strongly and effectively supportive of education is put in a school where most pupils do not come from such homes, his achievement will be little different than if he were in a school composed of others like himself. But if a minority pupil from a home without much educational strength is put with schoolmates with strong educational backgrounds his achievement is likely to increase" (Coleman, et al., 1966, p. 22).

Himmelweit and Swift (1969) conducted a longitudinal study in England and concluded that information about the type of school that a child attended would enable better prediction of his later (it was an eleven-year follow-up) behavior, outlook, values, and attainments than would information about his I.Q. or his family's social background. They emphasize the importance of the school as a socializing agent.

There is also evidence (Bronfenbrenner, et al., 1965; Schmuck & Van Egmond, 1965) that teacher behavior and attitudes are equal to or even more salient than those of the parents with respect to influencing the child toward certain value positions.

Glidewell, et al. (1966) in their review present convincing evidence for a strong relationship between the child's position in the classroom social structure (based on emotional acceptance, personal competence, and social power) and his personality traits and behavior (without attributing causality to the classroom social structure).

All of the above are cited to substantiate the proposition that entrance into the classroom social system has a powerful impact on the child's problem-management.

As the child is faced with new information, values, and expectations, he must adjust these new influences to the old influences of his family system. He must, often, develop a process of compromising, of somehow fitting different, even mutually exclusive, expectations together.

The nature of the intersystem accommodation contributes to the individual's problem-management (IPM). For exmple, if Billy's kindergarten teacher expects him to be able to tie his own shoe laces, put on his own coat, etc., i.e., to be less helpless and dependent than his family system prescribes, then the nature of the intersystem accommodation is competitive. This then hampers his problem-management, particularly in the control problem-area. He must make adjustments in his family and/or his classroom system assignments, and perhaps his control Idealized Problem Solution. In the classroom system the discrepancy between the Idealized Problem Solution and his Realized Problem Solution will have been enlarged. This enlarged discrepancy will increase his feelings of intrapersonal discomfort. In some cases the child must subordinate the demands of one system in favor of another. This will, of course, incur certain "costs" in the lower-priority system. Thus, Billy might have to endure a certain degree of ridicule and chastisement in the classroom for his dependent, helpless behavior. In most cases, however, the child would in a sense negotiate with each system in order to bring about changes in both assignments. With regard to many behaviors the child will be assisted by social norms which call for different role behaviors in different settings and at different ages.

It is difficult for some persons to grasp or to accept the concept of intersystem accommodation. I think this is in part due to our tendency to "believe what we can see." That is, we are captured by our immediate sensory experiences, and what we cannot experience directly we tend to hold suspect.

Basic to the concept of intersystem accommodation is the assumption that an individual is affected psychologically by an environment he is not *in* physically. The individual carries the forces from this "not-present" environment with him—it is sort of a handbag of psychological forces. In our observations of such an individual, we would be unable to see these forces. For the individual, particularly a child, these forces are often so implicit, so unarticulated, that he himself is often not clearly cognizant of these forces or their origins. He too is more caught up in his immediate physical environment.

If you are willing to entertain the above assumption you may well ask just what exactly these "forces" are. I would include here values, expectations, task demands (broadly conceived), and habituated complementary interpersonal behaviors, which coalesce into a very implicit, largely unverbalized, set of rules. These rules serve as a kind of "sticky atmosphere" which clings to an individual long after he leaves the social system physically.

Our immediate sensory experience of being part of a social system is typically to see other separate individuals, unconnected and independent of one another and ourselves. We dc not "see" many of the system *qua* system characteristics. We do not see the implicit rules, the "sticky atmosphere" which psychologically binds these individuals into interdependent relationships. As a child these implicit rules become as familiar as the wallpaper; we are exposed to them constantly but rarely attend to them, rarely call attention to them, and rarely have them pointed out to us.

Of course, in addition to these implicit rules, social systems have very formal, explicit rules and public prescriptions and these are also part of the atmosphere or forces that we carry with us from the "not-present" system.

As a graduate student I became intrigued with family styles and family interaction patterns, particularly as they related to or caused psychological disorders. This interest, plus some experience as a family therapist, seemed to sensitize me to previously "unknown" characteristics of my own family. Gradually, during visits with my parents, and particularly when my sister was also present, I became aware of a pattern that marked our interrelationships. I played my parts naturally, relating this way to one, that way to another. I had certainly "learned" the rules although I had not "known" them in any explicit way before. These rules explained, I felt, much of my own interpersonal style or behavior. They also made me better aware of some of my own behaviors as a parent and of where those behaviors had originated. I had carried these rules unkowingly for many years and many miles distant from their source.

Status Passage. Secord and Backman (1965) use this concept to describe the changes which are prescribed by social norms for an individual's age or role progression. Social norms require different system assignments for different ages. This is a circumstance in which social norms *cause* personality change (see also Kahn, 1968, for a discussion of role changes in organizations and resulting behavior changes).

For example, consider the passage from childhood to adolescence for a girl in this society. The affiliation area becomes salient. The peer group system becomes increasingly important, the relationship with the family system may correspondingly become more troublesome. Previous system assignments in the family now no longer fit so well. Her preferences for problem solutions and her strategies are changing. Particularly, her Ideal Problem Solutions for affiliation and control are being modified. As a sexual object the adolescent girl becomes more protective of her body privacy from the male members of her family. She becomes both more wary of and more interested in the behavior of male peers. Also, her parents, teachers, and friends begin to value and expect more adult-oriented behaviors from her.

Status passage interacts with genetic characteristics (physical attractiveness obviously is an important resource for the affiliation area, for example). It also interacts with social system assignments and intersystem accommodation. The social system which can modify its assignments to be compatible with social age norms and which can provide some of the new resources needed for new demands will facilitate its members in their status passage. If her family can accept changes in dress, make-up, and in her behaviors toward them by the adolescent girl, and can offer such supports as compliments on her looks and accomplishments, can increase responsibility, and can decrease restrictions, it will be working *with* the social norms and will facilitate the girl's adaptation to the changing social norms.

DEGREES OF PSYCHOSOCIAL ACCORD

What are the implications of this conceptual framework for a definition of psychological adjustment, or maladjustment?

I believe the concept of "psychopathology" or any definition of a "disorder" exclusively within the person is misleading and not helpful. I would propose rather that each of us is in varying degrees of psychosocial accord with each of our social systems and in our total social systems network (I am indebted to Bob Silver for his help with this idea). Psychosocial accord is the degree to which the individual's problem-management preferences, as he sees them, and his unique set of resources are facilitated, enhanced, or supported by his social system assignments and the intersystem accommodation among those assignments. Psychosocial accord would then refer to the degree of "harmony" between the person's requirements and his network requirements. Such a condition would rarely reach an optimal match and even then it would be perfect only momentarily. Each of us must negotiate, try to improve our own problem-management program, try to change our systems to fit us better, or try to find new systems that will fit us better. This view is generally in agreement with the "engineering" conception of adjustment by Sechrest and Wallace (1967), although theirs attributes less responsibility to the environment.

For the individual for whom there is a low degree of psychosocial accord, or for whom there is a "discordant" fit, the *causes* lie in the relationship between the person's requirements and resources and the requirements of the social systems network. The *results* of such a discordant condition may be psychological discomfort; ineffective or unsuccessful functioning according to system requirements; or a "lack," lack of enjoyment, love, good fellowship, sense of achievement, etc., a condition of blandness, a chronic lack of really good feelings about oneself or others.

Persons with more limited resources or more atypical problem-management programs will have less choice of systems; there will be fewer systems that can provide them with good fits. For example, if persons labeled as "schizophrenic" are found to have physiological conditions that make them more vulnerable to stress than most people, their resources and problem-management program will require a low stress systems network. The cause of the problem is still located in the discordant fit, and the reduction of the problem is to be found in more consonant person-system fits.

This is not to deny that in the case of some discordant fits, the situation can be improved by strengthening the individual's resources or by changing his problem-management program, this is frequently the first response. However, in order to effectively change the individual so that he fits better, the requirements of what he is to fit into, of his systems network, must be well known (Murrell, 1971a). And, before a social system or systems network can be changed to be more facilitative of consonant fits, the IPM requirements of its population must be well known.

Kelly's Ecological Approach

The view that so-called "pyschopathology" is in actuality a condition of "bad-fit" is well described in James E. Kelly's work (1966, 1968). Kelly suggests that the aim of a community psychologist's interventions should be to rearrange the interrelationships between the social system structure and the individual. In one place (1968), Kelly discusses four variables relevant to the individual-system relationship: (1) individual coping styles, (2) adaptive role functions, (3) social setting structure, (4) environmental (population) characteristics. Kelly studied the interrelationship between high school students' coping styles (high versus low exploratory coping styles) and the rate of annual population exchange of the high school (or the number of new students coming in and old students going out each year). Kelly's premise was that students with high exploratory styles would adapt better to high exchange environments while students with low exploratory coping styles would adapt better to low exchange environments.

Thus, neither the kind of coping style nor the type of environment is "psychopathological" or "psychopathology-producing" *in itself*. The relationships between these two variables and the expected result are presented in Figure 4.

Now we shall look at commonly occurring limitations on psychosocial accord and some general strategies for improving it.

Limitations on Psychosocial Accord

No system can be all things to all men, and no individual can adapt to all systems. There are limiting conditions in both

| Individual | Environmental Characteristic | |
Characteristic	High Exchange	Low Exchange
High Exploratory	Psychosocial Accord	Psychosocial Discord
Low Exploratory	Psychosocial Discord	Psychosocial Accord

Figure 4   Individual and environmental characteristics and the psychosocial result for the individual. From Kelly

individuals and systems which act to impede good fits. Among these limiting conditions are individual resources.

Individual Ascribed Statuses.   One limiting condition which makes it difficult or impossible for an individual to get out of a psychosocially discordant network is his ascribed status: his skin color, his sex, his age, etc. It is difficult for a child to escape some form of classroom social system. An ascribed status can "lock in" an individual to a network discordant for him.

Individual Natural Abilities.   Individuals may have skills, physical qualities, aptitudes, intellectual styles, etc., that are inappropriate for the formal achievement task and role expectations of a system. A college president might be discordant as a prison warden. A psychotherapist might be discordant as a drill sergeant.

One's natural abilities may restrict one's choice of changing one's problem-area priority. If one has limited verbal and abstracting abilities, academic achievement would not be a realistic first priority problem-area solution. Cognitive abilities may also relate to an individual's effectiveness in assessing information from the environment, and in modifying his priorities, solutions, and strategies.

Individual Previous Experience.   Interrelated with his other resources are the individual's past experiences in other social systems which shape his expectations, priorities, solutions, strategies, and qualifications. These experiences are not assumed to be fixed and unchangeable, but they can act as both constraints and aides. They can act to prevent movement into or out of networks. They can affect one's degree of comfort in a social system.

Social systems also have a number of limiting conditions.

Heterogeneity of Population. The more diverse the IPM (individual problem-management) preferences of its population, the more difficult it is for the social system to provide opportunities for good fits for all. The greater the heterogeneity of population, the greater the resources and flexibility needed by the social system if it is to provide good fits.

Lack of IPM Sensors. Another network limitation is that there are often no mechanisms for providing accurate information on IPM preferences to the network power structure. There typically are not built-in ways to regularly and comprehensively assess system-population accord.

Conflict with Formal Achievement Tasks. Most social systems do not exist exclusively to respond to IPM preferences. They typically have a product, and a task assigned to them by some superior system. The requirements of the formal achievement (FA) task will often not correspond to IPM requirements, or at least to those of all individuals. At the same time the formal achievement task itself, and the survival of the social system, are very important to the IPM of some individuals. The task of the intervener is usually to improve responses to IPM requirements without totally disrupting the FA task or threatening the survival of the system. However, some modifications of the FA task requirements may still be possible within these constraints. In some cases a totally new system may need to be established with its FA task requirements tailored from the start to fit the IPM preferences of a certain group or population.

Strategies for Improving Psychosocial Accord

In view of these limitations, what steps can be taken to improve individual-system fits? A detailed discussion of different kinds of interventions will be presented in Chapter Six. For now, the following different strategies are suggested as possible general responses to the above limitations.

1. Improvement of individual or population resources. One strategy is to change the individual so that he fits better into his present network. This could include such efforts as education, job training, psychotherapy, remedial reading, behavior modification, medication, etc.

2. Relocating the individual. Another strategy is to relocate the individual into a different system that can be more facilitative of his IPM requirements. This might include residential treatment settings, special education classes, foster-home placement, etc.

3. Modify system responses. A strategy for a particular system that creates psychosocial discord for many of its members unnecessarily (that is, its obstructions are not required by its FA task requirements) is to replace the discord-producing responses with those that fit its population better. To teach child-care techniques to mothers with little formal education, a child-development center may need to change from the lecture method to demonstration and role-play methods.

4. Modify system structures. For a long-lasting improvement, changes in the social system's structure would be advantageous. This might include building in new sensors or mechanisms that could routinely provide specific feedback on IPM concerns.

5. Create new systems. Special populations to which no present social network is now sufficiently responsive may need new systems especially suited to their characteristics. People migrating from rural Appalachia to Cincinnati may need special receiver systems to help them adapt to the urban habitat.

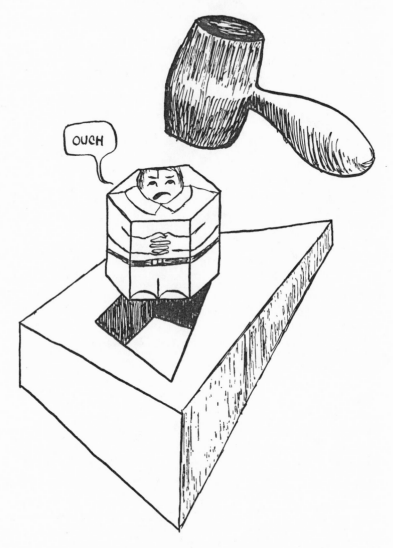

Figure 5   A discordant fit. Artist: Roseanne Reed

4. POPULATION—
SOCIAL-SYSTEM TRANSACTIONS

When the community psychologist plans an intervention he is concerned about the person-environment fit, about the fit between individual problem-management preferences and resources and the obstacles and opportunities presented to the individual by his social system network. However, for many practical reasons, when *implementing* an intervention the community psychologist must consider the fit between *population* and social systems. Population variables and social system variables and their interaction will be the focus of this chapter.

Social systems will be discussed at two levels in this chapter: (1) the stable face-to-face group and (2) the comparatively larger and more complex organization which would include more than one face-to-face group and a differentiated power hierarchy (some groups are subordinate to other groups). Population variables will include both group characteristics and the previously discussed Individual Problem-Management (IPM) variables.

The conceptual foundations for this treatment will include general systems theory, organizational psychology, and Barker's ecological psychology.

GENERAL SYSTEMS THEORY

From the viewpoint of General Systems Theory, a system is viewed as an organized whole unit which includes the interactions of its interdependent component parts and its relationship to the environment (Buckley, 1967). This emphasizes that the system functions as something other than the mere sum of its component parts; its *organization*, the relationship of its components to one another, must be recognized. This notion in itself is not new, having served as a basic postulate for Gestalt psychology, but it has been revitalized with the impetus of cybernitics and information theory.

Open and Closed Systems

Of particular importance is the distinction between "open" and "closed" systems. Open systems are "open" with respect to their environment; they exchange information, materials, energies, etc., with their environments. "A system is closed if there is no import or export of energies in any of its forms such as information, heat, physical materials, etc., and therefore no change of components, an example being a chemical reaction taking place in a sealed insulated container (Hall & Fagen, 1956, p. 23)."

Common Characteristics of Open Systems. Katz and Kahn (1966) list a number of open system characteristics. Among these are:

1. Importation of energy. There are inputs to the open system from its environment. By virtue of being open the system can receive materials, people, etc. Of particular importance to social systems is the import of information. In a sense, information in a social system is somewhat analogous to energy in a physical system.

2. The through-put. This refers to the activity of the system upon the energy, material, or whatever as it passes through the system. Via its work on the input, the open system reorganizes it, changes it, and thereby produces an output different from the input.

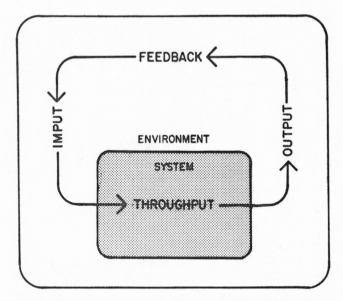

Figure 6   Systems as cycles of events. Artist: Robert Eurie

3. The output. The open system delivers an output or a product to its surrounding environment.

4. Systems as cycles of events. The idea here is that a system's product provides a link in a cycle which eventually leads back into the system. The output contributes energy or material that leads to the maintenance of the system's inputs. Ford sells cars, the money it receives helps buy steel (input) which is used to make cars, which are then sold, etc. See Figure 6.

5. Negative entropy. The concept of entropy is associated with a universal law of nature that all forms of organization move toward disorganization and death. Von Bertalanffy (1962) has argued that this law does not apply to open systems which tend toward greater complexity and differentiation by virtue of bringing in more and changing inputs from the environment. The open system can store energy for survival, it can adapt to changes in its environment.

6. Steady and dynamic homeostatis. The steady state of an open system is not a rigid equilibrium but there is enough stability to preserve the character of the system. To preserve the character of the system and at the same time be successfully adaptive to the environment, the open system is continually making gradual adjustments to try to keep constant the ratios and relationships of parts within the system. A too abrupt change in any one part of the system threatens the basic character of the system and therefore will require a counter action from some other part. The planning of social system interventions must be guided by this principle.

7. Differentiation. A special characteristic of open systems, as compared to closed systems, is that they become increasingly more complex and differentiated over time. Early in their development the process is the one discussed above of dynamic interplay among parts—a change in one part will require an adjustive change in some other part. Later in their development, however, a different process evolves which von Bertalanffy (1956) calls "progressive mechanization" which uses fixed regulatory feedback mechanisms. Neither Katz and Kahn nor von Bertalanffy are very clear about this process. My understanding is that as social systems become very large and very complex, certain relationships among system parts predominate at the expense of others. These relationships are probably a function of the power distribution in the social system. Subsystems which have no influence upon these dominant relationships, then, cannot cause system-wide changes but are confined and ineffectual. This may relate to Forrester's (1969) view that only a very few parameters in large complex social systems are "sensitive," that is, that only changes in these few parameters will provoke system-wide changes.

Equifinality. Another feature of an open system is represented by the term equifinality. This means that different initial states or causes may result in the same end-condition.

Two organizations, each of which has a warm, friendly, supportive climate, may have reached that stage from very different initial states. For example, one may have passed through a series of crises which demanded close cooperation and strong commitment from all members, the other may have had smooth sailing all the way and obtained its climate as the result of its management philosophy and style.

An open system possesses equifinality potentialities because it is continually receiving influences from the environment which serve to gradually modify it.

This concept has particular significance for the task of diagnosis of social system problems. An analyst cannot assume a previous event on the basis of a present "symptom." Different social systems can get to be the same way (e.g., rigid, inefficient, unresponsive to its members) for very different reasons. This concept also implies that a system's history does not necessarily prevent it from changing, or even exclusively determine the direction of the change. Because it is an open system, it is always susceptible to events and forces in its environment.

Inputs

Berrien (1968) makes a useful distinction between two kinds of inputs. Maintenance inputs serve to keep the system in operation, signal inputs are those which are operated upon. His example is the computer: the electricity which is necessary for the computer to run is a maintenance input, the program and the data fed into it are signal inputs. A system can tolerate more fluctuation and change in its signal inputs than in its maintenance inputs. Any system will be extremely wary of any change or proposed intervention which threatens its maintenance inputs. In social systems, maintenance inputs relate to power variables, while signal inputs relate to task variables.

Not all inputs are necessary or helpful to a social system. The system which is superior to it, the suprasystem, may make excessive demands regarding task production, it may send inappropriate supplies or inferior quality raw materials, or it may send confusing or contradictory information. Such harmful inputs put additional stress on throughput operations and in turn upon the population of the system.

Outputs

A system's product or output determines its value to the environment. This degree of value determines the flow of inputs and consequently the survival of the system. If outputs are not acceptable to the environment, and more specifically to the suprasystem, this may result in a reduction or cessation of inputs. If no one buys its cars, Ford will have to go out of business. Some outputs are simple waste, they are inefficient in that they use up inputs and are not proportionately transformed into new inputs. But unacceptable or threatening (to the suprasystem) outputs critically endanger the life of the system. The output of student demonstrations and violence has been assessed as having negative value by university suprasystems (state legislatures) with resulting reduction of inputs to universities in some cases.

In organizational psychology, those who have been primarily concerned with increasing productivity have been more concerned with outputs than with personnel satisfaction. Those emphasizing the satisfaction of individuals have directed their attention at throughput operations.

Throughput Operations

Throughput operations are given little attention by some system analysts. These may be considered simply as "black box" operations in which the analyst has little interest. For example, an analyst with limited time and resources might analyze the effectiveness of a large university by looking only at inputs and outputs without trying to examine each internal component as Schools or Departments or faculty-student relations, etc.

For our purposes, however, the throughput stage is particularly important since it is the place where social system and population "meet" with the greatest impact. Much of this chapter will be at least implicitly located at the throughput stage.

Feedback

Another concept utilized in general system theory is that of *feedback*, which is the core concept of cybernetics. Feedback refers to information-return and may be either positive or negative. If a system sends out information and receives back information of the same sign, it receives a *positive* feedback; if it receives back information of a different sign, it is *negative* feedback. Cybernetics is primarily concerned with negative feedback. A time-worn example of a system governed by negative feedback is the household furnace thermostat. The negative feedback stemming from a deviation counteracts it and maintains the system within a certain range (e.g., when room temperature goes down the thermostat activates the furnace, when room temperature goes up the thermostat deactivates the furnace, keeping room temperature at an even level). Positive feedback amplifies a deviation and serves to speed a system along its course, e.g., "run-away inflation" or economic depressions follow this process. Each increment adds further force to the "initial kick." The mutual causal process which is deviation amplifying, whose elements have mutual positive feedback between them, has been referred to as "morphogenesis" and has been referred to as "the second cybernetics" (Maruyama, 1968). To take a simple example, if a child receives punishment for his academic performance he has less motivation for academic performance; as his motivation further decreases, his performance is further lowered and the punishment continues to increase; this even further decreases his motivation, and so on.

However, the function of feedback is more complex than the usage of the term often implies. Feedback, as information from the environment, is crucial for making decisions. There is in the system a "sensor" or decision-making mechanism. How the feedback is used depends on the set or task of this decision-maker, and the existing current state of the system. Feedback is only information, it in itself does not make decisions.

To return to the thermostat as an example, assume that its existing current state is FURNACE-OFF. Assume further that the decision-making set is morphostatic, it is geared to maintain a steady state of temperature between 71.5 degrees and 73.5 degrees. The question to the decision-maker, under this state, is: is the room warmer than 71.5 degrees? The feedback may be either yes or no. As long as the decision-maker receives YES . . . YES . . . YES messages, the system remains in the same condition. It is receiving old information. Old information functions to maintain the system in the existing current state.

Eventually the decision-maker will receive "new" information, it will receive messages saying NO . . . NO . . . NO. This activates the decision-maker to activate the furnace and this in turn changes the existing current state to FURNACE-ON. Under the new state the question posed to the decision-maker is: is it cooler than 73.5 degrees? The feedback answers of YES . . . YES . . . YES again serve to maintain the system's current direction or state.

Most social systems have the two different (and often competing) sets: *morphostatic,* which seeks to maintain a steady state; and *morphogenetic,* which seeks growth. For survival, a social system must both be stable and be able to grow and change in ways that are adaptive to its environment (Berrien, 1968). Feedback contributes to both sets, but its usage is determined by the decision-maker mechanism. In groups and organizations there are usually identifiable factions which vie with one another, the one being concerned about maintaining and preserving the organization (the organization is the end), the other trying to move it toward faster and greater growth (the organization is the means). In politics, the conservatives and the liberals in a general way typify these two sets respectively. Morphostatic factions are essential for stability, morphogenetic factions are essential for growth and change. The absence of either would usually eventually doom an organization. Either can be maladaptive if not counterbalanced by the other. If the system maintains a too narrow range of sameness, or if the growth rate is too rapid, in either case the system is in trouble.

Mutual Causal Relationships

A central conception of general systems theory is that since the component parts of a system are interdependent, any action upon one component will have effects on other components. In my family I can't give my son a piece of candy without it having an effect on my daughter. It is a common experience among therapists working with whole families to find that when the symptoms of the identified patient are given up, often another family member will begin showing symptoms. While this conception seems simple enough, it is often not recognized or clearly understood. The effects of pollution upon our ecological system is another example. The idea that one could not poison insects and weeds without also poisoning birds and cows was not recognized. In a system, every change has a trade-off cost.

Not only is the multiple casual relations idea applicable to *intra*system relationships, but it also applies to *between*-system relationships. Any attempted change in a focal system will affect and be affected by its relationship to other systems—its suprasystem, other systems with which it cooperates and competes, etc. One cannot introduce behavior modification into a classroom without also affecting other classrooms, the principal, and parents. The topic of intersystem relationships will receive more attention in the next chapter.

To further describe the implications of mutual casual relationships, here are some of the ideas of Garret Hardin, a biologist, who adds a fresh clarity to these general orientations. Hardin points out that scientists wish for single causal agents which will have one single effect. He then describes how things simply do not work out that way. With reference to the effects of drugs, he points out:

> "When we think in terms of systems, we see that a fundamental misconception is embeded in the popular term "side effects" (as has been pointed out to me by James W. Wiggins). This phrase means roughly "effects which I hadn't foreseen, or don't want to think about." As concerns the basic mechanism, side effects no more deserve the adjective "side" than does the "principal" effect. It is hard to think in terms of systems, and we eagerly work our language to protect ourselves from the necessity of doing so" (1968, p. 456).

I would offer that the social sciences are still at the point of expecting to find single causal agents which will have single effects. Hardin suggests that the myth of our time is built around the dream "of a highly specific agent which will do only one thing" (1968, p. 457).

> "The moral of the myth can be put in various ways. One: wishing won't make it so. Two: every change has its price. Three (and this one I like best): *we can never do merely one thing.* Wishing to kill insects, we may put an end to the singing of birds. Wishing to "get there" faster, we insult our lungs with smog. . . ." (1968, p. 457).

With respect to changing a system or building a new one, Hardin suggests:

"A system analyst need not, when confronted with a new invention, reject it out of hand simply because "we can never do one thing." Rather, if he has the least spark of creativity in him, he says, "We can never do merely one thing, *therefore we must do several* in order that we may bring into being a new stable system." Obviously, in planning a new system, he would have to examine many candidate-ideas and reexamine our value system to determine what it is we really want to maximize. Not easy work, to say the least" (1968, p. 457).

Implications of General System Theory

What help does general system theory provide to the prospective intervener? Here are some suggestions.

1. General systems theory can provide something of a "big picture perspective" for the preliminary analysis. It can help to free the analyst from being "hung up" on single parts as either villains or heroes if he views their activities as determined largely by the set of the system. The particular individual who appears rigid and resistant to change may merely be enacting the morphostatic set of the particular social system.

2. It alerts the prospective intervener that he cannot alter any one part of a system without provoking responses from other parts of the system. In a system in which the decision-makers have a morphostatic set, their responses will be to choke off further "deviations." Sarason (1971) has described the behavioral and programmatic "regularities" in schools which appear to serve a morphostatic function. In a morphogenetic set, the change may have a ripple effect and the system may get "carried away" and take the change farther into areas not anticipated by the intervener.

3. An exception to the above can occur in large complex systems in which the intervener mistakenly chooses an "insensitive" or encapsulated area or variable, which has so little relevance to decision-makers that there is no response at all. An instructor in a university may develop an innovative and ef-

fective way of teaching art history, but not receive any responses from his department or university administration. However, if that instructor then attempts to set up a new department based on his method, he may very well get responses (probably of a restraining type since universities seem to generally have morphostatic sets).

4. The input-throughput-output model can be helpful in evaluating the efficiency of a social system. A comparison of input usage and resulting outputs will indicate the effectiveness of throughput operations, and comparisons with other systems performing similar tasks will provide a comparative evaluation of that system.

5. The input-throughput-output model can be helpful in organizing the complexity of a large number of variables in social systems. It can be applied to a wide range of possible systems.

6. Should the intervener be involved in the design of new social systems he will need to recognize the criticalness of both stability and change for that system and should try to build in feedback mechanisms that can facilitate change without undue disruption of stability. In other words, he should try to provide for both morphostatic and morphogenetic activities.

ISSUES IN ORGANIZATIONAL PSYCHOLOGY

The term "organizational psychology" generally refers to the study of the psychological and social aspects of large scale organizations (Leavitt & Bass, 1964). This area might be roughly divided into the following three ideologies or positions.

Classical Position

The classical approach, which has included such people as Frederick Taylor and Max Weber, promotes narrow job latitude, close supervision, and a rather authoritarian tone. It tends to see the individual as the "bad guy" trying to get out of work and therefore as being untrustworthy. This position is well known for its introduction of time and motion studies.

Human Relations Position

This position, which includes people such as Argyris, Bennis, Likert, Maslow, and McGregor, advocates job enlargement, greater autonomy for workers, wider participation in decisions, less close supervision, closer attention to group characteristics, and more trusting attitudes toward the individual worker. The individual tends to be the "good guy" and the organization is the "bad guy." This group is perhaps best known for its introduction of T-group training.

Integrating Position

The third position is less clear-cut. It has been called the integrating position by Lichtman and Hunt (1971). It eschews the absolutist stances of the other two and takes more of the middle ground regarding "good guys" and "bad guys." It takes into consideration situational factors to a greater degree than the other two. Systems approaches such as that of Katz and Kahn (1966) and those examining roles such as Hunt (1967) and Cyert and MacCrimmon (1968) would be examples of this position. It recognizes the interaction between organization and individual, it assumes wide variation in individual motivation (e.g., not all workers are primarily motivated by self-actualization), and it gives more importance to structural properties (e.g., size of the organization).

Comparisons

While the above oversimplifies each position, it does give the highlights of their central orientations.

Who is winning? Well, the classical group was being battered rather badly by the human relations group for awhile, and Bennis (1969) predicted its demise. It might be best described as weakened but not dead. The human relations group has had only partial success in proving its claims, for example, Hulin and Blood (1968) have found the job enlargement issue more complex than the human relations people had suggested, and a T-group training effectiveness has been sharply challenged on empirical grounds (Campbell, 1968, 1971). To date the integrating group appears to be emerging as the most persuasive and accurate of the three groups.

Now some of the dominant issues in organizational psychology will be examined using the views of these groups and reference to some of the available empirical evidence.

Flat Versus Tall Structure

The issue here is, what type of system structure will interact best with its inhabitant population as far as productivity and personnel satisfaction are concerned?

A "flat" organization has fewer hierarchical levels between the lowest person and the highest (in terms of power) than the "tall" structure, and there tend to be more persons working under one supervisor. This issue, then, also includes what is called "span of control," or the number of subordinates per supervisor. The human relations position favors the flat over the tall structure and the wide over the narrow span of control. This would allow more autonomy for the worker and it would convey more of a trusting attitude toward the worker. The classical position, for the opposite reasons, would favor the tall over the flat structure and the narrow over the wide span of control.

Porter and Lawler (1965), in a review of three studies, concluded that there was no evidence that a flat organization structure produced greater job satisfaction or improved job performance. The size of the organization seemed to make a difference. In small organizations (5,000 people or less) a flat structure did appear to be related to higher need satisfactions of managers, while in larger organizations tall structures were related to higher need satisfactions and productivity.

Worthy (1950) has argued that a wide span of control would allow for greater opportunities for individual initiative and development. However, there has been little research directed at this question. Porter and Lawler found only one empirical study, that by Woodward (1958). Woodward studied the span of control of first-line supervisors in several different English companies which varied in their method of production and found the most successful companies having larger spans of control than considered optimum by classical theorists. Thus Woodward's study gives some support to Worthy's thesis, but, as Porter and Lawler point out, the study is limited to first-line supervisors and so cannot be generalized to other hierarchical levels; moreover, the method of production was found to be an important variable in determining the optimum span of control.

The evidence, scarce as it is, tends to slightly favor the integrating position in that structural and situational factors appear to play an important part. Certain tasks, for example, may require the close coordination and communications provided by a tall structure (such as an airline), while other tasks (teaching at a university) may not.

This issue, which seems to involve the variables of task requirements, power, and communication, relates to the individual problem-area of experienced control most closely. An individual with a strong internal control orientation (who feels that he controls his own destiny) who wants to determine his own performance may fit much better into a flat than tall structure, whereas the person with an external control orientation (who feels his destiny is controlled by factors external to himself) may be very comfortable in a tall structure.

Job Enlargement

There has been a strong recommendation for "job enlargement" in industrial organizations by such human relations writers as Argyris (1957), Kornhouser (1965), Likert (1961), McGregor (1957), and Whyte (1955). Their position has been that job specialization or simplification, or the narrow job assignment, leads almost inevitably to job dissatisfaction and nonproductive behavior patterns. Hulin and Blood (1968) review the research in this area. They define job enlargement to include allowing individual workers to set their own working pace, giving them responsibility for their own quality control and for the maintenance of their own equipment, and allowing them to choose their own methods. After reviewing a broad range of studies they conclude that the case for job enlargement has been drastically overstated and overgeneralized. They point out that the whole issue is considerably more complex, requiring a recognition of special characteristics of the population involved and the surrounding community and their interrelationships with job enlargement and job satisfaction. They propose a model to account for the differences in the literature they reviewed. They suggest that job satisfaction will increase with job enlargement for white-collar workers and non alienated blue-collar workers. For alienated blue-collar workers, or those in plants located in communities (urban) that would develop alienation from middle-class norms, job enlargement would be expected to decrease job satisfaction. The point made here by Hulin and Blood is similar to the one made in the previous chapter: some individuals prefer high structure and do not prefer increased responsibility.

The main thrust behind the human relations theory of management that recommends greater flexibility, greater responsibility, greater participation, and less structure, authoritarianism, and supervision, is that the individual can then better actualize himself and will be more satisfied. As has been pointed out by Strauss (1963), these theorists tend to be university professors, and they may too much expect all men to desire the independence, flexibility, and potential for individual expression which is possible in the occupations they have chosen. As community psychologists, we must be watchful that we do not impose or recommend system conditions simply on the basis of their attractiveness to us personally, or to our pet conceptions as to what is good for all men.

Job enlargement, or more generally for my framework "assignment latitude," would seem to be closely related to the individual problem-areas of achievement and control. Opportunities for job enlargement would likely be desired by individuals with high achievement strivings and an internal control orientation, while clarity of task and repetitive routine might be desired by external control, low-achievement oriented individuals.

Distribution of Decision-Making

This issue involves the relationships between different units of the population, and the relationship of the face-to-face group to the suprasystem. The human relations group has advocated the decentralization of decision-making, i.e., that individuals at all levels of the organization be given opportunity to participate in decisions which affect them. This recommendation found its way into the OEO's antipoverty programs requiring "maximum feasible participation" by the disadvantaged and more recently into the Department of Transportation's programs requiring citizen participation in decisions regarding federal expressways. Likert's model for decentralization of decision-making was one of the earliest to explicitly advocate this position and deserves greater detail.

Likert's Model. Likert studied differences between managers and concluded:

> "The supervisors and managers in American industry and government who are achieving the highest productivity, lowest

costs, least turnover and absence, and the highest levels of employee motivation and satisfaction display, on the average, a
different pattern of leadership from those managers who are
achieving less impressive results. . ." (Likert, 1961, p. 97).

However, the more successful managers had not developed
principles or articulated theories regarding their methods. This
Likert tried to do, using as a basis the extensive research
generated by the Institute for Social Research at the University
of Michigan. One way of very briefly introducing his
model would be to say that it tries to integrate the formal
achievement task (FA) and individual problem-management
(IPM) contributions so that the two are complementary
and mutually supporting.

Low-producing managers, in keeping with classical methods,
exercise narrow span of control and high authority. In their
systems: "Jobs are organized, methods are prescribed, standards are set, performance goals and budgets are established.
Compliance with them is sought through the use of hierarchical
and economic pressures" (p. 99-100).

High-producing managers appear to interact with their
subordinates in a supportive, positive way. They tend to
respond to employees as human beings and not merely as tools
to do the work. Research has indicated that subordinates see the
high-producing manager as supportive, friendly, respectful, and
trusting. He is seen more as a person who helps, rather than a
person who punishes. Likert has developed, from this general
finding, the *principle of supportive relationships* which suggests
that an individual works better if he experiences his work and
relationships as contributing to his sense of personal worth and
importance. He also works better if he feels supported by other
people with whom he works. And therein lies the importance of
work *groups.*

Likert proposed that management utilize effective work
groups and suggested that group participation in decisions

would generally lead to greater satisfaction and better implementation of these decisions. He also suggested that using
groups rather than man-to-man organizations would reduce
competitive conflicts, increase loyalty, and increase communication distribution.

A major contribution is Likert's *linking pin model*, in which a
representative of each work group in the organization is also a
member of a group at the next highest organizational level (see
Figure 7), and in which staff groups and committees overlap
levels and groups. By formalizing and using such member
overlap, the organization allows for better communication,
better information flow, and perhaps most important, it makes
upward influence more possible.

In most organizations, influence from the top down is typical.
The boss typically can influence his subordinates. However, for
the subordinate to influence his boss is more improbable. There

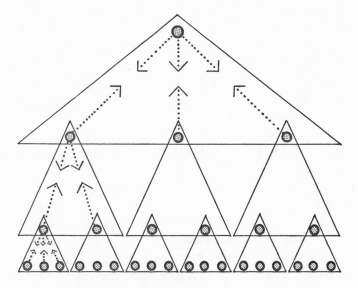

Figure 7   Likert's linking pin model. From *New Patterns of Management* by Rensis Likert, 1961. Used with permission of
McGraw-Hill Book Company. Artist: Robert Eurie

is research evidence which suggests that being able to exert an influence upward improves morale, satisfaction, and productivity (Pelz, 1951, 1952; Katz, et al., 1950; Likert & Willets, 1940). Also, the over-all functioning of an organization could be potentially improved as greater information from lower levels moves upward, thus providing the decision-makers with more and better information.

Evidence for Wide Distribution of Decision-making.   Morse and Reimer (1956) attempted to measure the differential effects of changes in centralization. They had hypothesized that decentralizing decision-making would increase job satisfaction and productivity. The experiment was conducted in one department of a large corporation which had four similar divisions, all approximately equal in job satisfaction, productivity, decision-making authority, type of work, type of personnel, and type of supervisory structure before the organizational change was introduced. This intervention prescribed that in two divisions the decision-making role of the rank-and-file members was increased, in the other two divisions their role was decreased. In the decentralized divisions, the rank-and-file employees had to assume the additional duties of the first-line supervisors, these supervisors had to give up their previous activities and assume the duties of departmental heads, and departmental heads had to function as top-management officials in coordination with other departments. These new roles were given legitimization by having an executive-vice president introduce the changes as new company policy.

The results of the study showed an increase in satisfaction in the decentralized divisions and a decrease in satisfaction in the centralized divisions. The productivity of both groups increased but the centralized divisions had a greater increase. The authors hastened to explain the superior productivity of the centralized divisions as a short-range effect due to the more impersonal method of reducing the number of clerks in the centralized divisions. Regardless of the productivity result, it is important for our purposes to note the contribution to IPM made by providing wider participation in decisions.

A study by Trist and Bamforth (1951) evaluated the effects of the introduction of the long-wall method of mining coal upon the productivity and absenteeism of miners. Under the long-wall method, miners had to learn to operate new machinery, they were more specialized, their wages were dependent on the individual task rather than group output, and they had less decision-making participation. Some mines, however, introduced a composite long-wall method which allowed for retention of former social groups, some decision-making authority, and job flexibility while at the same time capitalizing on the new machinery and procedure. Trist and Bamforth found the composite-long-wall pits to be superior in productivity and to have less absenteeism than the conventional long-wall pits.

Porter and Lawler found two studies that revealed no statistical differences in attitudes of managers in decentralized versus centralized organizations. One study (Carlson, 1951) found that executives spent less time "taking decisions" and less time giving orders in decentralized organizations as compared to executives in more centralized organizations. The other study (Weiss, 1957) found trends, but not statistical differences, in which decentralized organizations had lower turnover rate, lower number of grievances, less absenteeism, and lower accident frequency and severity. Porter and Lawler conclude by suggesting that the effect of decentralization of decision-making will depend to some extent on the *nature of the organization's task*. If the task requires close coordination and communication and involves interdependent meshing of different activities, e.g., auto assembly lines, a high degree of centralization may be essential for the success of *the task*. Whereas, if the task allows for a great deal of independence, in that the task of one individual is not linked and dependent upon that of another, decentralization may be both possible and desirable.

Individual Satisfactions Versus Organizational Productivity

This is perhaps the dominant concern of organizational psychology: throughout its literature runs this conflict between the organization's formal task requirements and the satisfactions of individuals within it. Berrien (1968) defines the opposing forces in his *formal achievement task* (FA) and *group needs satisfaction* (GNS) and declares that there must be a balanced FA/GNS ratio for the system to function properly. Homans (1950) defines these forces as the *external* group which poses the system's requirements for behavior, and the *internal* group made up of the individuals in the system who combine and pose requirements for behavior in reaction to the demands of the external system. Miller and Rice (1967) describe a boundary model which distinguishes between the *task* group which involves activities necessary to transform inputs into outputs, and the *sentient* group to which individuals commit themselves for emotional support.

The human relations people, in reaction to the classicists, have argued that being more responsive to the satisfactions (largely social and self-actualizing) of groups will result in better productivity. This view was founded largely on the Hawthorne studies (Mayo, 1933; Roethlisberger & Dickson, 1939) which appeared to show that social concerns were often more important than economic concerns in determining productivity. Human relations people have offered specific management approaches: Likert (1961, 1967) has advocated the "System 4" leadership style which emphasizes trust and wide participation in decision-making; Blake proposed a 9-9 management style, i.e., one that has optimal concern for both people and production and provided dramatic evidence of the efficacy of management training based on his grid approach (Blake, Mouton, Barnes, &

Greiner, 1964), although their results have subsequently been questioned by Greiner (1967) because of situational factors which may have contributed to the changes.

A complication is the frequent finding that job satisfaction is unrelated to job productivity (Vroom, 1965) which has led Katz (1964) to conclude that the two are independent of one another.

Writers fitting more into the integrating camp have emphasized an interaction between the individual's needs and organizational variables. Illustrative of this approach is the proposal by Schneider and Bartlett (1968) to use insurance agents' preferences for agency climate, ratings of agency climate by that agency's population, and the prospective agent's aptitude scores for the prediction of subsequent agent performance. Both individual and organizational variables would be quite specific to the particular situation.

Also falling within the integrating camp, Lawrence and Lorsch (1969) have noted that the individual enters into his organization assignment with a past history that influences his behavior and perceptions, but that the nature of the organizational context also interacts with that individualized unique system of values, perceptions, and motives. Lawrence and Lorsch illustrate this interaction from their experiences as consultants to assist a corporation in increasing its sales effectiveness. This organization manufactured, sold, and serviced highly technical equipment for hospital operating rooms. The consultants compared four successful sales district offices with four average offices. Their methods included interviewing salesmen and managers, administering TATs and CPIs (California Psychological Inventory) to salesmen, and administering a questionnaire regarding organizational climate (Litwin & Stringer, 1968). From the interviews, the consultants learned that the sales task was a long-term one; a salesman might spend from one to fifteen years before a sale at a hospital meeting with physicians and hospital administrators; this time was necessary to learn what they needed and wanted and to elicit their trust and confidence. Once the sale was made the salesman also continued the contact as part of the delivery, installation, and service contract. Thus, the salesman might go for long periods without a sale when his major activity was meeting with prospective clients. From a comparison of TATs, the consultants found that *successful* salesmen were generally higher on need for affiliation (McCelland's categories) and lower on need for achievement than the average (less successful) salesman. On the CPIs, the successful salesmen had higher "capacity for leadership drive through independence and flexibility" (p. 74). From the questionnaire on organization climate it was found that in the successful sales offices members perceived their organization in a more favorable light than those of the average districts, particularly in their perception of a "friendly team spirit." Other findings suggested that the successful organizations were perceived in such a way that members expected satisfaction of needs for achievement.

From these data, the consultants concluded that in order for a district to have a successful sales record it should have an organizational structure and management style which produced an expectation of satisfying needs for achievement. Behaviorally, these managers were more participative, set higher goals, and gave more coaching. The successful organizational structure also should produce an expectation of satisfying a need for affiliation which was particularly relevant to this sales task. This sales task allowed for the satisfaction of the needs for affiliation through repeated contacts with prospective clients and with service personnel, and may have been less satisfying for the "average" salesman who needed frequent sales for his higher needs for achievement but who was not as much compensated by affiliation need satisfactions. The task also required independent functioning and flexibility which matched with the correspondingly higher capabilities in these areas by the more successful salesmen.

In short, for the highly successful district offices there was a fusion between the organizational climate, the needs and capabilities of the individual salesmen, and the requirements and satisfactions of the particular sales task. The particular task demands fit well with individual priorities. In addition, needs for achievement, which were not being satisfied through frequent sales, could be satisfied to a degree by the nature of the organization's structure and climate. The three areas of task demands, individual needs, and climate complemented one another.

This issue of people versus productivity seems to involve particularly the variables of task and power. It also emphasizes that membership in groups and the characteristics of these groups mediate the individual-organization relationship. Somewhat indirectly, the importance of group or organizational climate has been suggested here.

Implications

Hopefully, the discussion of these issues has highlighted what goes on in organizational psychology. It also should reflect the large numbers of variables involved. From this array I have selected four broad variables that would seem to be important for preliminary analyses and subsequent interventions in different kinds of organizations: they are task, power, communication, and climate.

SELECTED ORGANIZATIONAL VARIABLES

Thompson (1966) in rather an understatement has referred to the organizational field as "variable rich." Stogdill (1966) in an attempt to comprehensively cover the dimensions of organizational theory found eighteen different conceptualizations of groups and organizations. Triandis (1966) presented some 55 variables and 43 hypotheses in a discussion of organizational design. Therefore, the problem here has been to select a *manageable* number of variables which are also among the *critical* variables in all sorts of organizations. While the four variables stated above are thought to be important in most organizations, it will remain for the intervener to select added or different ones most appropriate to his task and particular organizations. These variables will be discussed with special attention to their relationships to individuals within organizations.

Task Requirements

Organizations are established to perform a task, to produce an output. This task is formalized, explicit, and public. This I have called the formal achievement (FA) task after Berrien (1968). Organizations, however, are also social systems. There can be no social system apart from the individuals which compose it. The task, the physical environment, a program, whatever, cannot exist independent of the people that operate or function within it. An organization, then, also has a "people" task; it must be, to some degree, responsive to its component members. This "people" task I have called the contribution of the social system to the individual's problem-management, or simply IPM. Successful organizational functioning requires a workable balance between FA and IPM functions. Problems in organizational functioning can often be traced to having at least part of their source in an imbalance between these two functions.

The FA task and IPM are highly interdependent. The successful achievement of the FA task can be very important to individual satisfactions. This is represented especially in the internalization of the organization's FA task by the individual so that it becomes a part of his own preferred solution, probably to his achievement problem-area. Katz and Kahn (1966) discuss two types of goal internalizations: job identification and organizational identification. Job identification refers to the person who gains a great deal of personal satisfaction from his work itself. For example, scientists or craftsmen may work long hours and be very happy with their jobs because of the personal significance to them. The second type of goal internalization, organizational identification, is not with the job itself but with either the goals and values of the organization, the general class of tasks or organizations, or with a subsystem's goals and values. An experimental psychologist may identify with the values and goals of teaching and research in universities. A social worker at Family and Childrens Agency may identify with the mission of that particular agency. An accountant may find resources in his specific subsystem (defined and established on the basis of the organization's FA task), e.g., the Purchasing Department within a university, that facilitates his problem-management in the affiliation problem-area. He then identifies with that particular subsystem and not necessarily with the larger organization.

The structure of the FA task will also affect the degree to which members *can* interact with one another and the degree to which they must depend upon one another. If the task allows for frequent interactions, this can contribute to solutions for the affiliation problem-area. If there is provision for a high degree of autonomy, this can contribute to solutions for the control problem-area.

A special kind of task conflict concerns what I think of as "bogus" FA tasks. These are essentially IPM contributions for a limited segment of the system which are ostensibly labeled as part of the FA task, but which are implemented at the expense of the IPM of other system members. Thus, under the guise of improving FA task performance, a foreman may fire another member whom he believes to be after his job. Most organizations continue to function despite bogus FA tasks until the effect becomes extreme either upon the FA task or upon IPM.

It will be of value to the intervener to know how the FA task is defined by both the organization and its inhabitant population and to know the relative importance of the FA task to the population.

Power

Power and Task. The distribution of power in a system serves to organize the component individuals and subsystems for their task functions. Power distribution also serves to structure the decision-making methods of the system. The locus of power designates relative responsibility for the performance of FA task activities. The individual who is designated to receive blame or reward for FA task activities typically is accorded powers to reward and punish component members who directly perform those activities. The designation of responsibility and power for FA tasks typically comes from the suprasystem; for IPM it typically comes from among the group of individuals that inhabit that system.

Distribution of Power. The wideness of distribution of power is significant for the productivity and stability of the organization. It is assumed here that in general if power is distributed too narrowly, so that only a small proportion of the population have power, then the task will eventually be adversely affected. The low power members will experience themselves as having low control over their activities.

There is evidence to support the advisability of relatively wide distribution of power. In addition to the work previously discussed, a review of studies of dispersal by teachers of emotional acceptance and power (participation in decision-making) has been provided by Glidewell, Kantor, Smith, and Stringer (1966). From their review, a wide dispersion of social power and emotional acceptance by teachers (as opposed to a narrow dispersion) had the following consequences: (1) more frequent pupil-pupil interaction, (2) wider dispersion of peer power as expressed in greater tolerance and resolution of divergent opinion, (3) greater self-initiative, independence of opinion, and responsibility, (4) reduced inter-pupil conflicts, (5) increased mutual and self-esteem and lower anxiety, and (6) an increase in the prevalence of adult-oriented moral values.

In our current era, it may be predicted that if an organization has too highly centralized power there will eventually be a confrontation between the high-power echelon and the low-power echelon. This may then lead to an instability in the system and disrupted FA task performance. On the other hand, the question of how wide power can be distributed before there is an adverse effect on the FA tasks has yet to be answered.

In an organization with highly centralized power, a conflict is even more likely to erupt if the low-power echelon sees the high-power echelon as working on a "bogus" FA task. High school students are more likely to rebel against a teacher whom they see as using punishment to exalt his own feelings of importance rather than to simply keep order in the classroom. College students are more likely to demonstrate if they perceive the university as being involved in bogus academic functions (e.g., military research, ROTC programs).

A related factor is the availability of recourse to punitive actions based on formal power. The availability of a high-power "place to go" has an important IPM function; it allows the component member a greater experience of having control over his own destiny within the system. Availability to recourse, as a built-in system structure, would serve to reduce the disrupting effects of power conflicts.

The power distribution in an organization helps to define the *system assignment* of the component member. One's allocated power defines one's relative position *vis-a-vis* other members in other assignments. One behaves differently to members of greater power than to members of lesser power. One's degree of power determines one's "accountability" for the performance of tasks and thereby affects involvement in task performance.

Degree of power also serves to define the degree of allegiance to the organization. Generally, the greater the individual's power the stronger his allegiance. And the degree of power determines the range of permissible behaviors for the particular assignment; the greater the power typically the more the latitude and variety allowed for appropriate assignment behavior.

If, as I hypothesize, high power correlates positively with commitment to task performance, allegiance to the organization, and wide range of allowed assignment behavior, the question again arises regarding the advisability of a wide distribution of power. If power in any social system is concentrated in a small proportion of members there will likely develop opposing subsystems, the high-power one which is highly committed to the FA tasks and to the organization itself, and the low-power subsystem with low commitment. It is likely that eventually this opposition will erupt in sharp conflict with damaging repercussions on task performance. Within limits of task requirements and organization size, a wide dispersal of power would be expected to result in better FA task performance since there would be greater system-wide commitment and increased IPM opportunities as the result of fewer highly restricted system assignments.

If, however, the dispersal of power is too wide, the effect is that of practically eliminating power altogether, and the resulting loss of control would likely adversely affect both FA and IPM.

Power as Control of Inputs.   I prefer, among the many available definitions of power, a relational one. Basically, the degree of power one system has over another, or one individual over another, is determined by the degree that he controls (or is perceived as having such control) inputs or resources that are valuable to the other. This is especially true for maintenance inputs. Emerson (1962) has defined power as residing in the dependency of the other. If Jim completely controls the job needed by Bill for his financial security, Jim has a great deal of power over Bill.

The individual's power relationships with his social systems and with other individuals is critical for his problem-management in *all* other areas because his degree of power will determine the availability to him of resources he requires for his problem-management.

For example, if John's affiliation solution is confined exclusively to an intimate relationship with Desdemona, then Desdemona has a great deal of control over him—she controls his valued inputs. On the other hand, take Fred whose affiliation solution includes hunting and fishing trips with "the boys," a weekly poker game with other "boys," a monthly visit to Mitzi at the local house of ill-repute, continued frequent contacts with his three brothers, and his relationship with his wife Beth. Beth, compared to Desdemona, has much less power over her man. To the degree that an individual has "all his eggs in one basket," that is, his valued inputs all under one source of control, his problem-management is extremely vulnerable.

The relationship of an individual to a particular social system will be clarified by knowing to what degree that system has what he wants, as compared to other social systems in his social network, and to what degree the individual controls what the system wants (such as a rare skill or expertise).

Within the next 25 years the major institutional change may well be a redefinition of power relationships within the family and consequently in sex and age roles in our society. The behavioral sciences have the potential to contribute to and ease the discomforts of such changes, if they now begin to anticipate and study changes in these power relationships.

For the would-be intervener it will be important to identify the power source of his change-target, whether this latter be an individual or a whole system. In many cases, approval of this power source will be necessary in order to gain access to the system. The intervener will also want to know the power structure within the system, the informal alliances and factions as well as the official chain of command. The intervener will also want to assess the distribution of power between and within systems.

Communication

Communication serves a linkage function. It links the various parts by information flow: individual to individual, individual to group, system to suprasystem, etc. Information in an organization can be viewed as its "life blood." It carries the essentials for system functioning, e.g., task directions, inducements and penalties, formal rules, informal rules, etc. The direction, amount, and nature of the information define the relationship of the system assignments for the source and receiver (or their relative place in the power hierarchy). The information exchange between the system and its external environment also defines that relationship and determines system adaptability and sustenance.

Frick (1959) has defined informational processes as selection processes. Information has utility only when the receiver is faced with a choice. If I know the road to Paducah I do not need a road map. However, to use the information for selecting a choice, the receiver must know the choices possible. A computer can "read" an incorrect input and send back such information to the operator, but only if the choices have previously been programmed for it. The wider the choice, or the larger the number of alternative choices, the greater the uncertainty. The greater the uncertainty the more information is required to make a choice.

From the total variety of information to which it is exposed, a system selects what it considers to be relevant, useful, or important information. It filters out the "noise." Information it considers unessential, or which may include material that would be disruptive or harmful to the system itself is considered "noise."

The role of information selection is essential in determining the adaptiveness and growth potential of the system. If the system's information filters are set too "tight" it does not receive sufficient information about its external environment to make appropriate choices and changes. With tight filters the system sets a process of very narrow deviation counteraction. This leads to little leeway for change to adapt to new demands in the environment or in its internal processes. The system becomes rigid and maladaptive and eventually dies.

On the other hand, if the filters are too "loose" the system is flooded with information, uncertainty is high, the number of choices becomes unmanageable, decisions become arbitrary and lacking in general direction. The organization of the system will then deteriorate, stability will be lost, task performances will be inadequate, and the system eventually would go out of control and be destroyed.

An analogy to the too tightly filtered system comes from the sensory deprivation studies (e.g., Soloman, et al., 1961; Bexton, et al., 1954). Subjects in these experiments were deprived of visual, auditory, and tactile sensations (information from the environment) to the degree that perceptual and cognitive functions were impaired. Some subjects in these reduced sensation conditions began to manufacture their own information and reported hallucinations. They were unable to maintain veridical ties to their environment.

An analogy for the too loosely filtered system would be a brain injured child who is exposed to a large amount of stimulation. A reaction of overexcitement and loss of control would be similar to the gross reaction of the system to large amounts of unselected information.

What determines the setting of a system's information filters? I would suggest that the filters are usually under the control of the high-power echelon which sets the filters according to its interpretation of the system's appropriate tasks. In one family, the parents may decide that information about sex would be harmful to the socialization of their children and work to prevent their children from being exposed to any sexual information. Such parents may work to prevent sex education in the schools. In another family, the parents may believe that exposure to large amounts of information on sex is important for the successful socialization of their children. These parents may expose their children to erotic books, movies, etc., and may even have the children observe the parents during sexual intercourse.

A not uncommon condition for many social systems is for the high-power echelon to interpret the FA task as that of maintaining the system in the status quo (A morphostatic set). Any pressure for change is interpreted as a threat to the continued existence of the system. For this condition the filters are set to screen out criticism, or evaluation, or suggestions for system modification from the environment. Also, information about the system from within is not allowed through the filter to the environment if this information is seen as having potential for "misuse," or criticism of the system. Likewise, pressure for change within the system is treated as harmful noise and is screened out.

Governmental agencies, public school systems, and social service agencies are probably particularly vulnerable to the status quo "tight filter" condition.

Haberstroh (1965) has discussed information systems in organizations as being of foremost importance in the structure of organizational design and in task modeling. One can draw the inference that an intervention in the communication network within an organization would create major structural changes. Katz and Kahn (1966) discuss five major characteristics of a communication network, these being:

1. Size of loop. This refers to the distance or numbers of people serviced by any particular informational channel. Does a

high school principal, for example, communicate information about policies and rules only to his faculty, or also to students, and also to maintenance and secretarial personnel?

2. Repetition versus modification in the circuit. Is the information sent in the same form to all levels of the social system or is it modified or translated at different levels. Does the principal send notices to teachers, and then the teachers interpret the information to their students? Or do all levels receive the same message in the same form?

3. Feedback or closure character. This refers to the nature of the response to the information. A feedback response not only acknowledges the receipt of the information but returns new information to the source. A closed response only acknowledges receipt of the information, it cannot modify, evaluate, disagree, or in any way change or add to the information sent.

4. The efficiency of communication nets. This refers to the contribution to the FA task. Katz and Kahn review several studies which suggest that networks with fewer links tend to be more efficient than larger networks with many links. However, Shaw (1964) in a more thorough review concluded that different kinds of networks are better for different kinds of tasks; the more centralized (fewer links) network is superior on simple problems but the decentralized network (more links) is better for more complex problems. Shaw also concludes that decentralized networks are more satisfying to their members regardless of the task.

5. The fit between the communication circuit and systemic functioning. This refers to the relationship between the FA task and the system's information processing, e.g., is the size of the loop too big in that it carries unneeded information to many people who have to take the time to process it; does the circuit conduct the information that is needed for solving problems (usually feedback processes are superior to closed circuits for system adaptiveness); do bogus FA tasks maintain small closed

loops protecting information from both the lower echelon and the suprasystem?

Climate

The climate concept is molar, global; in a sense it includes some aspects of organizations that have been discussed above. This broadness makes it difficult to define, for example:

> "What to call the desired conceptually integrated synthesis of organizational characteristics has been a problem for many researchers. The term organizational climate has been used by several of them, although the term means different things to different writers. We shall use the term . . . to refer to the set of characteristics that describe an organization and that (a) distinguish the organization from other organizations, (b) are relatively enduring over time, and (c) influence the behavior of people in the organization." (Forehand & von Haller Gilmer, 1964, p. 362).

> "The concept of climate describes a set or cluster of expectancies and incentives and represents, we propose, a property of environments that is perceived directly or indirectly by individuals in the environment" (Litwin & Stringer, 1968, p. 29).

Fortunately, Litwin and Stringer constructed a questionnaire to measure organizational climate and the dimensions of that questionnaire serve for a more specific definition of climate. These are:

1. Structure: the number of rules, regulations, and procedures, the emphasis upon "red tape" as opposed to a loose, informal atmosphere, and flexible, changeable procedures. An illustrative questionnaire item would be: "The jobs in this organization are clearly defined and logically structured."

2. Responsibility: the degree of autonomy, of being able to perform task functions without continually checking with a

supervisor. An illustrative questionnaire item would be: "We don't rely too heavily on individual judgement in the Organization; almost everything is double-checked."

3. Reward: the feeling of receiving positive rewards rather than punishment and perceived fairness of pay and promotion opportunities. An illustrative item would be: "In this Organization the rewards and encouragements you get usually outweigh the threats and the criticism."

4. Risk: is the organization a conservative, play-it-safe outfit or does it take large risks? An illustrative item: "The philosophy of our management is that in the long run we get ahead fastest by playing it slow, safe, and sure."

5. Warmth: the perceived degree of positive social interaction. Item: "A friendly atmosphere prevails among the people in this Organization."

6. Support: the perceived degree of helpfulness from others in the organization. Item: "When I am on a difficult assignment I can usually count on getting assistance from my boss and coworkers."

7. Standards: the perceived level of required performance standards. Item: "Our management believes that no job is so well done that it couldn't be done better."

8. Conflict: the perceived tolerance for disagreement and expression of opinions. Item: "We are encouraged to speak our minds, even if it means disagreeing with our superiors."

9. Identity: the perceived degree of belonging to or pride in the organization. Item: "People are proud of belonging to this Organization."

(All illustrative items were taken from the B form, Litwin and Stringer, 1968, Appendix B, pp. 204-207.)

Climate and IPM.   Litwin and Stringer correlated preferred climate measures with three individual measures: need for achievement, need for affiliation, and need for power. Among their findings were: a high reward climate was preferred by individuals with high achievement needs; there was a significant negative correlation between preference for highly structured climate and need for affiliation; there were strong positive correlations between preferences for warmth, support, reward, and identity and need for affiliation; individuals with high need for power preferred highly structured climates, high responsibility, and high conflict (opportunity to express oneself).

ORGANIZATIONAL VARIABLES AND IPM: SELECTED HYPOTHESES

In order to illustrate in a more concrete fashion the relationship between organizational variables and IPM and the resultant level of psychosocial accord, a number of hypotheses will be presented here. They are not intended to be comprehensive or exhaustive but to represent an approach the intervener can use in his preliminary analysis.

For these hypotheses individual problem-management will be examined along preference dimensions of affiliation, achievement, and locus of control. It should be recognized that different IPM variables may be more important for a particular system or population and the particular intervention task. For affiliation I will assume members of a social system will fall along a dimension defined by a preference for high social interaction at one end which I will label sociopetal and a preference for low frequency of social contacts at the other end which I shall call sociofugal (these terms were coined by Osmond, 1959). For achievement we will assume a dimension defined at one end by individuals who are high strivers for achievement and at the other end by low strivers. For control we will use Rotter's (1966) dimension of internal to external locus of control ("internal" representing an experienced control *by* self, "external" representing almost total control *of* self by external factors). These dimensions are, then:

Sociopetal _____ Sociofugal
                        Affiliation

High Strivers _____ Low Strivers
                        Achievement

Internal _____ External
                     Locus of Control

Task Hypothesis

1. Social systems with heavy relative emphasis (an imbalance) on the FA task (relative to IPM contributions), with highly structured task requirements and narrow assignment niches will be more satisfying (relatively speaking) to sociofugal than to sociopetal preferences; to low strivers than to high strivers; to externals than to internals.

If after analysis it was found that the members of the system were highly internal and highly sociopetal *as a population,* then intervention efforts would be made to change organizational variables, e.g., add coffee breaks, enlarge assignment niches, provide for more individual responsibility and autonomy, etc. If it was found that for the large majority of members these variables were in a good match but that three members were in a poor match, then the relocation of those members to another system might be the preferred intervention.

Power Hypotheses

2. Social systems with narrow concentrations of power and decision-making will be more satisfying to externals than to internals; more satisfying to low strivers than high strivers; and neutral with respect to affiliation. (Narrow will be operationally defined here as consisting of 5% or less of the

members of a face-to-face system of 40 members or less making all decisions for the system and having exclusive reward-and-punishment power over the other members.)

3. The converse would be true for systems with wide distributions of power and decision-making. (Wide would be defined as consisting of 20 percent or more of the members of a face-to-face system of 40 members or less contributing to some decision and having some form of reward-and-punishment power over others.)

For social systems "in the middle" on this variable I would be unable to make predictions.

4. To the degree that a system provides for recourse to punitive action, or a high-power-echelon "place-to-go," the more satisfying that system will be to high internals.

Communication Hypotheses

5. The larger the size of the loop of the information channel, i.e., the greater the number of people in the system who receive information, the more satisfying will that system be to high strivers, internals, and sociopetals.

6. To the degree that a system's norms and expectations encourage modification and translation of information within the system the more satisfying that system will be to high internals and high strivers.

7. To the degree that a system provides for and actively encourages upward as well as downward information flow and encourages a feedback response as opposed to a closure response the more satisfying that system will be for high internals, high strivers, and sociopetals.

8. Highly centralized information networks will be more satisfying to high strivers, externals, and sociofugals.

Climate Hypotheses

(An hypothesis about "structure," and "responsibility," two

of Litwin and Stringer's climate dimensions, was made under the task hypothesis, number 1; an hypothesis about "conflict" was made under an information hypothesis, number 7.)

9. A social system having a climate of being rewarding rather than punitive will be more satisfying to high internals and high strivers.

10. A social system having a climate characterized by warmth, support, and identity will be more satisfying to sociopetals.

THE IMMEDIATE ENVIRONMENT

Organizations are often so big that many individuals within them never see each other. Also, organizations are typically subdivided into groups which very directly hinder or help the individual's IPM efforts. This section will discuss concepts of Barker which seem relevant to person-environment fit, and will look quickly at group-*qua*-group characteristics.

Barker's Ecological Psychology

Barker "sees" human behavior in a radically different way than most psychologists. He codes it in larger, more molar units defined by characteristics of the environment and over longer periods of time. Or, he sees behavior via the method of observing the natural behavior of individuals in different settings over several hours or even days. Contrast this with counting the number of times a person says "yes" or "no" when presented with dots of light at different intensities. This latter method represents a definition of behavior by the focus on specific discrete stimuli and presumably related responses —it is molecular, brief, and occurs in a contrived (by the experimenter) situation.

The scope of the work of Barker and his colleagues is difficult for psychologists to comprehend. For example, they studied 119 children in a small Kansas town in such settings as drug stores, classrooms, playgrounds, Sunday School classes, 4-H club meetings, football games, etc. This would amount to about 100,000 episodes of behavior each day! Among their findings (Barker, 1968): (a) children's behavior changed dramatically from one setting to another (this should not be surprising, consider the difference between classroom behavior and playground behavior); (b) especially significant was the finding that the behavior of a child could be predicted better from knowing the setting he was in than from knowing his individual characteristics, or to put it another way behavior settings were more important than stable individual "traits" in predicting that individual's behavior; and (c) the child's behavior tended to conform to the over-all demands of the setting over a course of time even when there was nonconformity within short time periods and with certain inputs from the environment.

This last finding needs further explanation. Consider Barker's example of a five-year old girl named Maud with her mother and brother in Clifford's Drug Store. During an eleven-minute period Maud's behaviors were coded into 25 episodes, e.g., *Pretending to Use Lipstick, Watching Girl Eat Soda, Eating Ice Cream Cone, Trying to Get Her Mother's Attention.* Also during that period Maud received 26 social inputs, mostly from her mother, which attempted to guide, direct, or control Maud's behavior. Maud conformed, or was congruent with these social inputs about one-third of the time. (An interesting sidelight: over all their observations Barker, et al., found children to conform to about one-half of all social inputs to them.) While Maud conformed to social inputs only one-third of the time, her over-all behavior was harmonious and appropriate to the drugstore setting: she had her treat and enjoyed it, she sat on her stool, she took her coat off when she arrived and put it on when she left, etc. As Barker put it, while Maud failed most of the items (social inputs) she still passed the test (her behavior was congruent with the setting).

From this process, a different-sized unit was discovered which was termed an "environmental force unit" by Schoggen (1963) and was defined as "an action by an environmental agent toward a recognizable end state for a person" (Barker, 1968, p. 152-153). This environmental force unit is bigger than a social input, it lasts longer and is more persuasive over the long run. It seems to be a heavily persistent pressure which is of low intensity so that while brief discrete behaviors seem to be deviations the end result is conformity.

Barker's findings can be interpreted as follows. A behavior setting has behavioral prescriptions built into it from a variety of possible sources: history, expectations, formal legal rules, norms, the constraints of physical structure, etc. The behavior setting contains these forces on behavior that are *extra-individual*, i.e., they apply to whomever appears in the setting. The population is at least implicitly aware of these prescriptions and would quickly recognize deviations. It is especially important for our purposes to recognize that these environmental forces are more than social inputs, more than interpersonal interactions, and exist independent of the identity of individuals in the population.

The fundamental unit of ecological psychology is the behavior setting which requires a rather technical definition before being operational, or before it can be measured. For our purposes certain characteristics will be highlighted. First, it occurs naturally, independent of the researcher. Second, it has time and place loci—it is known by its inhabitants by its location and appointed time. Third, it includes both behavior and milieu. The milieu surrounds and encompasses the behavior and they are structurally complementary. They fit together. Fourth, there is a standing pattern of behavior that exists even when the individuals change. However, if the standing pattern changes it is no longer the same behavior setting. Fifth, the individual in the behavior setting is at the same time a component contributing to the behavior setting and a whole to whom the behavior setting is only a part.

Barker's work also emphasizes the influence of physical structure upon behavior. A classroom with all chairs facing the teacher encourages teacher-to-pupil communication and discourages pupil-to-pupil communication. An expressway dictates a necessarily high degree of conformity of behavior by those driving on it. A path across a yard seduces the stroller to use it.

Implications.   The behavior setting can be viewed as a social system located in time and space that has an effective and persistent pressure for behaviors consistent with a recognized and accepted purpose or task. It is not determined by the characteristics of the population inhabiting it at any one time. It will contribute to the individual's problem-management in one way or another, but it is only one of many systems in a series or network. A change in any particular behavior setting will change the modal behavior of the *population* but may have only a modest effect on a given individual. The effect of behavior setting change on IPM would be expected to vary depending on the importance of the setting to the individual. The impact of the setting on IPM is over and above the impact of group-*qua*-group characteristics of the population.

Group Characteristics

A review of small group theory and research will not be attempted. A number of generally recognized small group variables will be briefly discussed and related to IPM contributions. These are: size, cohesion, heterogeneity of members, permeability, leadership, and status congruence. These will be considered as properties of the population and as separate from behavior-setting forces.

Affiliation. For the individual whose preferences are for belongingness and frequent positive social interactions, the small, cohesive, homogeneous group would enhance his opportunities. His preference would be enhanced even more if the leader is relationship-oriented rather than task-oriented i.e., the leader both encourages and participates in social interaction. Cohesion and homogeneity are more likely if the group is relatively impermeable (group membership is stable with few new members in or old members out), and if there is status congruence (status in the group is consistent with other statuses outside the group). Obviously, such a group will be irrelevant or even discordant for the person who prefers infrequent social contacts and independence.

In the literature of organizational psychology, social relations have been emphasized as critical to the worker's job satisfaction by the human relations group. Social satisfactions are often described as being in opposition to demands for productivity by the organization. While there is evidence to support this position, beginning with the Hawthorne studies, it should not be taken to mean that job satisfaction is exclusively dependent on positive social relations for all individuals. If that were so, there would never have been "rate busters" in the Hawthorne studies.

Achievement. For the individual whose preferences include high achievement strivings, a task-oriented leader providing clear task structure will be desirable. A small cohesive homogeneous group which sets low productivity standards would be discordant for him if his strivings are in the direction of the organization's task (a high striver for position and power in the union, of course, would have quite different directions). Heterogeneous groups would tend to be more creative and generate more potential solutions to problems but these groups also have greater difficulty in agreeing upon final solutions

(Triandis, 1966). Whether or not this characteristic were enhancing, then, would depend upon the nature of the group's task. Triandis (1966) suggests that when there is heterogeneity, group effectiveness (productivity) demands a clearly defined task structure.

When the high striver identifies with the group and with the group's achievement, then pride in the group is in accord with his preferred achievement problem-area solutions. Hemphill and Westie (1950) suggest that low permeability of a group often is an indication that membership in the group is difficult and possible only as a result of a particular level of achievement—this builds a feeling of pride among these achievers. Pride is also more probable if members are homogeneous with respect to goals. These goals must have high value to promote pride. Goals which are easily attainable soon lose their value. Goals which are never attained lose value since they are never reinforced and become viewed as hopeless.

Control. If the individual prefers a dependency solution in this problem-area, he will be in accord with a high task-oriented leader who prescribes the exact nature of each member's activities. If the preference is for independence, the reverse would be true. The independence-oriented individual may work better in a less cohesive, large, heterogeneous group that has less pressure for conformity to group norms.

If a group is composed of a large number of independence-oriented persons it may frequently oppose the constraints and regulations of the organization or other systems. However, being composed of such persons may make it difficult for the group to organize and agree on strategies.

Implications

The prospective intervener doing a preliminary analysis to

examine the person-environment fit in a system will need to know the forces from the behavior setting which prescribe and prohibit behaviors. He will also need to know the characteristics of the group and recognize that what may be a resource for the IPM of one person may be an obstacle to the IPM of another person with different preferred solutions.

POPULATION—SOCIAL-SYSTEM RECIPROCATION

In this section I will offer a schema for viewing the relationship between population, social system (small), and organization. The population of a social system is seen as being different from the social system but not as independent of it. The intervener will often by practical necessity be directing his efforts at the *population*-environment fit, hoping to enhance the psychosocial accord of many of the individuals in that population but being unable to do so equally for every individual.

The term "social system" offers some difficulties because it is not limited in size. In the following discussion "social system" will refer to a behavior setting of the size such that all inhabitants have frequent face-to-face contacts, that has a clear formal achievement task, that has existed long enough and is permanent enough that the population has established stable group characteristics, and which is within an organization of other social systems one of which is in a superior power relationship to the given social system. An elementary school classroom, a university physics department, the personnel section of an industrial plant, the day shift headquarters section of a police department, all would be examples of a social system of this size. The system that has formal power over the social system, the suprasystem, would be the principal, a Dean, the plant owner, and the chief of police (and their respective staffs), in these examples.

Social System as a Pliable Tunnel

A *social* system is not physically bounded, although the physical structure may be an important influence upon it. A social system's structure is formed by verbal definitions: a written constitution, a task designation on an organization chart such as "Personnel," an informal task definition such as "we've got to organize to oppose busing our children out of the neighborhood," etc. It is also formed by norms, traditions, and attitudes developed over a period of time—everyone who lives in Oskaloosa has a similar attitude as to the proper task and behavior for Clifford's Drug Store. Task requirements are especially important in forming the structure of a social system. These task requirements and environmental force units determine, if you will, the "shape" of the social system— different social systems have different shapes and structures.

While social systems do not, in fact, have physical boundaries, for the sake of this schema the reader is asked to imagine the social system as a tunnel made of pliable material (such as soft rubber). See Figure 8 for a representation. The exact shape of the tunnel (round, square, triangular, etc., but don't take this analogy *too* seriously) is formed by task requirements and environmental force units, but the shape can be changed to some degree by the population without destroying the character or existence of the social system. There is continual interchange between system and population which results in gradual but continual modifications in system shape and structure.

The tunnel is linked to other systems—the most critical of which is the suprasystem. The suprasystem has a direct power line to the tunnel that provides basic support and keeps it from collapsing. Another "line" is the communication link between the tunnel and other systems, including the suprasystem.

The population "flows" through the tunnel (very slowly). The population exerts pressure on the inside of the tunnel. Characteristics of the population may demand expansion or shape alterations, or allow contraction—population requirements will force system changes but will also be constrained by system shape and structure. Characteristics of special interest in this regard are group-*qua*-group variables

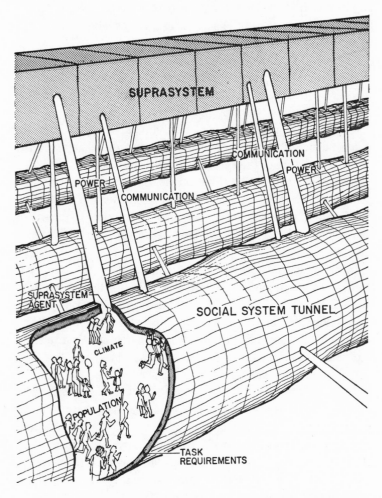

Figure 8   Social system as a pliable tunnel. Artist: Robert Eurie

(e.g., cohesiveness, heterogeneity, etc.), and the collective IPM preferences of individuals in the population. These combine to contribute a population climate. This schema attempts to illustrate the give-and-take between population and system, how they are different yet not independent. The fit between population and system is assumed to largely determine the individual's degree of IPM success and his psychosocial accord with that system.

Individual Problem-Management as a *population* variable is simply an aggregate of individual preferences. Suppose a measure were developed which would give the relative priorities for the individual on the problem-areas of opportunity for achievement, opportunity for affiliation, and opportunity for independence. This measure would then be administered to the entire population of the system. If the results showed that 75% of the population had affiliation as their first priority and achievement as their last, this would be considered a population requirement. It is obvious that this population requirement would demand push-and-pull negotiations with the system's task requirements.

In designing a new social system, whether it be an experimental classroom or a New Town for 100,000 people, the more information the designer has about the prospective population the better the chances are for a good population-system fit, if those population characteristics are then used in designing the shape and structure of the new system.

As with any analogy, complications arise. All of the population does not "flow" through at the same rate. For example, the professionals at a mental health center are in the mental health center longer than most of the clients and typically have a more intense impact upon system structure. In systems with such differences between flow rates, there are basically different subpopulations which may have very different, even opposing, requirements.

Suprasystem Agents

Some individuals in the population are more properly a part of the social system. These are the persons who serve as agents of the system's structure and more particularly as agents of the suprasystem. The shop foreman, the classroom teacher, the platoon sergeant are examples of "enforcers" of suprasystem task requirements. They serve as power and communication inserts into the population. These agents will usually have the greatest investment in the focal social system: more than the population, more than the suprasystem. For these agents, their IPM is closely wedded to the social system's task, structure, and survival. They are at the pressure point between population requirements and suprasystem requirements. They control to a large degree the communication between population and suprasystem. They contribute significantly to population climate. They control the intervener's port of entry into the social system. They are neither villains nor heroes, they are simply the single most critical component of the social system.

PRELIMINARY ANALYSIS:
KEY AREAS AND METHODS

In this section key areas for the preliminary analysis will be listed along with possible methods and measures for information collection. But first, why is a preliminary analysis necessary? Here are some reasons.

Reasons for a Preliminary Analysis

First, almost any intervention will be only as good as the information upon which it is based. The necessary information for intervention purposes is the *match* between population variables and social system variables since it is to the "poor fits" that interventions need to be directed. The analysis is necessary to point up the harmonies and disharmonies. Such collection of information should not be considered "research," at least not with its typical connotations in laboratory-oriented psychology. The rigor typically associated with that term is often not possible or necessary for the preliminary analysis. But methods developed in research can serve in the collection of intervention-relevant information.

Second, in cases where the disharmonies are quite obvious at the outset and may even be the reason for the intervener's interest in the system, a preliminary analysis is still necessary to reconnoiter, to get the "lay of the land," in order to uncover other less obvious disharmonies and to scout out possible booby traps that would obstruct the intervention. An intervention can be "bushwacked" in many and subtle ways.

Third, the preliminary analysis itself, in some situations, may turn out to be an intervention. As one example, two students in my community psychology course, Patricia McCarthy and Roseanne Reed, as part of their social systems analysis of a high school, administered a questionnaire about the school to students, teachers, and administrators. They tabulated the results and wrote up a report which so impressed the principal that he decided to use it as the basis for small group discussions at an all day in-service training program with Miss Reed and Mrs. McCarthy serving as consultants. The report and the program served as a catalyst for changes: students began drafting a new student behavior code, teachers decided the school needed a clearly defined philosophy of education, and the beginnings of a crisis prevention and response program was started. Among other examples, Sylvain Nagler has reported the change-facilitation effects of a community survey. Pierce, Trickett, and Moos (1972) reported changes in ward environment after feedback sessions with staff about the results of the Ward Atmosphere Scale (Moos & Houts, 1968).

Fourth, in order to evaluate the effects of the subsequent

intervention some base-line, some "before-intervention" information, must be available. Comparing this information with that collected during and after the intervention will help to show what worked and what did not, and if unanticipated effects occurred. For long-term interventions the collection of information should be built into the intervention design itself to provide constant feedback as to the effects on the system and population

Now on to methods. There is no one best method. The choice of methods will be dictated by such practical considerations as the "contract" with the host social system (what it will allow), the purpose of the intervention, and the resources of the intervener. Aside from these kinds of practical considerations, though, any method selected will have some disadvantages (and the information obtained will always be to some degree incomplete). The value of the method chosen must ultimately rest on its appropriateness for the population and social system involved and the purpose of the intervention.

Following from the conceptual framework of this book, here is a list of key areas for a preliminary analysis:

1. Identification of the most relevant problem-areas of the population.
2. Measurement of priorities of preferred solutions in the most relevant problem-areas for the total population.
3. Assessment of group characteristics.
4. Measurement of system requirements, particularly the opportunities or obstacles in the relevant problem-areas.
5. Identification of disharmonies between system requirements and population requirements.
6. Direct measures of population satisfaction.
7. Assessment of the system's relationships with other systems.

The first six will be discussed here and the last key area will be taken up in the next chapter. The methods suggested are, of course, not restricted to any one key area. The same method may obtain information for several key areas. For the discussion below, a review of methods and measures of human environments by Rudolf Moos (1972c) was very valuable.

Identification of Problem-Areas

To find out which areas of concern have the most relevance to the population, open-ended methods have the advantage of not imposing the analyst's preconceived notions upon the information. Some first-hand experience in the system would be especially helpful, simply observing what goes on and even participating in these activities if this is appropriate. Open-ended interviews, of either a formal or informal nature, can quickly give a great deal of information about the population's primary concerns. Also, from this kind of information the prospective intervener begins to develop hypotheses about population-system disharmonies.

For example, suppose the system were a high school. The analyst might have formal appointments to talk with the principal and guidance counselors about the school. Then he might spend three or four mornings observing in classrooms, study halls, and the lunch room. He might talk with teachers informally in the teacher's lounge and chat with students during their lunch. He would ask what these people thought about the high school, what they liked about it and what they did not like about it. On the basis of this information, the analyst might conclude that the major areas of concern were about control (degree of autonomy allowed or guidance provided to both teachers and students), and achievement (some push for curriculum change and some controversy over maintaining academic standards).

Measurement of Population Priorities

Having an idea as to which areas are of primary concern, the analyst can then proceed to measure the preferred solutions and strategies in those areas.

The analysis could decide to develop his own measure. He could devise items reflecting different solutions and offer them in a forced-choice, paired-comparisons questionnaire which would yield a priority listing among solutions for the population, and for subpopulations. This would tell him what the population wants most. In the high school example above, the analyst could obtain priority lists for students, teachers, and administrators.

Or, the analyst could decide to use measures already developed that related to those areas of concern in that kind of system. Below is a sample of possible areas and kinds of measures.

Kelly and his associates (1971b) have developed a number of measures of exploratory preferences by the population which are then related to high school characteristics, particularly student population turnover. These measures include an exploration preference questionnaire (Edwards, 1971); a semiprojective test which presents exploration situations to the subject and then asks him to choose among multiple choice alternatives as to what he would most like to do in that situation (McClintock & Rice, 1971); a peer rating form of exploratory behavior (Roistacher, 1971); a biography form designed to get at the socialization experiences which had been important in the development of exploratory preferences (Newman & Gordon, 1971); a case study of differences in help-giving by two student subpopulations using observations of behavior, interviews, and questionnaires (Todd, 1971); and a questionnaire designed for black students to measure alienation (McGee, 1971).

Moos and his associates have developed questionnaires which measure perceived climates in such systems as psychiatric wards (Moos & Houts, 1968), community-oriented treatment programs (Moos & Otto, 1972; see Appendix B), correctional institutions (Moos, 1968b), university student residential units, primary work groups, and junior high and high schools. In the treatment programs the questionnaires are answered by both staff (suprasystem agents) and patients. A comparison between the actual climate and the ideal climate scores would yield a satisfaction score (Moos also provides some explicit satisfaction items).

Holland (1966) has developed a model for vocational choice which is especially pertinent to measuring person-environment fit. He describes six model environments and six personality types along the same dimensions: realistic, intellectual, social, conventional, enterprising, and artistic. One could then measure both the system and the population on the same dimensions.

Assessment of Group Characteristics

Here the analyst may feel he has enough information about group characteristics either from his open-ended, in-systems stage, or from his population measures, so that he needs no additional information.

If not, he might be interested in group measures of attraction (e.g., Newcombe, 1960), or cohesion (e.g., Seashore, 1954), etc. He might check the history of the group to assess such characteristics as permeability. He can also assess status congruency, heterogeneity of members, etc.

Measurement of System Requirements

Here, of course, the organizational variables of task, power, communication, and climate would require examination. For example, in assessing task efficiency such measures as achievement tests, sales, number of patients seen, number of patients terminating prematurely, number of trainees successfully placed in jobs, etc., can serve as relatively "hard" indicators. For power, discerning who actually makes decisions through observation, finding out who has the reputation of having power, assessing power distribution, and checking back on who made previous decisions may be useful. For communication, the actual following of messages from their sources to their eventual receivers and noting what happens to them enroute may reveal a great deal about the communication network. For climate, the Litwin and Stringer questionnaire is a good measure and adaptable to many different kinds of systems. In addition, other climate indices may be available such as absenteeism, turnover, strikes, equipment loss and damage, etc.

For assessing behavior-setting characteristics, the work of Barker and his associates should be consulted. Others have also attempted to measure or categorize aspects of social environments. Wolf (1964) studied the degree of intellectual "press" of the environment and its relationship to general intelligence. He specified a number of environment variables among which were: opportunities for verbal development, the nature and amount of assistance given when a child was having academic difficulties, activity level, etc. Mischel (1968) has suggested that it would be possible to do an "incentive analysis" of systems to define what behaviors are reinforced, and which reinforcers are the most effective. One could count the kinds of responses to behaviors in the population by suprasystem agents, e.g., positive reinforcements, negative reinforcements, ignoring responses, etc. The analyst might profitably have system personnel themselves chart these behaviors and responses (e.g., Tharp, Cutts, & Burkholder, 1970).

A number of instruments have been developed which seek to measure the environment in terms of the perceptions of the population. Halpin and Croft (1963) have developed a questionnaire to assess the climate of elementary schools on both teacher and principal dimensions. They identified six different school environments, e.g., open, closed, paternal, autonomous, etc. These sound as if they would describe system requirements of the population. A number of instruments have been developed for university systems. Pace (1969) has developed a scale for assessing five different dimensions of college environments. Peterson, et al. (1970) developed a scale for faculty and administrators which allows for measurement of different beliefs about the proper purpose of the institution; this would relate directly to the task variable. Astin (1968) developed an inventory to measure environmental stimuli in universities in four categories: peer environment, classroom environment, administrative environment, and the physical environment.

In the case of large-scale interventions and ample resources, the use of computer simulation can be valuable. This method handles a large number of variables at one time and can analyze their interrelationships over time. Forrester (1969) has used computer simulation to study urban systems and discovered that in large complex systems the variables affect one another in "counter intuitive" ways. That is, our everyday experiences with simple systems lead us to expect cause-effect sequences just the opposite of what actually occur in large complex systems.

It will often be important to assess community attitudes and perceptions toward the system in question. Selecting representative random samples and then surveying them either by telephone or by door-to-door interviews will provide valuable information.

It will also be critical to examine the relationship of the system to other systems, particularly its suprasystem. These issues will be the topic of the next chapter.

Identification of Population-System Disharmonies

In order to specify these disharmonies, which would then serve as targets for the intervention, the analyst will have needed to measure dimensions or variables of both system requirements and population requirements which were commensurate with each other, such as Holland's model attempts to do.

In a social systems analysis of elementary school classrooms, several of my students devised a paired-comparisons questionnaire including items related to affiliation, achievement, control, and survival, which was then administered to pupils, parents, and teachers (with slight modifications in the items). This gave the problem-area priorities for each subpopulation. They also devised another companion questionnaire which asked questions directly about these problem-area opportunities in the system, e.g., "Do you have opportunities to be a leader in your class? . . . Do you have enough opportunity to socialize with your colleagues? . . ." The results then indicated whether there were adequate opportunities in high priority problem-areas, from the viewpoint of each subpopulation. Such questionnaire measures could profitably be supplemented by directly observing and counting the number of opportunities in these areas.

Population Satisfaction

After locating disharmonies the analyst may wish to follow up with direct measures (interviews or questionnaires probably) to assess the relative degree of dissatisfaction these disharmonies produce. This may aid him in further pinpointing the targets for the intervention. It can serve as something of a check on his disharmony information as well. There is the risk, of course, that members of the population will feel that it is unsafe, in some respect, to express their opinions and gripes, even anonymously. Their perception of the analyst and his role will be important determinants of the validity of this information.

The above merely scratches the surface of the many available instruments and approaches. Typically lacking now are methods which provide either commensurate dimensions for both populations and systems (as Holland attempts), or a method that directly links the two sets of variables. Hopefully, such methods and measures will evolve with greater experience in studying person-environment fits. Until then, the prospective intervener must manage even with information gaps, he must make hypotheses and test them, he must make do with the instruments that are available now.

In addition to the issues discussed above, there are, of course, many practical problems involved in the collection of such information, such as gaining access and cooperation. Some of these practical considerations will be dealt with in some detail in Chapter Six.

JUST WHEN DID YOU NOTICE THIS GROWING
INABILITY TO ACCOMMODATE CHANGE ?

Figure 9   Analysis of a social system. Artist: Roseanne Reed

5. INTERSYSTEM RELATIONSHIPS

No less than an individual, no system can function independently of other systems. This chapter will look at these interdependent ties among systems, a rather neglected topic heretofore. We are used to thinking of systems under single categories. Our university training programs are divided neatly into academic categories with very few interlinkages. Our governmental agencies, funding sources, political platforms, physical planning, etc., all tend to see social problems in single-system terms. Health, mental health, education, recreation, police, welfare, etc., are single-system answers to multi-need problems. How about having police activities under the public health department? This suggestion usually produces a startled response and immediate arguments against it, all based on single-system perceptions of those two services.

This chapter will try to point out features of intersystem relationships that will be relevant to a preliminary analysis and to interventions. It will also examine service system networks in relation to the requirements of users of those services.

The outline of possible key areas for a preliminary analysis in both this chapter and the previous one attempts to be comprehensive but manageable. In practice, however, it is unlikely that a prospective intervener will have the resources to fully examine all the areas suggested here. He must choose those areas most relevant to his target system and the purpose of his intervention, and according to his available resources. It is not intended that all of the variables discussed are *must* variables, i.e., that they are essential for each and every intervention project.

INTERRELATIONSHIPS AMONG ORGANIZATIONS

Evan (1966) has noted that social science research has neglected the area of *inter*organizational relations partly because organizational theorists generally are preoccupied with internal relations. He cites such theorists as Taylor, Weber, Barnard, and Simon as exemplifying this *intra*organizational focus. Evan proposes the concept of "organizational-set" which refers to a set or network of organizations. In analyzing an organizational-set, Evan would consider the relationship between this set and a particular constituent organization, the "focal organization," with respect to the following areas: (1) the role-sets (the complex of roles and role relationships possessed by occupants of a particular status) of boundary personnel or those at the interface of interorganizational transactions; (2) the flow of information; (3) the flow of profits or services; and (4) the flow of personnel. To put it somewhat differently, Evan is suggesting that the analysis of the focal organization will be improved by carefully examining its relationships with other organizations. Such an analysis of the focal organization's environment would help explain, suggests Evan, the following: (1) the internal structure of the focal organization; (2) the degree of autonomy by the focal organization in decision-making; (3) its degree of effectiveness in attainment of goals; (4) the kind and distribution of information exchange between the focal organization and its organizational-set; and (5) the forces upon the focal organization which would cause it to cooperate or compete, to coordinate, to merge, etc., with other organizations within its organization-set.

Dimensions of Intersystem Relationships

Evan provides a list of dimensions of organization-sets which suggests a number of variables to consider in a preliminary analysis of intersystem relationships.

Degree of Dependence.   To some extent, each organization within a set is in an interdependent relationship with other organizations. This "interdependence" has been defined by Litwak and Hylton, in their discussion of interorganizational analysis, as meaning "that two or more organizations must take each other into account if they are to accomplish their goals" (1962, p. 401). Evan points out that a focal organization relates to input organizations and to output organizations within its organizational-set which are crucial in determining the focal organization's degree of dependence. The greater the concentration of its inputs, the more dependent the organization. For example, if Family and Children Service relies upon the United Fund for 90% of its budget, it is in a highly dependent relationship. This degree of dependence defines the power characteristics of the intersystem relationship. As described by Emerson:

> "Social relations commonly entail *ties of mutual dependence* between the parties. A *depends* upon B as he aspires to goals or gratifications whose achievement is facilitated by appropriate actions on B's part. By virtue of mutual dependency, it is more or less imperative to each party that he be able to control or influence the other's conduct. At the same time, these ties of mutual dependence imply that each party is in a position, to some degree, to grant or deny, facilitate or hinder, the other's gratification. Thus, it would appear that the power to control or influence the other resides in control over the things he values, which may range all the way from oil resources to ego-support, depending upon the relation in question. In short *power resides implicitly in the other's dependency*" (1962, p. 32).

Or: to the degree organization A controls the inputs of organization B, A has power over B. Before organization B agrees to any intervention program, it will carefully investigate the possible effects upon A, and upon A's provision of B's inputs.

Interorganizational Member Penetration. Within an organization-set, there is an overlap of membership. When a realtor sits on a school board, for example, he is simultaneously a member of the authority system of the public educational enterprise and a member of the real estate profession. In this instance, the public school's authority system has been "penetrated" by the real estate interests. The realtor's profession fully retains its potential to reward and constrain him on behaviors within school board affairs. The same relationship holds, of course, for other organizations. A banker on the school board intrudes the values of banking, a black school board member may act as a penetrant of black citizen groups, a member of the League of Women Voters would singlehandedly link her organization as well as womanhood and motherhood. The behavior of the individual penetrant, then, is to some degree a function of the nature of his intersystem accommodation and the relative strengths of the forces from these different systems.

One rapid and fairly easy way to map out the interpenetrations of community organizations is to obtain membership lists of lay boards, for example, those of the United Fund, YM-YWCA, Family Service, etc. After finding out which organizations these members represent, the community analyst will have a better idea as to the composition of the "interlocking directorate."

Such a preliminary "mapping" should not, however, be taken as a definitive analysis of the community's power structure, which is an altogether much more complex undertaking. For one thing, the method used will affect the nature of the results

(Aiken, 1970; Freeman, Fararo, Bloombert, & Sunshine, 1970; Walton, 1966, 1970). Freeman, et al., for example, used three different methods in attempting to identify powerful community members: (1) *decision-making* —30 community issues which had been resolved by decision were selected, interviews were then conducted to identify those members who had participated in the decisions; (2) *reputation* —questionnaires were administered which invited the respondent to list in his opinion the most influential members of the community; (30) *social activity* —the same persons also responded to questionnaire items covering frequency of their social activities. The results showed the top leaders found by one method were not necessarily the same as those found by another; in only one comparison did two methods concur in more than 50 percent of their identified leaders.

Similaritiy of Task and Competitiveness.   Conflict between organizations is taken as given in interorganizational analysis by Litwak and Hylton (1962). Evan suggests also that organizations with similar goals and functions will typically be competitive. If system A has outputs which are similar to those of system B, then, obviously, they will engage in a competitive relationship with each other; but then what? Will each "try harder" to please the consumers of their outputs? Perhaps, but their efforts more likely will be with respect to the organization that dispenses their inputs. Social service agencies, for example, may put more of their competitive energies into convincing their funding agencies of their value than into improving their services (since funding agencies control their maintenance inputs and users of the services typically do not).

This point may have implications for intervention programs. If the cooperation of an organization is needed for the intervention programs, it may pay the intervener to assess the attitudes and activities of that organization's competitors and chief input organizations. The intervener may then convince the organization that cooperation in his program will enable it to equal or surpass its competitors in this area, and that the input organization (suprasystem) would favor such activities.

Suprasystem-Subsystem Relationships

In any community there is the permanent issue of autonomy for subgroups versus the requirements of the larger system as a whole. This is illustrated by the demands by blacks that they be in control of their own community, that they control their schools, police, businesses, etc. The same issue is illustrated by the desire of the accounting department in a large corporation to set its own coffee-break time rather than having top-level management make that rule.

This is a crucial and enduring issue. If the subsystems are *too* independent, the suprasystem will be destroyed. The loss of organization and coordination could result in anarchy. On the other hand, too little autonomy allowed to subsystems will also lead to conflicts which will eventually explode and have the potential to destroy the suprasystem.

We return again to Berrien (1968), who has neatly portrayed the situation of balance and conflict using his proposition that the two chief products or outputs of a social system are: (1) formal achievement (FA) and (2) group need satisfactions (GNS). He offers that the ceiling of formal achievement and the floor of group need satisfaction are under the control of subsystems, while the floor or formal achievement and the ceiling of group need satisfaction are under control of the suprasystem (see Figure 10).

This means that the suprasystem has a minimum level of FA task performance that it requires and it will not tolerate anything lower; likewise the population of the subsystem has a lower limit to its level of GNS task satisfactions that it requires. Conversely, the population of the subsystem has upper limits to FA task demands which it will tolerate; and the suprasystem

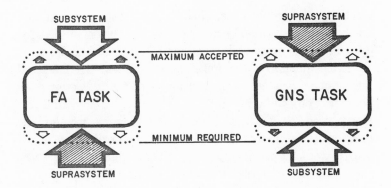

Figure 10   Balance controls of the GNS/FA ratio

will tolerate only a certain level of GNS task satisfactions. Beyond certain extreme limits, the GNS/FA ratio is no longer negotiable by either one side or the other.

For any given social system a GNS/FA ratio within mutually acceptable limits is necessary for effective system functioning. When that ratio is out of balance, one or the other system is apt to take drastic action. For example, suppose the members of the police force (subsystem) spend their time in cafes drinking coffee and socializing, satisfying social and relaxation needs (GNS), to the point that increasingly large numbers of citizens complain to the mayor (suprasystem). The mayor is likely to take drastic action (to prevent the FA task level from dropping further) by, among other things, sharply curtailing coffee breaks (lowering GNS), and thereby rebalancing the GNS/FA ratio. If, however, the mayor's reforms are too strict (requiring too high FA task performance), or his punishments too severe (forcing GNS level too low), then the members of the police force will react drastically by quitting, striking, or sabotaging operations, and by devising alternative means of meeting their socialization-relaxation needs.

As Berrien describes it, the ratio will vary somewhat in the normal course of time, alternating in both directions. The first reaction to a FA imbalance, when it is still small, is recognition but no concerted action by members of the subsystem; it is too difficult to organize all members since the imbalance is relatively small. As the imbalance increases, the increased impact upon each member makes organized counter-action more possible. The state of the ratio (which task area predominates) at the time the deviation begins will determine whether the reaction by the subsystem will be organized or disorganized. If the FA task performance is higher than GNS, (e.g., management introduces automation and then begins laying off men in small lots and individually) the rebellion would be fragmented and disorganized. If the GNS is high relative to the FA (e.g., a Governor calls in the National Guard after protesting students have developed high feelings of cohesion, while academic operations and performance have been disrupted) the solidarity of the subsystem grows and organized rebellion can more likely result. (The assumption here simply stated is that the higher the GNS in the subsystem, the more likely the members are to unite and make an organized opposition possible. If the GNS is low, relative to the FA, when the imbalance is precipitated, the members will not, at least at first, become united and organized.)

In the previous chapter, reference was made to the recommendation for participation by lower-echelon workers in management decisions. Placing this recommendation into Berrien's model, it would appear that increased participation would have the effect of tying GNS more closely to FA, so that the worker who experiences formal achievement as part of his own satisfaction can have high GNS only if the FA task is performed effectively. This would make rebellion nearly impossible. For example, if college students are given a significant part to play in university operations, the university's achievements (which would also certainly be modified to some degree by the students) become their own achievements, and again rebellion is less likely.

Berrien emphasizes the part that excessive dominance by suprasystems plays in these intersystem conflicts and in potential damage to the entire network. It also logically follows that an excessive dominance by the subsystem population guarantees conflict and seriously menaces the life of the larger network (witness campus riots). Social scientists have on the whole neglected the subsystem's part in such conflicts in favor of finding suprasystem villains. The interaction and mutual dependence of such intersystem struggles has not been sufficiently recognized.

In analyzing intersystem relationships, power relations are the first priority area the analyst must decipher. When approaching such an analysis it is helpful to keep in mind the strengths and vulnerabilities generally of suprasystems *vis-a-vis* subsystems. The strength of the suprasystem lies in its organization and its ability to reward and punish. It is vulnerable precisely in its dependence upon subsystems for performance of the FA task. The strength of the subsystem is complementary—it is most powerful in its potential to disrupt the FA task (a work strike, for example, is a powerful weapon). The vulnerability of subsystems lies in their lack of reinforcements that they can grant or withdraw, and their lack of organization. As Featherstone (1969) has commented in reference to urban black poor—they have only the two perennial weapons of the underdog, the power to disrupt and the appeal to humanistic values.

Community Inputs

It is necessary to recall that the suprasystem and subsystem are not "fighting it out" in isolation. There are inputs from the environment external to the organizations which interact with these power relations. One source of these inputs is the *attitudinal context* of the community. Another is the attitudinal context of society at large. The activist student subsystems in universities were able to be bold and assertive, even though they were a tiny majority of student bodies, because they had wide, if often passive, support from the student body at large. Groups of black welfare recipients—again a subsystem possessing little formal power and who are acutely vulnerable— have been willing to directly and publicly accuse welfare officials of injustices and to demand their rights. Such behaviors have been possible because of supporting attitudes in the community. Whites seem to have an acceptance of such protests as more or less "part of the times." In black communities there seems to have arisen a new norm which calls for bold declaration of rights and demands for equality, and a united effort toward positive self-attitudes.

In addition to attitudinal inputs, the community may also have a direct part to play in intersystem relationships via supports and sanctions from the high-power echelon of the community. This high-power echelon may be able to provide, withdraw, or withhold money, political support, supplies, and information from various organizations. For example, if a Human Relations Commission is putting pressure on a community industry to hire more blacks and Mexican-Americans, and if that industry has contributed substantially to the mayor's election, and if the Human Relations Commission is funded by the city council, then the power relationship between the commission and the industry is directly affected by the relationships of each to the high-power echelon (in this case elected city officials) of the community. This should not be oversimplified by assuming that it is specific to the particular person of the mayor. The mayor represents the community and to some degree reflects its general set of values and expectations. (Of course, the high-power echelon of the community is not always the formally designated governmental body.)

The unique history and set of traditions of a community further affect the intersystem power relationships. For example, consider a community whose population is composed largely of persons "born and raised" locally, with comparatively little influx of new people. This history may contribute to attitudes favoring "life-long residents" and established institutions and customs over newcomers, strangers, or "outsiders," and traditional methods over new ideas. Such an attitude may generalize to subgroups (e.g., mental health professionals) which contain a high proportion of "newcomers." The "old-timers" and established institutions will hold this community-derived power advantage, then, in any contest with "newcomer" types who desire change in institutional status quo. (Such "newcomer" change agents would do well to "woo" the oldtimers; having them with you will make things far easier than having them against you. Oldtimers are not always rigid and opposed to change.)

Klein (1968) provides an example in which lack of awareness of community values and traditions led to a program failure. The task was to explain a new community development program to community residents. A committee chairman proposed organizing a series of informal coffee klatches at which the program would be explained. However, this organization never got off the ground. The committee chairman was a relative newcomer and was not aware of the community attitude, revealed to Klein by a long-term resident, that meetings in individual's homes were viewed with suspicion and as taking advantage of personal friendships.

Power in the Community: An Example

For its illustration of intersystem power relations, we will now examine in some detail a study by Donald Bouma (1970) of the power position of a real estate board. Bouma defined social power, following Useem (1950), as "the concentration of influence and authority within a social system for making, legitimizing, and executing decisions which have consequences, intended or unintended, on the social chances of the members of that social system" (p. 367).

The real estate board in question had been particularly active and uniquely successful in influencing community affairs in a midwestern city (population approximately 200,000) pseudonamed Grand Valley. On all issues which had been taken to the voters, the alternative preferred by the real estate board had prevailed. In one instance, a referendum on public housing, the real estate board was opposed by the Chamber of Commerce, the county council of churches, some 32 organizations including unions and social welfare groups, and by both daily newspapers. The outcome favored the real estate board by a margin of 3 to 2.

Bouma's purpose was to analyze the factors in the board's social position. Why had the board been so successful in determining community decisions? What generalizations might be drawn regarding the development and maintenance of a strong power position' vis-a-vis other community organizations?

Methodologically, the problem was approached in four ways. First, the history of the board was reviewed in order to better understand the roots of its present structure and its development. Second, the methods used by the board in influencing community decisions were examined via newspaper accounts and official records of the board. Third, Bouma was a participant observer. He was involved with community issues, appearing on panels and radio forums, and on at least one issue was in opposition to the real estate board. (Bouma does not state the sequence of these methods, so it is unclear whether his personal involvement may have affected subsequent data availability.) Fourth, individual realtors and other community leaders were interviewed, meetings of the board of directors and of the entire membership were attended, and the minutes of these meeting were examined.

The inputs into the real estate board were chiefly money, membership, and information. The basic source of its power position was that no other organization in the community had any control or influence over these inputs. The board owned a multiple listing service, the only such service in the community, by whch all members of the board were free to try to sell any house listed. To use the service, a realtor had to be a member of the real estate board. In order to make a living as a realtor, it was virtually essential to belong to the board. By its control of the multiple listing service the board thereby insured the continuance of membership and money. The dependence of individual realtors on the board also assured the board of full membership support and availability of hands for campaign work. The nonprofit board also acquired more money than was needed for board maintenance and therefore had a considerable amount left over for community campaigns. These inputs to the board were well protected.

With respect to information inputs, realtors were particularly knowledgeable of zoning laws, assessments, property taxes, and other such technical information of relevance to community decisions such as school bond proposals. Additionally, Bouma concluded that the real estate business is a good way of maintaining a close tag on the social values of the community. Realtors usually have frequent contacts with their clients, and these contacts touch all segments of the community, cutting across racial, economic, and ethnic lines (however, one would expect underrepresentation from nonproperty owners, e.g., minority groups, poverty groups, young people). At the very least, the board seemed in a better position than most other organizations in the community to obtain this kind of information.

At the same time, one of the few restraints upon the board's social power developed from this value information. The board would not go beyond certain points in their community participation if their value information suggested strong opposition attitudes by the public to their anticipated position.

Another source of power development and maintenance identified by Bouma was the strengthening effect of having many members of the board in appointed and elected authority positions in the community. Realtors thus "penetrated" other organizations which could not command the same degree of allegiance as the board. For many years two of the three state representatives from Grand Valley were members of the real estate board.

Bouma also described what he called a *cumulative* factor in social power. By being powerful and successful in determining decisions in the past, the board became increasingly *the* organization to have on your side, and as a result was frequently approached and consulted. Such conferences gave the board additional opportunities to influence community affairs out of the public's eye. Such "wooing" sessions also provided the board with access to additional information. To slightly rephrase an old adage, it would seem that "it takes power to make power."

To summarize Bouma's findings: the board's inputs were virtually independent of other organizations; the board's outputs were extremely valuable to other organizations; it maintained effective internal controls since its component members were strongly dependent; the board managed a high degree of penetration into other organizations; the board had access to and actively processed a large amount of relevant information (it had relatively loose information filters); yet despite this nearly invulnerable power position the board was careful to maintain a compatible relationship with the prevailing value systems of the community.

INTERSYSTEM NETWORKS AND USERS

Here the focus will be on the goodness-of-fit between a network of human service systems, e.g., mental health, education, health, recreation, etc., and the requirements of the population which uses those services. To what degree does the network provide opportunities or obstacles to the IPM of users? And what intersystem exchanges are helpful or harmful to this goodness-of-fit? At this level of complexity, of course, the very fabric of our society is intimately involved and the sources of difficulty are typically so large or so ingrained that they are beyond the resources of any one intervener. Changes that need to be made are often beyond what community psychologists alone can make, but we can contribute to these changes.

Inappropriate System Responses to Users

The assumption behind service system organization appears to be that the requirements of the user population are divided along the same lines as professional training. You can't expect a school to be concerned about a child's health, or a hospital to be concerned about a child's emotional response to separation from his parents! Service systems provide *single* services based on professional training while users very often have multiple and interconnected service requirements. And typically there is not adequate coordination among these single service systems or effective methods of referral.

An example of an effort toward a multiple service approach is the Bedford-Stuyvesant project in New York initiated by Robert Kennedy. "We must grab the web whole," said Kennedy in a 1966 speech. The initial plan included coordinated programs for jobs, housing improvements, a community university specially planned for drop-outs, plans for better health and recreation facilities, a community center and town hall, and a campaign to persuade new industry to locate in the area.

At the start of the project Kennedy said, "An effort in one problem area is almost worthless. A program for housing, without simultaneous programs for jobs, education, welfare reform, health, and economic development cannot succeed. The whole community must be involved as a whole."

Chief among the problems of this project as it evolved were power conflicts between users, financial backers, professionals, and among different user groups. In short, there were intersystem obstacles.

System Priorities versus User Priorities

All too often service systems are organized for administrative convenience and without regard for user resources or requirements. To expect a distraught mother with a third grade education to navigate the impatient, impersonal, indifferent, poorly labeled administrative maze of a large city hospital is expecting too much. Service systems too often are organized and operated with the security and comfort of delivery personnel as the first priority, with responsiveness to users as typically secondary (for example, most users have daytime jobs, yet compare the number of appointments provided at social service and mental health agencies during the day with those provided in the evenings or weekends).

Too often there are competitive and wasteful (from the point of view of the user) exchanges among service systems. Service systems are often in competition for maintenance inputs from such input sources as United Fund agencies, governmental agencies, charitable organizations, etc. They may view coordination efforts as a threat to those inputs, or even to the survival of their agencies. Coordination agencies may be viewed by service systems as potential threats to autonomy and maintenance inputs. The result of such weak coordination is that separate, unconnected responses to users prevail, often leaving gaps in service. There may be overlap of some services, those having promise of greater inputs (e.g., in the current year drug abuse programs are good for potential funding, in other years it has been manpower training programs, juvenile delinquency, mental retardation, etc.), and underprovision of less promising services. The type of services are determined not by user requirements, but by service system desires for increased inputs. Service agencies are eyeing and vying with one another, each trying to improve its power position and increase its maintenance inputs, which takes energy and time away from programs for the user.

Service systems inputs are usually not under the control or even influenced by users. This may have the effect in some service systems of the IPM of delivery personnel being facilitated at the expense of user IPM. Some agencies are "agency-centered" (major decisions are made with the goal of building and maintaining the agency), others are "program-centered" (decisions are made on the basis of user requirements rather than the security or maintenance of the agency). The best example I know of a program-centered system is a subregional mental health center in Bloomington, Illinois (state supported) directed by Ann Menz, under the regional directorship of Lew Kurke. This agency was continually developing new programs to improve their responses to their clients. Furthermore, their avowed purpose as an agency was to go out of existence! They continually tried to get local agencies to take more and more responsibility for mental health services. They were glad to have their own staff hired away by local agencies. All of their decisions, it seemed to me, were made on the basis of user requirements, not agency enhancement.

The present organization of service systems in most communities places the control of maintenance inputs to the system out of reach of direct control by users. User outputs, or user satisfaction with programs, have no formal vehicle for directly impinging upon system inputs, at least not until user dissatisfaction reaches extreme levels. As a consequence, delivery personnel quite prudently are more responsive to their input sources, i.e., their middle-class boards, government agencies and officials, civic leaders, etc. (who usually are not users), than to their users.

At this point the exasperated critic may be exclaiming, "All right, Murrell, what solutions do you suggest? After all your subjective criticism of present service systems, what would you do to improve this "fit" you are always talking about?"

Fortunately, I have something of an answer, but do not claim a solution. In the process of designing an over-all system of human services for the Louisville New Community project (more about this in Chapter Six) I had occasion to grapple with these issues. Very briefly, we designed a community network of service systems in which a variety of service systems were under the same source of inputs which could then convincingly influence coordination and collaboration among systems. We prescribed intersystem working relationships that aimed to combine educational, health, recreation, and social services through joint appointments, through locating them in close proximity, through their sharing of support personnel, and through the provision of physical space controlled by the community (these agencies would not own their spaces). The key to such coordination must be the control of inputs to the different service systems. We also designed a new and separate elected governance body whose specific tasks were to monitor the programs of service systems, to facilitate communication between delivery personnel and the community residents, and to administer a biannual "habitability survey" which allowed users direct power over the heads of each service system.

It is not assumed here that users are always right and delivery personnel are always wrong, self-serving, or disinterested. On the contrary, many individual professionals are deeply committed to their clients and have very high standards for their own service activities. However, under the present intersystem organization of service agencies and their lines of accountability, the first priority of service *agencies* is not to user requirements. To improve programs in the direction of increased satisfaction of user requirements, users need more power with which to negotiate.

PRELIMINARY ANALYSIS FOR
INTERSYSTEM RELATIONSHIPS

What are the key intersystem areas to examine for a preliminary analysis? One could approach this task from two directions. One could first study the entire population of potential users and gain estimates of their requirements. Then one could compare this information with what systems do in fact provide. For a community-wide intervention, the goal would then be to provide new systems to respond to unmet requirements, and to terminate those systems which were not responsive. A second approach would be to examine present systems, their relationships with one another, and their user populations, examine the network-user fit, and then try to modify the different systems and their relationships to improve this fit. Either approach is a big order, but comparatively the second approach would require fewer resources and less authority. Since it is more realistically within reach of more interveners, the second approach will be discussed here.

Definitions

First, some definitions are needed. The following are offered with the view of being of some pragmatic value for the preliminary analysis.

Focal System.   This term designates the particular social system that is to be studied. Other systems are then defined in terms of their relationship to this focal system. This system might be a family, university, high school, etc. It is defined by the focus of the intervener.

Suprasystem.   The suprasystem is the next highest system having direct power or control over the focal system (it is assumed here that most focal systems will have suprasystems). The suprasystem includes the focal system and probably other social systems as well. If the focal system is Mrs. Johnson's fourth grade class, the suprasystem would be George Washington Elementary School. If the focal system is George Washington Elementary School, the suprasystem would be Unified School District Number 105. The suprasystem always has direct access to and authority over the focal system; there is no intermediary system.

Community.   The term "community" will be used here in a specialized way, specific to the purpose of a preliminary analysis. Community will refer to that environment (usually of people) which has some significant functional relationship to the focal system and suprasystem. This relationship might be with respect to user qualifications for service by the system. A mental health center's catchment area, the population for which it is to provide mental health services, would be an example. I am presently in the process of doing an evaluation of a parent-child center which serves only a specific census tract. That census tract would be the functional community for that preliminary analysis. Or, the community might be the population-environment which had some form of political-legal authority over the suprasystem and focal system. If the focal system were the central administration of a school district and the suprasystem were that district's school board, the community would include the residents of that school district which elected that school board.

To put it in measurement terms, the community would include the population most relevant to survey for attitudes toward and opinions about the focal system (e.g., residents within the catchment area, parents within the census tract, and voters of the school district). In this context, the term "community" is always related to the intervention target.

Implicated Systems. This term refers to social systems which are interdependently involved with focal systems. At the focal system level of analysis, if the focal system were the West Central Mental Health Center, implicated systems would include other social agencies which made referrals to the Center (e.g., police, Juvenile Court, etc.), or which received referrals from the Center (Louisville General Hospital, Central State Hospital), or systems which had a direct advisory capacity but no direct power over the Center (e.g., Jefferson County Mental Health Association).

The relevance of implicated systems for intervention programs is reflected in the experience of Fairweather, et al., (1969) with creating a new subsystem for "chronic mental patients" within a larger community. One of the principles advanced by these authors was: *"Any created social subsystem must be compatible with the environment in which it is implanted"* (p. 325). Fairweather, et al., describe in detail the arrangements made with various organizations and individuals that would be related to the small group living-work unit for discharged patients. A few of these organizations were the hospital, the University, a nonprofit corporation which would hire some of the ex-patients, and labor unions. In this terminology, each of these would be an implicated system.

Many community-oriented professionals have, in their efforts to effect changes in social institutions, encountered what appear to be "hopeless" systems which are uncooperative with change or efforts at greater responsiveness to the IPM of their users. Examples might be county welfare offices and public schools. Because of their apparent "hopelessness" (and typically different values and ideology) the prospective intervener may decide simply to ignore these systems but to persist with other more compatible systems.

The position taken here is that the effects of all implicated systems are important, that such "hopeless" implicated systems cannot be ignored or simply by-passed, but rather that their effects be carefully evaluated and their potential responses to proposed change programs anticipated. Hopefully, in some cases, a careful assessment of such an implicated system will reveal a vulnerable area, susceptible to certain inducements, and thence forebearance if not enthusiasm may be obtained for the intervention program. In short, these "hopeless" systems are avoided at the peril of the intervention. Realistically, however, it is true that some systems will remain change-impregnable even after exhaustive evaluation, or at least that such systems will remain invulnerable given the resources and power of the intervener. This possibility, however, does not warrant *premature* pessimism.

Comparison Systems.   For the purpose of evaluating the effects of an intervention program, it is important to identify systems which could serve as control or comparison groups. Preferably, the comparison system would have the same FA task and be under the same suprasystem as the focal system (e.g., two different high schools within the same school district). A preliminary analysis of the comparison system, examining the same variables as those under study in the focal system, would provide for a post-intervention comparison of the two and a possible evaluation of intervention effects (see discussion of Kelly in Chapter Six).

In some cases the intervention may be the establishment of a new (and presumably improved) alternative system, such as a classroom managed by behavior modification techniques (e.g., Tharp, Cutts, & Burkholder, 1970). Special care needs to be taken to identify an appropriate comparison system having a population very similar to that of the proposed new system (e.g., socioeconomic level, IQs, aspiration levels of students).

Focal Community Feature.   A focal community feature is a characteristic, not confined to any one social system, of the community which is the proposed target of the intervention. As a community *feature* it typically involves a number of different systems, affects them differentially, and represents a problem or potential problem for the community. Examples of such feature tasks are: increasing the feelings of competence in elementary school children, reduction of the number of high school drop-outs, increased feelings by residents of having some degree of control and participation in their environment, developing a service to provide effective responses to drug users, etc. This typically involves the development of multi-system responses to a target population.

Two-System Relationships

First, a number of key areas will be discussed that would often be useful in a preliminary analysis of a focal system and its relationship to other systems.

Linkage. Glidewell (1971b) has pointed to the linkage characteristics of complementarity and reciprocity. Complementarity means that the systems exchange resources that each needs from the other. Reciprocity means that the complementary exchanges are of equal value. Each system's input from the other equals its output to the other. These resources may be material (money, raw supplies, etc.), they may be ideas, skills, feelings, motives, information, etc. Resources of particular importance would be power (related to maintenance inputs) and communication (signal inputs). These are represented in the "links" between the focal system and the suprasystem represented in Figure 7 in Chapter Four. Task functions and climate are internal system variables that affect what is exchanged.

It is proposed that intersystem relationships are potentially, if not always actually, oppositional struggles. Each system is either trying to ensure reciprocity or to gain the upper hand over the other. Such relationships need to be examined to determine which struggle has been intensified or resolved, or the degree to which one system dominates, blocks, supports, or tolerates the other.

Task. The following task areas would be important to assess:
1. The degree of agreement or disagreement between the two systems as to: (a) the definition of the system tasks (is the definition of the foreign relations task by the State Department the same as the President's?); and (b) the evaluation of the importance of the tasks (does the value placed upon increased production by the foreman equal that assessed by the worker on the line?).
2. The degree of collaboration between systems with respect to task-relevant operations (does the suprasystem adequately supply the focal system with necessary supplies, resources and support in general, or does it impose restrictions which impede the focal system's operations?). This variable might be viewed as a dimension running from a collaborative relationship, through to a midline defined as indifference, and then to the other extreme of an opposing relationship.
3. The FA/IPM task ratio. Does the intersystem relationship contribute to a balance or imbalance between the FA task and IPM contributions? This variable applies particularly to the focal-system—suprasystem and to the population—focal-system relationships. For example, if a teacher maintains strict discipline through ridicule and demeaning remarks, she creates an imbalance of FA task (maintaining orderly classroom) over IPM contributions (feelings of self-esteem and confidence) for the students.
4. The similarity of system outputs and degree of competition. This variable will refer particularly to relationships between implicated systems. To what degree are they responding to the same user population? To what degree are they dependent upon the same source for inputs?

Power. The following power areas seem particularly important for analysis of intersystem relationships:

1. The degree to which the systems are dependent upon each other. This variable defines the power relationship between the two systems. Of particular importance is the degree of control by one over the maintenance inputs of the other.

2. To what degree is responsibility and decision-making centralized, as opposed to being widely distributed? For example, does the school district superintendent prescribe that all teachers in his system will teach reading phonetically (centralized power) or does he dispense the authority of choosing the method to the teacher (wider distribution of power).

3. The degree to which the structural and procedural mechanisms of the intersystem relationship provide routinely for subordinate system inputs to decisions which directly affect it. To illustrate, consider the following: the focal system is a county mental health center, the suprasystem its lay board. The decision takes place at the monthly meeting of the lay board and center executive staff on the matter of collecting unpaid fees. The members of the lay board routinely invite staff members to its meetings and routinely consult with them on all decisions made. In this particular relationship, then, the subordinate system does have broad opportunities to participate in decisions affecting it.

4. The degree of member penetration. This variable refers to the number of individuals who have overlapping membership between the systems. This is most likely to occur between implicated systems (e.g., the school superintendent serves on the United Fund board). Organization A has power over B, relative to B's reciprocal power over A, to the degree that it has more of its members penetrating B than B has members penetrating A. Evan (1966) has suggested that for organizations of similar task functions, overlapping membership may serve to reduce competitiveness.

5. The degree of cumulative power. This refers to the history of

the power relations between the systems. To the degree that system A has been successful in exerting control or influence over system B in the past, it holds a power advantage in the future. If it is a new relationship, the system which has built up the higher cumulative power in the community has the power advantage.

Communication. Three variables are presented here as being particularly relevant to an intersystems analysis.
1. The degree to which information from one system is disseminated to the other system. This variable includes both the amount of information distributed, and the significance or relative importance of that information. Generally, this variable reflects the relative openness of information filters at the interface of the different systems under study.
2. Whether or not there is a provision in the structural procedures of the intersystem activities for the exchange of negative feedback (remember that "negative" here refers to *new* information or information that is different from the information already in the system; it does not necessarily mean that the content of the information will be critical or derogatory). This is an all-or-none variable, it does not include the amount of negative feedback exchanged, it only designates whether or not there is provision for negative feedback exchange between systems.
3. The relative access to relevant information. This variable is also a power variable. One system may have better access to information because it has control over the information source. In other relationships, one system may have better access because its information filters are more active and open. In a relationship between competitive implicated systems, other things being equal, the system with better access to information has the power advantage.

Climate. The following intersystem comparison pertaining to climate could be important.

1. The degree of discrepancy of climate between the systems. My hypothesis is that in general the greater the difference in climates between any two systems the greater the conflicts in their relationship. Differences in climate will often also reflect differences on task, power, and communication variables. Individuals from a formal, highly structured, authoritarian suprasystem would perhaps find it difficult to objectively assess the task effectiveness of an informal, loosely organized, equalitarian subsystem.

Figure 11 offers a summary of these key intersystem areas.

Intersystem Obstructions to Users

From a somewhat different angle, areas of intersystem relations in a service system network that pose problems for users will be discussed.

Task	Power	Communication	Climate
1. intersystem agreement on task	1. relative reciprocal dependence	1. amount of information exchange	1. discrepancy of climate between systems
2. intersystem collaboration on task	2. distribution of power by suprasystem	2. provision for negative feedback loop from subsystem	
3. FA/IPM balance	3. subsystem participation in decision-making	3. relative access to information	
4. comparison of input suppliers and output users	4. reciprocal penetration		
	5. relative cumulative power		

Figure 11   Key areas for a two-system preliminary analysis

Contradictory Demands.   The demands of different systems upon a common user population may be contradictory. This is a state of competing intersystem accommodation for the user population. One example of this is the subculture demand in Amish communities that their children not be required to go to high school in opposition to the state's education requirements. The users, the adolescent population, are caught between competing system demands. Or, black children may be caught between the norms and expectations of youth programs in their neighborhoods which emphasize black pride and awareness and refusal to knuckle under to white exploitation, and the expectations of their middle-class white teachers.

For the preliminary analysis, the task definitions and the environmental forces of the competing systems need to be examined and compared. The major points of conflict need to be identified as targets for an intervention. Also, the presence or absence of communication procedures between the competing systems needs to be scrutinized with the aim of improvement.

Uncoordinated Services.   This situation does not involve active conflicting demands but rather is the absence of a facilitating fit between systems. In systems that are related to one another vertically, the lack of coordination may leave the users inadequately prepared for entry into the next higher system, e.g., family to school, head start classes to regular classes, junior high to senior high, etc. Systems related to one another in a horizontal fashion may give the users misinformation about the procedures or tasks of the other. Examples of such horizontal relationships include a welfare agency making a referral to a mental health center, an outpatient clinic referral to an inpatient unit, an employment agency referral to a mental health center, etc. The result is to leave the users baffled, frustrated, and unserved.

Here it will be important to examine the definitions of FA task by the suprasystem and by the delivery personnel. Is there a discrepancy? If so the intervention might require discussion with the suprasystem to exert pressure for change on its delivery personnel. Particularly with referral mess-ups, the communication between the systems needs to be studied. The communication malfunction may, however, be due to competition for inputs, to mutual avoidance of certain user groups, or to personality conflicts between respective delivery personnel. Sometimes inadequate referral may not be due to intersystem relations but to the inadequate task performance of one of the systems. Here the relationship between delivery personnel and the suprasystem agent (the FA boss) will be critical.

Gaps in Services. This refers to the situation where the service system network as a whole may be missing important systems for user requirements. The job training program may do the training and find jobs but there is no transportation for the users. Mothers may have jobs and transportation but no day care services. "Mental patients" may have psychotherapy, drugs, jobs, but no opportunity for involvement in social groups. Practically speaking, the intervener will usually focus on only one user characteristic (given that single service systems predominate) and closely examine user requirements and preferences relevant to that characteristic. For example, he would study the trainees in the job training program, and the systems in which they participate. The gaps then would be reflected after a series of these system-population analyses.

DIRECTIONS FOR INTERVENTIONS

An intersystem network is as dangerous as a jungle. The intervener can expect to be distrusted. Systems will expect that their legitimacy or adequacy are being questioned, that the intervener is trying to "horn in," to get more than he gives, and may perceive him as an "undercover agent" for some other system. He can expect outright refusal to let him in, passive resistance if he does get in, and booby traps or sabotage of his intervention. For the brave and hardy soul who still desires the challenge, here are some suggestions.

First, it is important that all systems that are to be involved are consulted about the proposed project at about the same time and from the beginning. They need to have opportunity to genuinely participate in the planning of the project. This will mean that the intervener often will have to compromise—a half loaf is better than none. He will have to be patient and willing to have his ideas resisted, criticized, and changed. He will need the patience of Job and will not have as powerful input support. Obviously, the more power the intervener does have the easier it will be for him.

Second, if the intervener is confronted with two conflicted systems his first step may be to approach their respective suprasystems. However, he must be careful to avoid an out-and-out power play if possible. Even with directives from above, systems can passively resist and find apparently legitimate reasons for being unaable to help even when they express a "willingness" to do so. The intervener wants to get approval and legitimacy from above, but also participative contributions from below.

Third, in cases of absolutely recalcitrant systems that will hear of no kind of intervention, the intervener may decide that it is necessary to help the users organize their own systems to fight for added or different services. This, of course, is the community organization approach which places the intervener in an advocate role (see Weissman, 1969). This role poses problems for the community psychologist as a scientist which will be discussed in the next chapter. Another alternative, particularly when the problem is one of a gap in services, is to work with other existing systems toward developing a new system that *will* respond to the gap.

Fourth, particularly when the problem is the lack of coordination between systems or inadequate preparation from one system to the next, the strengthening of linkage functions may well be the focus of the intervention. Glidewell (1971b) in discussing some of the discontinuities between a mental health system and an educational institution suggests the following (translated into our terms) for improving linkage functions: (a) overlapping role incumbents, such as counselors who hold joint apointments in both systems; (b) intermember penetration of suprasystems, such as educators serving on the mental health center board; (c) direct interaction in the other system by delivery personnel, such as mental health consultants working in the schools (e.g., Iscoe, et al., 1967; Rae-Grant & Stringer, 1969); and (d) increased participation and utilization by users, such as using parents in the treatment of children, or having this year's high school sophomore class help prepare and orient next year's sophomores.

The intervener himself may play an important linkage function by listening to members of different systems and distributing information among them. Particularly when the delivery personnel of competing systems have difficulty talking to and hearing each other, the intervener can be important as an intermediary. Of course, as an intermediary he can be caught in a cross-fire, so his is a delicate mission.

A final word. No matter how well he performs his preliminary analysis or plans his intervention, a great deal of the intervener's success depends on his interpersonal style *vis-a-vis* members of these host systems. He has to relate to individuals rather than to systems in the abstract. These interpersonal skills are a prerequisite; not everyone is suited to this activity. My view is that it is particularly important for the intervener to relate in a genuinely collaborative way. The arrogance of the expert role, the vocabulary and superior manner of the intellectual who desires to give instruction to the system, or the indignant and self-righteous air of the social reformer, are all counter-productive in the long run. One really has to feel as if one is a *partner* in the intervention enterprise.

At the same time, the intensity and immediacy of relating to individual members of these systems can prevent the intervener from also seeing them as being affected by their system, as representing important functions for their systems. If they appear as "villains" remember that there are environmental forces from the system which at least in part contribute to their behavior.

6. INTERVENTIONS

The purpose of this chapter is to provide help for the actual operation of an intervention. It will include a discussion of six levels of possible interventions, a detailed description of five actual interventions, and finally a listing of thirteen intervention guides.

The broad definition of "intervention" that will be used here is simply any systematic effort at introducing a change in individuals, social systems, populations, or networks of social systems, which has as its desired end the improvement of the individual-environment fit. "Intervener" will refer to the one person or group that bears the greatest responsibility for initiating the change. It is to present and future interveners that this chapter, indeed this book, is directed.

First, the variety of possible interventions needs to be considered.

SIX LEVELS OF INTERVENTION

Clearly, interventions may have all shapes and sizes. Here the objective is to reduce the indefiniteness of the term without aspiring to precise delineations or to an exhaustive taxonomy of all possible interventions. Six types of interventions, differing in complexity and ambitiousness of purpose, will be briefly described. The bulk of the chapter will provide detailed examples of the latter four.

Level One: Individual Relocation

No one individual can harmonize with all social systems and no one social system can facilitate the problem-management of all individuals.

When the relationship is incompatible to the degree that improvement is beyond the capability of one or both sides, then the individual should be relocated into a system more compatible to his problem-management. Examples would be: relocating a mentally retarded child out of a regular classroom and into a special education class; relocating a child from his natural parents when they are incapable of caring for him to a foster home; relocating a man into an employment training program and then into a new job situation out of a job situation whose demands were incompatible with his intellectual resources.

This intervention is probably most effective when the "inharmonious" fit is limited to characteristics of the one specific system, rather than general characteristics of many systems within the network. If John, for example, finds Desdemona to be bitchy and bossy, and therefore anticomplementary to his interpersonal requirements, he may easily choose to "relocate" and begin a new relationship with sweet and submissive Rebecca, since Desdemona's characteristics are not exclusive among all his possibilities.

Also, this intervention is probably more effective when the individual's inharmonious characteristics conform to, in Sarbin's terms, *achievement* statuses rather than *ascribed* statuses. For men with good educations and employment histories it is relatively easy for them to change their jobs and increasingly improve their individual-system fit. However, being a member of a minority group, being female, being young (all ascribed statuses), etc., may well contribute to inharmonious relationships in the relocated system as much as in the original.

This intervention is also unlikely to be effective over the long term if the relocation system is to be a temporary "helping" one, as has been pointed out by Glidewell (1968). For example, systems such as those for protection (prisons, mental hospitals, etc.), for therapy, for rehabilitation, etc., have the expectation that the individual will soon return to the original inharmonious system. More precisely, the ineffectiveness here is not in the method itself but rather in the current inability of such temporary systems to modify the individual's resources, preferred solutions, and strategies sufficiently to allow the individual to readapt back into the unchanged original inharmonious system (prisons, for example, typically have recidivism rates of around 70 percent).

Furthermore, as Glidewell points out, even if the temporary system does bring about changes in the individual, these changes may be such as also to be disruptive or tension-producing when the individual returns to his old system. That is, the changes are those appropriate from the temporary system's point of view, which is not necessarily that of the original system. This is more likely the more isolated and different the temporary system is from the original one.

Level Two: Individual Interventions

Here the effort is to change or add to the individual's resources and strategies so that he can remain in and better accept his system assignment (as it is) and can execute it in a manner more acceptable to the system. Examples would be: technical training, behavior-modification programs, outpatient psychotherapy, crisis-intervention therapy, medication, physical exercise, etc. Clearly, this method works best if the individual himself chooses to be changed or improved, i.e., he wants to stay in the system.

The effectiveness of this intervention depends upon how specifically relevant the method is to the individual's bad-fit characteristics (i.e., it must be related to system requirements):

psychotherapy will not provide new job skills, job skills will not control diabetes. Again, if the bad-fit characteristics are ascribed statuses, this intervention will be inadequate.

Level Three: Population Interventions

Here the effort is to change, prepare, or provide added resources to a population that is or will be in an inharmonious relationship with its social systems. Prevention programs in mental health are good examples of this kind of intervention (e.g., Cowen & Zax, 1968). Programs characterized as "anticipatory guidance" (Bloom, 1971; Caplan & Gruenbaum, 1970) try to prepare a population for future crises, such as preparing late-middle-aged people for retirement; preparing parents and children for the initial entry of the child into school (e.g., Kellam & Schiff, 1966; Klein, 1961; Murrell, 1969; Rae-Grant & Stringer, 1969); premarital counseling; the Head Start program; enrichment programs for infants (e.g., Gordon, 1969) and many others.

Glidewell (1968, 1971) emphasizes that population-directed "prevention" and early detection programs in public health have relieved much pain and distress but have not reduced the incidence of the disease. He emphasizes the need to modify *environmental* systems as critical to the real prevention of behavior disorders.

A major difficulty in implementing many such population-focused programs is getting the target population to volunteer to participate. First, the population has to know why it needs such a program. Second, participation in such programs must be seen as nonaversive, not as labeling one as deviant or requiring one to admit that one might have socially undesirable problems. Third, the population has to be motivated to do something about typically nonimmediate, nonurgent problems (e.g., premarital counseling would take place before those involved had experienced many of the anticipated problems).

Level Four: Social System Interventions

These methods attempt to make enduring changes in social systems themselves to the end that they are more facilitative of individual problem-management. An intervention generally will be more enduring and effective if it affects the *structure* of the social system (e.g., rearranging the power hierarchy) rather than simply adding new tasks or activities within the old structure.

Among the possible kinds of social systems interventions are the following:

Change in Key System Personnel. Perhaps the best known methods for social system change involve changing the behaviors of key system personnel. Consultation (e.g., Iscoe, 1967; Rae-Grant & Stringer, 1969; Caplan & Gruenbaum, 1970), direct training of teachers in behavior-modification techniques (Tharp, Cutts, & Burkholder, 1970), training police in crisis-intervention techniques (Bard, 1971), and many other efforts directed not at the target population itself but at changing system responses to the target population, are examples of one kind of system change effort.

Increasing Assignment Latitude   This refers to the expansion of "niche breadth" so that the individual has more leeway to execute his system assignment in a manner more acceptable to himself and which gives him more opportunity to make adjustments in that assignment to better fit the demands of his assignments in other systems. This would mean, for the system, that it could tolerate greater diversity among its members. The greater the diversity in an environment, according to a principle of ecology (Kelly, 1968), the better able are more diverse species to adapt to it simultaneously.

The critical constraint upon assignment latitude is the system's formal task requirements. This task will require certain behaviors and forbid other behaviors. As Glidewell (1968) has pointed out, in general it is a fundamental requirement by institutions that there be *some* limits to one's niche breadth— for the sake of the institution's continued production and maintenance. The aim, however, should be to allow variation in style and approach to prescribed tasks by different persons even though the tasks are generally similar.

A note of caution: wide-latitude assignments provide less structure and guidance. To individuals whose solutions and strategies require closer guidance, such wide-latitude assignments will hinder their problem-management. Therefore, a system should be able to provide an assortment of assignments which vary on this dimension of latitude and then attempt to place the person in the assignment which fits him best.

Increasing assignment latitude, in and by itself, will only provide greater *opportunity* for the individual to utilize his preferred strategies toward his preferred solutions; it does not change his resources, or lack thereof, which may be critical to the inharmonious relationship. It also will not help if the disharmony is network-wide, e.g., allowing wide assignment latitude for a black delinquent within a residential institution, but being unable to change his assignments in his home, school, or employment situations will not improve those relationships after he leaves the institution.

Increasing Assignment Variety.   In addition to providing assignments of differing degrees of latitude, a social system network will enhance psychosocial accord if it can provide a variety of ways in which very different individual resources and strengths can be maximally demonstrated.

Foa (1971) has presented an intriguing and convincing position with regard to his *resource theory* in relation to urban environments. Foa empirically arrived at six classes of resources which vary on the dimensions of concreteness and *particularism* (the latter being of major concern here): love, status, services, information, goods, money. Love would be the most particularistic resource, money the least particularistic (or the most universalistic). I can easily receive money from anyone and in many forms. I can receive love from only a few people and it will need to be expressed in ways especially suited to me. Foa points out that the size of metropolitan populations and the tendency of our social institutions to each specialize in a narrow range of resources require responses to individuals that are ineffective because they are so universalistic. Our urban institutions, often under the excuse of administrative efficiency, typically do not recognize population diversity as relevant to their tasks, they do not accommodate a wide range of different individual resources; you either fit their narrow range or you do without.

The aim suggested here is to increase a system's ability to provide particularistic responses to its members. Examples would be: a high school changing its hair and dress code to allow greater diversity; a university faculty department having wide variation among its members in terms of teaching loads, research loads, and community service loads; an industrial organization changing work assignments so that they allow for greater variety, responsibility, and autonomy (which has been found to increase satisfaction and productivity, e.g., Trist & Bamforth, 1951).

For example, over the past 15 years or so there has been an accumulation of evidence that different students need different kinds of teaching methods or approaches, that one method may be best for one type of student, another method for another type of student (Pervin, 1968). Grimes and Allinsmith (1961) compared a relatively structured method of teaching reading (phonics) with a less structured approach (the whole word or the "look and say" approach) with third grade children who differed in amount of compulsivity and anxiety. Highly compulsive students did better in structured than unstructured classes. Highly anxious students did more poorly in unstructured schools than in structured schools. Children in unstructured schools appeared to be better socially adjusted. The authors conclude that there is an interaction effect between personality and teaching methods. Beach (1960) found that students low on sociability perform better in large lecture section whereas more sociable students perform better in discussion groups. Amidon and Flanders (1961) found that dependent children performed better under indirect than direct teaching methods, while more independent children performed equally well under either method. Further studies attest to differences in performance or satisfaction due to differences between teacher-student "fit" (Bay, 1962; McKeachie, 1961; Patton, 1965). Katz and Sanford (1962) concluded with vigor that there is no one universal curriculum that is best for every student and then berated institutions and administrations for making such a "convenient" (for them) assumption.

The intervention being suggested here, however, goes beyond recommending more variety in teaching approaches. It recommends that the social network intentionally strive to *tailor* assignments to fit individuals. This would mean that children whose resources were stronger in physical or motor areas would be given system assignments that would provide for expression of those skills, that would legitimize those skills, and that would reward those skills. A child who had trouble reading but was a whiz at carving would receive tasks involving carving and would receive praise and recognition for his carving: he would be the class carver, not a slow learner. Boisterous and athletic boys would be singled out for special attention not for their disruptiveness but for their athletic prowess, their strength, etc. In other words, a social system should not provide only a set of square holes (even if of different sizes) and try to fit each individual in; it should strive to recarve the holes so that they fit both the individual's idiosyncratic "shape" and the system's formal task requirements. Such a condition will not result from mere good intentions but will require active administrative commitment and action. In the case of the educational setting, for this example, it may sometimes require a modified definition of the system's formal task.

Designing Experimental Systems.   These efforts set up new systems that possess changed social system variables and then compare these new systems with old systems that have the same formal achievement task and perhaps the same population. Fairweather, et al., (1969) provide a prototype for this kind of intervention in their design of a system for housing and employing mental patients following their release from mental hospitals and then comparing the effects of the new system to old methods (e.g., visits to a mental hygiene clinic while living at home).

Such efforts are rare. They obviously require large amounts of money and manpower. They provide the community psychologist with a particularly attractive operating base, providing him with legitimate expertise power due to his research training and at the same time giving him considerable autonomy.

Interventions in Systems and Feedback.   As Buckley (1968) has pointed out, social systems are both stable and in a continual process of change. This makes intervening in social systems something like trying to mount a running horse. Since the system is always changing, an intervention initiated at time 1 and having positive and expected effects may, at time 2, have negative and unexpected effects. This suggests the necessity of building a mechanism into the intervention itself for continuing feedback about its effects. Thus, if an interventionist were to design changes in the reinforcement contingencies used by a classroom teacher he should also design and provide the teacher with methods to measure their behavioral effects regularly over time.

Level Five: Intersystem Interventions

Methods at this level involve more than one system, typically systems with different formal achievement tasks. They may be directed at reducing conflicts or smoothing transitions for individuals who are in simultaneous transactions with the different systems. They may represent efforts at attacking community-feature social problems with coordinated action from many different systems. Implementation at this level becomes more complex because typically the intervener has no authority or clear role with all of the systems involved.

Intersystem Assistance Programs. Social systems should strive to ease abrupt transitions into new systems and to reduce conflicting intersystem accommodations by devising programs that enlist both (or more) systems for a combined effort. For example, schools should strive to actively engage families of children entering school for the first time both to communicate expectations and to understand the values and expectations of these families. This information then should be used in receiving the particular child and in designing his system assignment. Another example would be to develop programs in hospitals which would reduce the possibility of serious psychological effects of hospitalization for young children. Caplan and Gruenbaum (1970) suggest several possible programs such as providing for mothers to stay with and help nurse their children, changes in hospital procedures and practices, stronger efforts to treat children at home rather than in a hospital, etc. Such programs require hospitals to consider, listen to, and in some cases yield to the other system—the family.

Intersystem Coordination Programs. These efforts attempt to mobilize the resources of a number of social systems having different formal achievement tasks toward a social problem which interfaces with each of these tasks but which is not the exclusive concern of any one of the systems. The collaboration of a number of different social service agencies to provide for a suicide prevention program would be one example. Another would be the collaboration of education officials, juvenile court probation officers, mental health professionals, church officials, and employment agency representatives to increase employment opportunities for adolescents as a deterrent to juvenile delinquency.

Community Action Programs. Most community action programs are of an intersystem nature (e.g., see Marris & Rein, 1967; Weissman, 1969; Zurcher, 1969) and are focused on one segment or issue of the community (rather than on the community as a whole which would qualify them as *network* interventions, see below). They are typically efforts at organizing subgroups within a population and related social systems to bring about changes in institutions or services. These institutions or services are frequently perceived or declared to be harmful or at least obstructive to the particular subgroup.

Level Six: Network Interventions

The efforts at this level are community-wide. The design of a new community that would enhance the community's psychosocial responsiveness to its individual residents (Murrell, 1971b) is one example.

These efforts are as yet rather rare but opportunities are increasing as "citizen participation" is increasingly recognized as valuable. In particular, interventionists in urban and regional planning commissions have opportunities to enhance harmonious relationships between the individual and his habitat.

ILLUSTRATIVE INTERVENTIONS

Each of the following interventions is one in which I had direct first-hand experience as the intervener. This precludes an objective assessment of the intervention's success, but it allows for the fullest access to the events and people involved and for a frank critique. This is, then, a chronicle of what has happened to me and what I learned from it.

The purpose of presenting these interventions is to illustrate guides for interveners. The intent is not to provide a comprehensive review of intervention programs in community psychology. There are available other books which have this as their major purpose, e.g., Carter (1968), Cook (1970), Golan and Eisdorfer (1972), Shore and Mannino (1969).

KINDERGARTEN POPULATION INTERVENTION

Overview

This intervention falls under level three, a population intervention. It was directed at all prospective kindergarten students in the Turner School District (Kansas City, Kansas) starting in the spring of 1967. It consisted of a series of talks by me to mothers of the prospective kindergarteners regarding how to prepare their children for entry into school. Each child came with his mother and was taken to visit ongoing kindergarten classes and then was given some tests to determine maturity and school readiness. Participation by mothers and children was voluntary. However, the school officials and PTA made a very strong effort to get all known children and their mothers to attend the preparatory program. Also, a series of meetings had been scheduled between the kindergarten and first grade and their families and the things teachers could be aware of and do. This was also to include discussions of problem children.

The major aims of this project can be summarized as:
1. To help the child get off to a good start in his school experience and therefore to help prevent social or emotional problems.
2. To detect social or emotional problems early so that treat-

ment could be more effective (we assumed).

3. To use Mental Health Center staff to start the project and then to assist and encourage the school system itself to take it over.

Preliminary Analysis

This project was based upon a preconceived notion of the problem, not upon any preliminary study nor upon any concrete evidence than there *was* a problem.

At the same time there was a wave of work in early detection and prevention programs (e.g., Cowen, Zax, Izzo, & Trost, 1966; Cowen, Gardner, & Zax, 1967). I was most specifically influenced by an article by Don Klein (1961) which discussed the work of Lindemann and his group and described the school-entry time as a period of potential crisis. Also, from my position as Chief Psychologist at the Wyandotte County Mental Health and Guidance Center (Kansas City, Kansas) I could see that we could never hope to provide enough treatment for everyone who needed it and that with many we were simply coming in too late to be of any help. So, because of practical clinical problems and because it was a progressive mental health activity I helped launch this program. (An earlier talk with Lorene Stringer had also been helpful and supportive and had provided impetus for moving in this direction.)

However, this project did not suddenly burst forth full-blown from me alone. It grew out of a series of consultations with counselors at Turner High School. Stemming from these meetings I had additional contacts with Martha Eislie, the head counselor, and we began talking the same language. She had a thorough knowledge of the personalities and politics of the entire school system. With her knowledge she was able to talk to principals and the superintendent and to clearly interpret and sell the proposed project to them. It was very handy for me and for the project to have an "agent" in the system. The disadvantages of having Martha as our agent were not clear at the time. They boiled down to this: Martha herself was not a neutral part of the system (probably no person can be, but Martha was rather outspoken), she belonged to one of two major factions. So, our project (and myself) became linked to this faction. Without any very clear understanding of these power relations I was *in* them. The effects on the project were that some of the reactions (either positive or negative) by other school staff to myself and the project had less to do with the merits or weaknesses of the project itself but more with the staff member's particular relationship to Martha and her faction.

Another example may show how inattentiveness to interrelationships within the system can foil an intervention. An arrangement had been made by Martha and the principal of one of the elementary schools for me to meet with the kindergarten and first grade teachers to talk about problem children. (It is important to note that the teachers themselves had not asked for my help.) After I arrived I soon realized that the principal planned to stay and attend the meeting. This fact, plus a few authoritarian remarks by the principal, set the tone of that doomed meeting. Feeling that their effectiveness as teachers was being evaluated by the principal and myself, the teachers very understandably had few problem children to discuss. I had not at all anticipated that the principal would attend or that this tone for the meeting would result.

Role of the Intervener

First of all, I was a representative of the Mental Health Center. I made sure that I kept Elizabeth Gray (the executive director of the Center) informed about all plans and problems associated with the project. She once told me how important it was for her to know about all aspects of the Center's operations so that she could answer the many questions she received from members of our lay board and other members of the community.

Clearly, since the Center paid my salary I had to protect my input lines there.

Second, I entered the system at a high-middle power echelon. My access was through Martha and through the central administration. I was an agent (unknowingly at first) of the central administration and of the faction to which Martha belonged. I was not an agent for the critical implementation personnel, the principals. In practice, this meant that the fate of the program rested upon the relationship between Martha and the principals.

Third, I was in the role of a mental health professional, having expertise in the eyes of most of the school staff. I was an outsider, a relatively nonthreatening outsider I think (i.e., Martha vouched for me), with a fairly logical proposal.

Resources

What were my resources? I had the presumed knowledge and prestige of the Ph.D. degree. I had the backing of the good reputation of the Mental Health Center which had been providing helpful and often successful service to referrals from Turner. This was my greatest resource in working with the principals since they could now feel free to call me directly regarding referrals to the Center and hope for perhaps special consideration. I had expressed interest in their problems and had offered my time at no cost. I made every effort to be a helpful collaborator rather than being the superior or judgmental expert consultant. Of course, Martha's backing was an essential resource. And, not to be underestimated, I offered a plan that apparently made some sense to the school staff.

Assessment of the Intervention

The weakest part of this intervention was the lack of a preliminary analysis. The intervention was not a response to data or to requests for help either from teachers, principals, or parents. And without a preliminary collection of base-line data there was no way to evaluate whether the program attained its first two objectives. The absence of a preliminary analysis also left me relatively ignorant of intrasystem power relationships which might have sunk the program before it set sail.

The Turner school system did continue the project the following year and carried it out with its own staff. This following year there also was a plan to follow up those children who appeared to be vulnerable on the basis of the readiness tests. This was basically a check of how well these tests did predict adjustment and academic problems. I left my position at the Center and the region and do not know if it was continued a third year or not.

On a more personal level, and in retrospect, the things I feel I did best as the intervener were: (a) I protected my inputs from the Mental Health Center very well which was essential since it was my greatest resource; and (b) with Martha I was able to sell the plan. The biggest weaknesses were: (a) my failure to involve the implementation personnel (the principals) earlier; (b) my ignorance regarding the covert alliances and conflicts of interests within the system; and, of course, (c) the already mentioned failure to obtain sufficient advance information upon which to design or evaluate the intervention.

HIGH SCHOOL
SOCIAL SYSTEM INTERVENTION

Overview

This was a level *four* intervention, an attempt to modify the structure of a system (it was directed at one particular *focal system*) in a way that would facilitate the psychosocial accord of its population. Of central emphasis was our effort to make this a truly collaborative program between the high school and the

Wyandotte County Mental Health Center staff.

This effort might be more aptly described as a series of interventions, many of which took place after I had left. I will therefore concentrate here upon the preliminary analysis and the work toward building a collaborative relationship.

Based upon my experience with the kindergarten project, I wanted to know what was going on in the system before developing an intervention. I would now articulate this as a cardinal rule for interveners:

Before you intervene, know thy system!

I also very definitely wanted the program to be responsive to the concerns of the implementation personnel.

It began on a fall morning in 1967 when I went to see Father Maher, principal of Bishop Ward High School, a catholic high school in Kansas City, Kansas. I had heard that his was an innovative, changing system and hoped it was accessible to us. My proposal to Father Maher went something like this:

At the Mental Health Center we are faced with many troubled adolescents. We see quite a few from Ward each year. By the time we see them, their family patterns are often rigidified. We find many of them are just not able to use psychotherapy. We would like to work with you to see if there are some things that can be done *in the high school itself* to be helpful to these youngsters. However, we don't know anything about a high school—we don't know what it's like to be a student here, or a teacher, or an administrator. So, first we would like to ask you to simply let us come in and look around, so that we can learn more about your high school. Then we would try to work *with* you to set up some helpful programs.

Father Maher, not knowing quite what he was getting into, nevertheless was receptive to the idea. Three other members of the Mental Health Center staff and myself spent several months observing and talking to people in halls, classrooms, teacher's lounges, cafeterias, and study halls. (This "walking around analysis" will be discussed in more detail below.) Following that period we made a presentation of our observations to the faculty and then discussed them in small groups. On the basis of these discussions we next offered alternative ways we might continue working with them and asked the faculty to indicate their preferences. Subsequent programs developed which included training in group discussion skills (which they perceived as being relevant to their FA task); joint staff discussions regarding discipline policy matters; group sessions with students, half of whom were on probation, half of whom were not; and a special consultation relationship with one of the black Center staff members regarding racial issues.

Throughout this early period there were continual joint meetings, followed up by letters which would attempt to nail down conclusions and state proposals specifically. An enduring issue in these meetings was the proper role of the Center staff. We wished to maintain the collaborator role, while with the high amount of initial ambiguity involved they wanted us to state clearly what we wanted.

Preliminary Analysis

Our first analysis actively involved what later I have jocularly referred to as a W.A.A., a "walking-around analysis." Our major problem was the lack of structure or guidance to our observations and questions. We did not know what to look for, and we did not have a good sense of what was and was not important.

At the end of this period, we collected our impressions into the following document which was distributed to all the faculty members and which served as the basis for the small group discussions.

SUMMARY OF OBSERVATIONS
AT WARD HIGH SCHOOL

When we, members of the Guidance Center staff, first approached the Administration of Ward, we expressed our interest in getting to know more about a high school setting. Since we see many adolescents at the Center we thought it would help us to know more about "what happens" in a high school. We approached Ward because we had heard that you were trying new things, and we felt you might be more open than other high schools in the area. From our experience this has been very true.

After several months of observation at Ward, we discussed our observations with some members of the administrative and guidance staffs. Following that we were asked to present our observations to the faculty. We have asked for the opportunity to meet with you in groups so that there might be opportunity for discussion of our observations, and for exploring areas that we can further work on together.

First, let us say we were very impressed with Ward. We have some knowledge of other high schools in the area and we were amazed at the efforts being made at Ward toward trying new things and trying to meet problems. We have learned a great deal from our experience and have come to view the problems of the administration and faculty from a more knowledgable, and more sympathetic, point of view.

I. *Atmosphere of change: reactions.*

A. *Students* generally seemed to have positive attitudes toward changes, e.g., modules, team teaching, free time periods in the cafeteria, etc. Toward the latter period of our observation (late fall) we began to hear more negative comments, e.g., the modules as being too short.

B. *Teachers* seemed to have more ambivalent reactions to changes. Some were very positive, excited, and proud of changes, others seemed skeptical of giving students increased freedom, skeptical of students' ability to be more responsible, and critical of teachers using less strict discipline.

C. It was our *guess* that perhaps some teachers were reacting to the loosening of control by administrative policies (as they saw it) by becoming tighter in other areas. For example, cafeteria supervisors making students studying in the cafeteria go out and come back at module change. This struck us as being rather arbitrary.

II. *Teacher-student relationships.*

A. Student opinions were varied. Some students said they felt free to approach their teachers, to talk with them, and felt teachers were receptive to them. Others felt their teachers were difficult to approach, were not receptive. We would imagine that this would be fairly typical in high school settings, that some teachers are more receptive and approachable than others, and that some students might find it easier to talk with their teachers than others. There might be ways, however, of making it more possible for more students to feel free to talk with at least some of their teachers.

B. Students feel there are too many rules and regulations. They generally don't like pink slips or their frequency of distribution, they feel that punishments are sometimes arbitrary. They don't think the system of pink slips is useful.

C. Some teachers also have doubts about the pink slip method.

D. Our impression was that there is wide variation among teachers in their sensitivity to and interest in students.

III. *Teacher-teacher relationships.*

A. We sensed some rivalry between male and female teachers.

B. There seems to be generally good relationships between guidance personnel and teachers. Our guess is that this is due, partly, at least, to a positive attitude toward guidance functions on the part of the administration. These relationships seem much better than those in other high schools we have worked with.

IV. *Teacher-administration relationships.*

A. Generally speaking, our impression was that the administration is quite open to the opinions and concerns of teachers. Criticism of the administration seems more possible to express by teachers in this high school than we had expected.

B. However, we gathered the idea that some teachers are skeptical of the administration's sincerity in asking their participation in developing new programs and policies. Some teachers seemed to be saying that they were not convinced, yet.

C. There were indications that some teachers experience difficulty in communicating upward, from teachers to the administration. Some seemed to feel that certain teachers had the ear of the administration, while others did not. Probably more efforts toward open communication will be necessary on the part of both teachers and administration.

V. *Student-student relationships.*

A. There seems to be a strong system of cliques of students, and the students are very aware of this. Some expressed dissatisfaction with this state of affairs.

B. We were not able to observe that there are students who are isolated from other students. However, we expect there are some students who do tend to be "loners."

VI. *Some over-all impressions.*

A. Ambivalence about changes in a system is probably to be expected.

B. There seems to be considerable concern about control, and this is clearly understandable with the large number of students in the system, there must obviously be firm clear rules and consistent implementation of the rules. On the other hand, students of this age need areas in which they can express needs for increasing independence and responsibility.

While firm control is necessary, it is our impression that forms of control which demean the dignity of the individual student are not necessary for effective control, and in fact breed resistance to reasonable controls. We have noted a few instances which seemed to be a use of ridicule toward students. We have noted the use of referring to boys by their last names, when more respect might be conveyed by using first names. We have noted instances where orders are given in a "hard" way, when it seemed to us that a friendly request would have been equally or even more effective, and would have carried less of a demeaning quality.

— — — — —

From these observations we would be interested in exploring some of these questions:

1. Are there ways of increasing communication between students and teachers, students and administration, and teachers and administration?

2. Are there areas in which students could participate more actively in policy decisions? Can they be brought into the problem-solving process more?

3. Are there ways to encourage more interaction between students and teachers and administration?

4. Can firm controls be maintained without subjecting students to conditions of disrespect and ridicule? If so, what could be done to reduce these conditions?

It is interesting that these observations tap climate and communication variables particularly, with some muted notice of power relationships. This occurred naturally, i.e., we had no *a priori* outline to guide us. Our relative neglect of task variables was partly related to a lack of awareness of them and partly to a reluctance to dabble in the high school's FA task, which we may have felt was none of our business.

The Mental Health Center staff members who were involved during this stage were Mr. Rod Bush, then a psychology graduate student at the University of Kansas who was with us on a community mental health traineeship; Mrs. Virginia Freeman, a staff social worker; and Mr Ronald Metzger, also a staff social worker. Soon after this meeting with the faculty I had accepted another position and knew I would be leaving within several months. From then on the direction of the Center's staff on this project was under Ron Metzger.

Programs

Following from the faculty meeting and from further meetings with administrators and counselors, three alternative ideas evolved for the participation of Center staff. These ideas were described and distributed to the faculty, who were to indicate their preferences. That document is as follows:

In planning for continued involvement of staff members from the Mental Health and Guidance Center with Ward High School personnel for next school year, several different ideas have been given consideration. We would like each faculty member to indicate the alternatives in which he or she would most like to be involved in after considering the three alternatives listed and discussed briefly below. Please rank the alternatives in the order of your interest in them. Place the number 1 after the alternative of your greatest preference, number 3 after the alternative of your least preference, etc.

To proceed with planning, we need your responses very soon. Please fill out and return to the office by _____ .

   Choice Number

Alternative #1 (Group Discussions)   _____

Alternative #2   _____

(Group Discussion Leader Training)

Alternative #3 (Encounter Group)   _____

Other   _____

(Please describe on back of this sheet)

Not Interested   _____

Descriptions of Alternatives

Alternative #1—Group Discussions

A given number of discussion sessions would be scheduled on a regular basis, perhaps weekly or bimonthly and each session would probably last an hour. Group members themselves would decide on the agenda or topics which would be discussed by the group. The group *could* consist of participants from various parts of the school system (teachers with administrators, students with teachers, students with guidance personnel and teachers, etc.) or all participants could be located in one part of the system (teachers *or* administrators or guidance personnel, etc.). This type of discussion group could potentially focus on topics ranging from "discipline problems" to "student-teacher communication," etc., and give participants opportunities to exchange ideas and learn from one another.

Alternative #2—Group Discussion Leader Training

This experience would entail two elements: (1) a brief academic orientation to leading group discussions and, (2) practical experience leading a discussion group, probably of students, with the trainer and perhaps some other "trainees" observing. All "trainees" and the trainer might be involved in ongoing evaluation-discussions of their practical experiences leading a group discussion. The groups of students who would participate as discussants (on topics of their choice, perhaps including "teenage relationships with their parents," "race relations," etc.) might also gain some training in discussion-group leadership from their experiences as participants and coevaluators of the discussion sessions.

Alternative #3—Encounter Groups (Sometimes called T-Groups or Sensitivity Training Groups)

As in alternative #1, participants could be from different parts of the system or they could all be from the same part of the system. There are two basic purposes of an Encounter Group experience:

(1) to provide opportunities for participants to increase their awareness of how self and others think, feel, and behave, and developing more behavioral flexibility and openness by looking at how self and others work together, and

(2) to gain awareness and understanding of processes which occur in group situations (or classes). Things such as communication, leadership, change, or problems encountered in a school situation would be focused upon by the group. This type of experience encourages participants to be themselves so they can test their effectiveness in various interpersonal situations.

The Encounter Group would involve various exercises or tasks assigned by the leader, as well as group discussions. Conditions will be created under which participants can gain new perspectives of themselves and others, of how they work with other people, of group dynamics and processes. Prospective participants should expect peaks of excitement and exhilaration as well as periods of apathy and frustration throughout this experience.

This group would meet regularly over a given period of time with the possibility of scheduling one or two extra long meeting times.

Teacher preferences on this survey were for Alternative #1, Group Discussions, and #2, Group Discussion Leadership Training. Furthermore, plans were made as a result of further meetings with administrators, guidance personnel, and teachers for Center staff to participate in the orientation meetings for both teachers and students at the opening of the next school year. The following letter summarizes the planning at that stage:

> Dear Father Maher:
> You may recall that at the last meeting regarding our consultation activities at Ward High, it was decided that we would suggest a possible way of providing an introductory learning experience for team teachers on the topic of "group discussion leadership." You were planning on this occurring the week of August 19th through the 23rd.
> We've given this considerable thought and wish to suggest the following for your consideration, reactions, questions, and comments. Certainly there is nothing mandatory about using this framework or format and we're interested in any suggestions from you.
> The experience, we estimate, would take roughly 2-1/2 hours of time, counting on a 15-minute break somewhere in the experience. The phases would be something on the following order.
>
> Phase 1. A 20-minute general presentation on the topic of group discussion leadership would be made by one of our staff members. This would touch on such areas as involvement and participation, roles in groups, leadership, control, decision making, etc.
> Phase 2. The large group of teachers (Did you say about 35?) would then draw numbers to break down into small groups. The size of each small group might be very different. For each group, a leader would be arbitrarily designated (by the number he drew), a topic for discussion would be assigned each

group, observers for each group would be designated. The observers would be instructed on what items of group functioning they are to watch for in the group they're assigned to observe. These small group discussions would go on for about 45 minutes.

Phase 3. Each subgroup would then discontinue discussion of the assigned topic and, for about 15 or 20 minutes, discuss with each other what had been going on in their specific group and their reactions to it.

Phase 4. A 15-minute break might then be scheduled for everyone except the observers, who would meet together with our staff members and try to pull together general group themes and issues.

Phase 5. Perhaps a 5-minute presentation of the observer's impressions could then be made to the total group by one of our staff members. This would be followed by a 25- or 30-minute *total* group discussion on any aspect of the experience, including content, to try to pull together "loose ends."

You had requested also that we participate in the general orientation the following week with all teachers and again during the first two days of school during the student's orientation. We're wondering if a general presentation to those two groups of what our involvement will be throughout the year and the implications that will have for each of their groups would be appropriate? Or maybe you have other thoughts on that.

I'll look forward to hearing from you soon.

Sincerely,
Ronald C. Metzger
Psychiatric Social Worker

During the next school year other Center staff members were also involved in the Ward Project: Mrs. Helen Bontrager, a psychologist; Dr. Charles Johnson, a psychologist; and Mrs. Carolyn Swift, a psychologist.

Another program included the guidance group program in which Mrs. Bontrager was a co-leader with a guidance counselor. The following reports on that experience.

GROUP GUIDANCE COMMITTEE REPORT

We have completed our first eight-session group project involving eight students at Ward High School. Four students were boys, four girls. Four were on probation and four were not. Four were juniors and four seniors. The sessions were un-structured—this was uncomfortable for both them and us but we learned to handle this. Attendance ranged from two to eight students. We had to remind them of the sessions. At the end of the last session they asked to continue for another eight meetings.

Issues Raised in the Student Discussion Group Included:
1. They feel they do not understand the rules or the reasons behind them. They feel the rules are in-consistently applied (Negroes favored; teachers chew gum, different teachers have different rules). They feel they are treated like children and state they hear lots of rumors about what school policy really is.
2. Because they do not understand the reason behind the rules, they (passive-aggressively) try to punish the school for rules which they see as silly and meaningless—this leads to a self-perpetuating cycle (e.g., gum chewing).

3.   They feel there is less freedom this year than last (e.g., assigned places and no talking in study halls). They felt there was not enough time to get to classes—if late then you have to get a note for being late and this wastes more time.

4.   They feel there is more trivia and less trust of them than last year.

5.   There is dissatisfaction with the system of student representation. They feel it is faculty controlled and they don't know who the representatives are, don't know how to get their questions answered or their opinions expressed and heard by the administration.

6.   They feel there is poor communication within the school and they have little representation in school policy. They feel they have less time to communicate with peers—thus poor morale, rumors, breakdown of social life in school (no class unity—cliques).

7.   They respect competent teachers who know how to lead kids but not incompetent teachers who try to throw their power around. They are very sensitive to this difference and really don't mind working hard for a teacher whom they respect and see as competent.

The Actual Experience and our Impressions:

It was a learning experience for both the students and the co-leaders. The students were enthusiastic and involved and covered a wide range of topics. We were unable to tell the problem from the non-problem student.

The students had a real desire to communicate with the administration.

The juniors seemed to care more about the school and expressed a more optimistic viewpoint verbally.

The seniors cared but didn't think too much could or would be done about it.

The seniors felt there were no distinctions between them and the juniors and the juniors felt there wasn't too much to look forward to as far as "senior privileges."

In evaluating the first group session we felt that 40 minutes was not enough time and there was difficulty scheduling the sessions and the room was not entirely satisfactory.

For our second group we will have 60-minute sessions and arrangements are being made for a different room.

The next group will involve students who are all on probation. They will be younger (freshmen and sophomores), are all male and more structure will be provided for the group. They will still be allowed to choose other topics. Since all are probation students we will have a more definite task from the beginning which could make a difference.

It is interesting to note that no student has ever refused to participate in the group. Apprehension was noticed about a mental health worker as co-leader.

In setting up the second group it was decided that Miss Godell would continue to really thoroughly develop her group leadership skills rather than have three successive leaders (Guidance Office personnel at Ward) who had just skimmed the surface.

Next year the co-leaders will be from within the Guidance Office at Ward with Mrs. Bontrager as outside consultant and observer throughout the year. It is hoped that this will eventually be self-sustaining if it seems a fruitful way of dealing with mild behavior problems.

The administration at Ward also solicited contributions from the Center staff on various school policies and issues. The following summary gives a flavor of that involvement.

Notes from the meeting of members of the staff of the Wyandotte County Mental Health and Guidance Center and the Steering Committee of Bishop Ward High School:

Dr. Charles Johnson opened the meeting by referring to the report from the Guidance Center and suggested we discuss the areas of concern rather than the report itself. He felt that we should concern ourselves with what is most important at the moment.

From the report it was obvious that a major concern was our Expulsion Policy and the Pink Slip System. Discussion followed on the Pink Slip and confusion seems to exist on this system of reporting behavior problems.

The following points were brought out in discussion:

1. Do teachers have the right to put a student out of class permanently?

2. Would the teachers be backed up by the Administration when issuing a Pink Slip?

3. Is there a need today for teachers to understand the differences in society and the make-up of the home?

4. Should we redefine the way we see our responsibility to the student?

5. Review Board—Do some teachers not accept this and insist on their own views of the situation?

6. Is the policy of the Pink Slip accepted by the teachers?

7. Is the policy uniform? Do all teachers follow the policy or do some ignore it and handle the matter in their own way?

8. Does the Pink Slip say that the student does not conform to the particular teacher's classroom standards rather than deviant behavior?

9. Do some teachers write the slips, turn them over to the Deans with the idea that it is the end of the matter as far as they are concerned? Or do some want to know the outcome?

10. Do the Pink Slips serve a wider purpose than just deviant behavior? Are they used as a means of monitoring behavior in the different classrooms or finding out if teachers are having problems with relationships to students?

Father Maher advised that a teacher does not have the right to put a child out of the classroom permanently. However, they may request that this be done. They would have the right to put him out on the spot but this would be a temporary measure. Sister Ann mentioned that the levels of tolerance differ on the teaching and administration levels. It also differs with each person.

The suggestion was made that teachers be involved more with the Discipline System as in parent-teacher conferences, etc. More of these conferences have been set up this year and it was found that the teachers do wish to be involved and their attendance has been high.

The question was asked, "do we need another name for the Pink Slip?" A suggestion was that two boxes be placed on the report, one marked "Records

Only" and the other marked "Action." The report could show: Offense, Interpretation, and Recommendation.

It was suggested that a small committee be formed. Their course of action would be: What is to be done regarding the Pink Slip and how it will be done.

Racials Concerns Committee:

Mrs. Freeman gave a report on her meetings with Negro students and Negro parents. She found that the Negro students needed a place where they could express their feelings, their gripes, their concerns and interest in Ward. She found that they wanted to be involved. In the racially mixed group, formed from the Leadership Group, she found them to be very honest in expressing their feelings.

Getting the parents involved was a good idea. Suggestions have been made of setting up more parents' meetings maybe with Mexican-American parents, small parish parents, etc. A committee could possibly set these up.

The Negro students have several questions to ask of the Administration. In what way could they help to have contemporary literature in our Library? How could they help Mr. Schubert set it up? Is there a budget for books, posters, etc.?

It was felt that a project handled by the Negro students themselves or, if they wish, by a mixed group, could be instrumental in helping them learn responsibility. Mrs. Freeman found that many of the students coming to see her had not taken responsibility for their absence from class. She felt that they must be helped to learn this responsibility. The anniversary of the death of Martin Luther King was suggested as a timely and meaningful subject for a Negro student project. However, they should initiate this project and then the Administration could help. An assembly would be the way for the Administration to recognize the project.

Dr. Johnson brought the meeting to a close with the questions, "What has the Guidance Center accomplished at Ward, and what about Ward in the future?"

Role

While we very consciously worked at being collaborators and coequals, were successful in eliciting inputs from the Ward staff, and faithfully carried through on their inputs (the group leadership training was entirely their idea and they did not accept the encounter group proposal which was our favorite), we did maintain the expertise element within our role. This was a good combination, I think. Basically we were trying to say: "We have some skills that might be helpful to you, but we need to work *with* you to see how they can best be used for *your* needs." We were not passive and nondirective, we offered ideas and made proposals; but we insisted upon their participation and that the ultimate decisions remained theirs.

Particularly at first, role clarity was difficult to achieve because it conflicted with their previous conceptions of Center staff as individual therapists. By our statements, by our efforts at avoiding that role (although we did at times give advice regarding individuals), and by our system-oriented activities, they gradually developed a view of our role more consistent with our own.

It seemed to help clarify our role and to maintain the collaborative emphasis if we committed ideas, proposals, and results of meetings to paper. This documentation seemed to help all of us know what we were going to do, and helped keep an open, nonsecretive air to our discussions. It also facilitated task performance by keeping everyone informed as to dates and decisions.

There was clarity as to whose agent we were. We were chiefly the agents of the Steering Committee which was composed of administrative personnel, guidance personnel, and teachers. We were clearly not the agents of the students, although in some instances we served liason or linkage functions with them. We did attempt at times to speak for the students and often tended to sympathize with the students' views in disputes between them and teachers or administrators.

Receptivity of the System

Clearly, this system was eaglerly open to our involvement (at least the high-power echelon was). Their information filters were open: they allowed us easy access to information about them, they were interested in receiving information from us. This accessibility also facilitated the collaborative model: we were not imposing an intervention from outside, they were not threatened by us (not as a system, at least).

Resources

We were fortunate in having the amount of manpower from the Mental Health Center, particularly in view of heavy clinical demands. This was due to the far-sighted leadership of Eliza- beth Gray, the executive director of the Center, and the support of Warren Phillips, the medical director of the Center. Without this critical support (from our input source) the project would not have been possible.

We were also fortunate in having staff members who were insterested in this kind of project and who had relevant slkills for it.

An issue of particular relevance to community mental health centers is that of money for such a project. We did not charge Ward High School for our time. This allowed for and facilitated a collaborative relationship. However, given the limited financial resources of such Centers they often cannot afford to provide such programs free. As with clinical patients, most often a consultation fee is charged. While such fees are often necessary (as a maintenance input), they make a collaborative relationship more difficult. We were fortunate that with the initial aspects of this program we did not have to charge a fee.

Assessment of the Intervention

We did contribute inputs to system change. We did develop new programs. We did learn a great deal about the system. We did establish an effective collaborative relationship with the system. At the *process* or implementation level we attained our objectives. But what about outcome? Did we improve the psychosocial accord for the individuals in the system? We do not know. We did not collect the kind of initial information that could be used for a pre- and postintervention comparison. Even if we had, the results would have been difficult to interpret since conditions outside the high school in the urban community, indeed the country, were affecting what was happening within the high school. Racial tensions were high in the Kansas City urban area in 1967-1968-1969. These tensions found their way into Ward, and a new militancy and forthrightness among minority students and their parents posed new conflicts. Hopefully, the presence of Center staff was helpful with regard to the handling of these added conflicts, but the intervention program itself cannot take either blame or credit for the *increase* of such conflicts during its operation.*

ADVOCACY SOCIAL SYSTEM INTERVENTION

In this intervention my role was that of an advocate. I have previously said I feel that the advocacy role is a difficult one for a community psychologist (acting as a professional) and I will

*Special thanks are extended to Ron Metzger for his advice on this section and for rounding up the documents.

try to illustrate the basis of that opinion here. I feel that there *are* social systems which are not susceptible to change by the community psychologist in his professional role—he is limited to systems that provide at least minimal access and willingness to change. Without these minimal conditions, a social system can perhaps be changed by the advocacy—political-battle approach. I believe the focal system to be described here is representative of such systems.   Let me warn the reader: because I was an advocate I have a very biased, partisan view of this system and the intervention. I will not pretend a documented, or necessarily fair account. And therein lies part of the problem for the advocate.

Overview

This also was a level four intervention, an effort to modify the structure of a particular social system in a way that would facilitate the psychosocial accord of its members—*but only some of its members*. Its objectives would be *counter* facilitative for members of the high-power echelon.

The short-run objective was to defeat a school bond proposal, then work for a better proposal. The long-run objective was to change the membership of the high-power echelon of the Kansas City, Kansas, school system; first the members of the school board and then the superintendent. We wanted a change to persons who would provide what we considered a better, different, and more just educational program (according to our views).

The intervention group consisted of an alliance among various organizations in the black community and a pre-dominantly white, liberal group which called itself "Project Concern" and an unofficial alliance with the Kansas City, Kansas, League of Women Voters (many of the Project Concern members had marital ties to League members). My discussion will center on Project Concern.

Our chief objections to the bond proposal were: (1) that it

would perpetuate existing de facto racial segregation; (2) that it was unimaginative with respect to possible education innovation since such things as educational parks and middle schools (which would also have meant more racial mixing) were not even being considered; (3) that the proposal had been written without consulation with or participation by citizens; and (4) that the proposal itself represented inadequate preparation (there had been only very limited outside consultation; some schools apparently were simply to be replaced by new buildings of the same size and type in spite of the facts of current overcrowding in some areas and under-utilization in others; etc.).

Our objections on the intellectual level were galvanized into organized action by our perception that the superintendent was evasive, arrogant, and at times rude when he was being questioned about the bond proposal (admittedly the questions were often direct and sharp). This behavior of his, particularly when we heard of it being directed at our wives, on top of our already deep-felt conviction that the quality of our children's education was seriously inadequate, was sufficient to energize and unite us for a campaign against the bond proposal.

Preliminary Analysis

Project Concern itself did not collect information, it was geared to political action. The information it used came primarily from a school study done by the League of Women Voters (the study served as the initial basis for questioning the bond proposal). In addition, even before there was any opposition to it, the school board and administration were loath to provide information about the system. Its information filters were "tight."

The long-run objective was very ambitious, that of replacing the majority of the current school board members and the superintendent with people whose views would be compatible with ours. Obviously, in a political struggle (or even in day-to-day dealings with uncooperative officials of other systems) when your path is blocked by some individual, say superintendent Jones, you find out who has power over Jones, or who controls his essential inputs, and then try to exert pressure downward on Jones. We were stymied here. The school board did have such power over the superintendent but he was "their man" and they themselves definitely represented and identified with the "establishment" of the community. An attack on the superintendent was interpreted as an attack on this establishment. These school board members also tended to be long-term residents while we tended to be short-term mobile professionals. The school board also had accrued cumulative power by an ingenious power technique. Over the years they had established the tradition that when any member wished to go off the board, he did so *during* his term, which allowed the remaining members to appoint a new member (who would, of course, have compatible views with their own) who then had the advantage of being an incumbent in the next election (when the incumbents ran as a slate). For over twenty years there had been only one instance of an outsider defeating an incumbent. In this way, similar value orientations were perpetuated on the board. Also, we became aware of an interlocking directorate (mutual interpenetration): the same "establishment" individuals tended to be on each other's boards, e.g., the YM-YWCA, United Fund, the OEO's citizen board, etc. (including that of my mental health center). The school board's power position was nearly as strong as Bouma's real estate board that was described in Chapter Five.

Therefore, without access to or leverage on individual input sources, we were forced to go to the board's ultimate source of inputs—the voters.

We did not know the attitude of the community toward its school system in general or toward the bond proposal specifically. A population survey of these attitudes would have been very helpful to us for both the short- and long-range objectives. We also found it difficult to communicate our views to the community since we could not get our criticisms aired in the two area newspapers. (We did get minor TV exposure from a Kansas City, Missouri, station.) I have subsequently lived in communities where newspapers were quick and eager to give equal and fair coverage to citizen criticism of public bodies (the Louisville Courier-Journal, Times is a good example) and am even more aware now as to how handicapped we were in this respect. However, subsequent events have suggested that the newspapers' lack of interest in our criticisms reflected the attitudinal context of the community.

Role

My opposition to the bond proposal and to the high-power echelon in general was based both on my observations and interactions in the Kansas City, Kansas, school system as a mental health professional, and on my views as a parent and a citizen. However, in any public statements that I made as a spokesman for Project Concern I was careful to speak only as a citizen, not as a psychologist. I could not legitimately base my opposition to the school bond proposal on my expertise as a psychologist.

A number of us at Project Concern were professionals in social agencies and this posed a problem for us. We did not want to embarrass our agencies or the lay boards of our agencies; some even felt that their opposition to the bond proposal threatened their jobs. The power (or at least the perceived power) of the school board was such that we were unable to completely protect our personal input sources. This was one reason we never had an official leader during the campaign and why we rotated as spokesman when public statements were required.

Gradually I assumed the role of a propagandist for Project

Concern. I wrote a radio spot announcement against the bond proposal, for example, which just bordered on but did not actually insert the issue of higher taxes. (We had always publicly maintained we were for new schools, and we were for spending money but that we wanted a better proposal.) And, in other speeches or announcements that I wrote I found myself "slanting" the truth as I knew it—not lying, not actually distorting, but clearly trying to persuade by nuance and word selection. Initially this was fun. It was a relief perhaps to get away from the strict adherence to evidence and the objectivity which was pounded into me by academic training. In the end, however, my training gained the upper hand and I felt, and still feel, uncomfortable with the "massaging" of the truth that I was involved in.

Resources

The resources of Project Concern were meager. We probably spent less than $500 in the entire campaign. Our prime resources were some intelligent, articulate (some of us at great length, and energetic people and a clear "cause."

For the over-all campaign the black community was very well organized. One black leader told us that it was the first time they had been able to unite the black community on the same side and they brought in a solid "no" vote.

Assessment of the Intervention

The bond proposal was defeated at the polls in October, 1967. That our initial objective was met is clear, that *our* efforts were responsible is less clear. Some "no" votes were very likely votes against the slightly higher taxes. In fact, Project Concern received a letter after the election from a citizen thanking them for helping to keep down taxes. However, several years later a bond proposal asking for even more money *was* passed in the absence of any organized opposition.

Following the defeat of the bond proposal the school board did set up a citizen's advisory board (as a counter to our criticism of a lack of citizen participation). They did bring in a group of educational consultants for the subsequent bond proposal (the first proposal had been criticized particularly by the League of Women Voters because there had been so few consultants involved) but did not follow the advice of the consultants. "Open" schools were planned and built after the second bond proposal passed. These were indications that we had had an effect on the board.

Our long-range objective of replacing the superintendent and school board members clearly failed. The superintendent is now at least as strong as ever and in subsequent school board elections individuals of an even more conservative bent have been elected. These events suggest that this superintendent, his school board, and the community's newspapers do reflect the dominant attitudes and values of the community. There is a possibility that our efforts contributed to a polarization of community attitudes or an awakening of the community's prevailing racial attitudes. It is more likely, however, that these events reflected society-wide concerns and attitudes of the time.

In short, this intervention failed to effect change in system structure.

ADVOCACY AND SYSTEM ACCESSIBILITY: SOME THORNY ISSUES

Advocacy presents many difficulties for the community psychologist in his professional role. First, his personal values as a citizen and his principles as a behavioral scientist may conflict at the level of actual practice. It is hard to be an advocate *and* a community psychologist within the same role. It is also hard to separate personal values as a citizen from professional values based on professional experience. The advocate may need to be a propagandist who "bends" the facts as he knows them; he is certainly not objective and he acts primarily on his values, not exclusively on the basis of evidence. The advocate must assume "good guys" and "bad guys" in fairly absolute terms, which does not mesh well with scientific theory. Scientific training can act as a constraint on the advocate. At the other extreme, the citizen can hide behind his scientific training to avoid any responsibility for social problems.

A second difficulty is the issue of misrepresentation. The political advocate who organizes a group of people to change a system through power pressure can very rarely justify his actions on the basis of his expertise and evidence as a psychologist. If he claims that a system should be changed on the basis of his knowledge as a psychologist, he may be misrepresenting himself. Obviously, he cannot separate being a psychologist from being a concerned citizen, and some of his action may indeed stem from his experiences as a psychologist. But his evidence is rarely of the sort that could be published in a psychological journal. No profession can legitimately legislate what its members do as private citizens, but it can, it seems to me, demand that when we declare ourselves as performing as psychologists that our actions and methods conform to its set of standards.

A third difficulty is whether as behavioral scientists we can make decisions as to which groups should be hurt to the benefit of another group. The adversary-confrontation approach usually aims at taking away the power from one group and getting it for another group, which means that the first group suffers. The advocate may claim that the first group *deserves* to suffer, or that its suffering would be less than that of the second group. But on what basis can he decide that? And who gave him the authority to make such decisions? Does the community psychologist, as a behavioral scientist, have the right or the mandate to make such decisions?

A fourth difficulty is that many systems are not open to change from the collaborator—behavioral-scientist approach. They will not let the intervener in. The community psychologist who restricts his professional activities to accessible systems is deciding that it is better for him to work as a collaborator from within. This means that he only works with systems that are at least somewhat open to change. The systems that would deny him entrance, that deny any need to change, may in fact have the most discordant effect on their populations.

These are issues that the field of community psychology must continue to examine. They are issues that each individual community psychologist must consider and resolve to some degree. I will offer my position, not as the right one, but as one alternative position which can then be compared and evaluated against other positions.

My view is that the political advocacy role does not fit comfortably within behavioral science. While it is probably a necessary method for change in some systems, I am convinced that community psychology as a field should stay very clearly within the constraints of behavioral science. I also believe that it is more effective over the long term to facilitate system change from within and from a collaborative relationship. I would say that at this time those systems that refuse even modest accessibility are not appropriate for the tools of the community psychologist. Community psychology cannot be a societal cure-all: it should not be expected to be able to intervene effectively in each and every possible system. I would leave the inaccessible systems to the political advocate but request that he not represent himself as a psychologist. Also, it seems to me that community psychology should strive to develop interventions that are "nonzero-sum games," i.e., it should seek changes that are facilitative to the IPM of *all* members. At least, no individual should sustain an irretrievable loss as a result of the intervention. People who think of change in adversary-confrontation terms have said that this is not practical. In my experience it is both practical and desirable. Alberts (1970) also subscribes to this view in principle while allowing the "compensation" idea in practice, i.e., that some may be worse off after a change but that if they are then fully compensated in some way for their loss (e.g., obtaining a different but equivalent job), then the benefits to others totals up to an improvement for the total community. Admittedly, it may not always be possible in practice, but it is a realistic goal.

My recent experiences are that there are plenty of systems that *are* open to change. There seems to be a growing acceptance that social agencies and schools should be evaluated and requests for such evaluations are increasing. There is plenty of work for community psychologists in accessible systems.

SMALL- VERSUS LARGE-SCALE INTERVENTIONS

The three interventions described thus far are what I would call "small-scale" in terms of objectives or resources. The kindergarten and high school projects are examples of focal-system interventions that a community psychologist based in a mental health center could carry out with limited resources. Before going on to discuss comparatively large-scale, community-feature interventions I would like to discuss some of the advantages and disadvantages of small-scale interventions.

As Intermediate Steps

Small-scale interventions may have short-range or minimal effects in and by themselves. However, they may serve as steps in a long-term path to system-wide or even community-wide changes.

Positive Side Effects

A small-scale intervention attempt which fails to attain its object, or one which attains only a short-term effect (it is probably in the nature of this imperfect world that no intervention is ever entirely successful), may nevertheless have been worth the time and effort because of the relationships established with members of that system and because of the information an intervener is certain to acquire in such a process. The kindergarten project, for example, helped the schools and the Center to work together more effectively on individual cases and provided the Center staff with important information about the effects of these schools upon individual clients with whom they might be working.

Multi-System Problems Demand Large-Scale Interventions

Small-scale interventions tend to be single-system efforts while many social problems have multi-system sources. For example, the Ward high school project could not be expected to eliminate drug abuse among its students since such an outcome would require the involvement of many other systems — the family, the drug suppliers, the medical profession, law enforcement, etc. To have an impact on poverty, a total community-wide approach would be necessary. Small-scale interventions against such problems are simply a waste of time and money. The next two interventions to be described are large-scale interventions.

JUVENILE OFFENDER
INTERSYSTEM INTERVENTION

The three intervention efforts already described took place before this book was started. The project to be described in this section began well after this book had taken shape and as a consequence there has been an interaction: ideas from the book have influenced the project and the project has suggested added ideas and provides some concrete examples of some of the ideas of this book.

Overview

This is a level five or intersystem intervention. It involves several systems as they affect a special population: juvenile offenders in Kentucky who have been adjudicated to a state institutional treatment setting. Its stage as of this writing is largely that of the preliminary analysis. It is the most complex intervention yet described, it involves the most resources, and it clearly is a large-scale intervention. I am implementing this intervention from a university base and from an applied researcher role.

There are five major objectives: (1) to develop an information-processing system for the state Department of Child Welfare which will continue and can be modified after the research project has been completed; (2) in the process of meeting this first objective a classification system for this population will be developed; (3) also as part of the information-processing system, follow-up information on the rehabilitation careers of these offenders will be collected and an empirical prediction table established that will provide information on how well different offenders (different categories of offenders) fare in different treatment settings or programs; (4) an analysis of each treatment setting will also be done and when combined with the prediction information will provide a basis for recommendations for changes in treatment settings. Of course, as personnel change and treatment programs change the original prediction data will become out of date, so there must be a constant up-dating. Therefore, the information processing system should become a part of the structure of the Department of Child Welfare, a part of its routine operations. This will provide the

Department with an information base against which to evaluate new treatment programs. As a consequence of this project it is hoped (5) that a *better fit* will result between offenders and their treatment settings.

Method

For the first four months of the project we surveyed the recent (last ten years or so) research in the vast and fragmented area of juvenile delinquency. An unspoken assumption which seemed to guide much of this research was that a juvenile delinquent becomes so because of a single variable. One study might examine child-rearing attitudes of the parents of delinquents, another the effects of social class, another the delinquent's self-concept, another his future time perspective, etc. With rare exception (e.g., Stein, Sarbin, & Kulik, 1971), these studies failed to examine natural patterns of variables (e.g., parent behavior and social class and self-concept and future time perspective interacting among themselves). Ours is a multiple-variable approach.

We have put together three sets or batteries of measures which are administered in three different systems. The first is the home environment battery which is administered in the home community to the offender and his family before he is sent to an institution. Its central instrument is based on the unrevealed differences task developed by Ferriera and Winter (1965, 1968) which I had used before (Murrell, 1971c) and which yields measures of family interaction.

The second battery is administered in the Kentucky Reception Center where the offender is first sent for evaluation. Part of it is administered to the juvenile offender and is directed at presumed stable intrapersonal characteristics, e.g., self-concept, locus of control, future time perspective, sociability, etc. Another part of this battery is filled out by the staff and includes Quay's (1971) behavior ratings and ratings based on the offender's history, as well as predictions by staff as to the offender's future adjustment in another treatment setting and after his release.

There were no existing instruments that we knew of which would give us a notion of the offender's priority of problem-area solutions.So we designed a new one! We called it the What's Most Important Test and included two items in each of five problem-area categories: opportunities for affiliation, supportiveness from staff, clear structure from the staff, opportunity for achievement, and opportunity for independence. All items are related to the Reception Center, so the priorities pertain to that specific system. Each item is paired with an item from another problem-area in a paired-comparisons format yielding relative preferences among the five areas. It is an example of a measure of IPM preferences.

The third battery is administered in the treatment setting (to which the offender is sent after about a three-week stay in the Reception Center) of which there are twelve. The major instrument here is the Community-Oriented Programs Environment Scale (COPES) developed by Moos (1972a) which is a 102 item, ten scale, true-false questionnaire designed to assess psychosocial aspects of treatment programs. The ten scales tap three general variables: *relationships* among patients and between patients and staff; *program* emphasis or orientations; and *administrative structure*. The scales are: (relationship) Program Involvement, Support, Spontaneity; (program emphasis) Autonomy, Practical Orientation, Personal Problem Orientation, Anger and Aggression; (administrative structure) Order and Organization, Program Clarity, and Staff Control. There are two basic forms of the COPES, Form C which is administered to both staff and patients for a description of the real program, and Form I which consists of the same items worded slightly differently for describing the ideal program. See Appendix B for the instructions and items of the COPES.

A comparison of the COPES scale profile for a given treatment setting with a given offender's problem-area priorities on the What's Most Important Test would yield a match between the individual's priorities (in this kind of system at least) and the relative emphasis to these areas given by the treatment setting. This is a definition in measurement terms of the goodness-of-fit between the individual and his social system that was discussed in Chapter Three.

The outcome or criterion variables include ratings of the relative successfulness of adjustment by the offender in the treatment setting by staff, adjustment ratings by probation workers after the offender has been released, number of runaways, and a measure of recidivism.

On the basis of the home environment battery, Reception Center battery, and various demographic variables, categories will be formed using a cluster analysis. Such a category would represent, then, a group of people who had a similar pattern on these many measures. Then on the basis of the outcome measures, a success rate for each category for each treatment setting can be established. Using this information one could predict the probability of success for a given offender of a given category for a given treatment setting. Then, by using information from the treatment setting battery, explanations for the different degrees of "fits" between categories and settings can be offered along with recommendations for new treatment programs or changes in old ones so that there is at least a good fit for each category with a treatment setting. (Hope for an optimal fit for every offender within a limited number of settings is not realistic at this time, but an improvement of the match between the over-all offender population and the available treatment settings is quite possible).

Intersystem Relations

The most difficult aspect of this project is working out agreements, making arrangements, and getting cooperation *across* systems.

The project began with Ben Mossbarger of the Division of Institutional services within the Department of Child Welfare telling me of the general interest of his division in establishing a different classification or diagnostic system and asking me if I would be interested in submitting a proposal. I was. (I had worked as a consultant with Ben previously on a smaller project.)

Ben had had preliminary discussions with a funding source and thought there was a possibility of obtaining grant money. An initial decision was whether I should apply for the grant directly or whether DCW should apply and give me a contract to do the project. DCW would be willing to do it either way. Knowing that the project would require a great deal of cooperation from DCW personnel at different levels and in different divisions, I opted for the grant going to DCW. This made it officially their project. I would be more of an insider this way and could more legitimately request assistance from the various divisions of DCW. The disadvantage was the added layer of bureaucratic machinery that I would have to go through. Thus far, however, this arrangement has been very helpful in conducting the project.

Although very obvious, it is worth emphasizing that it is essential that there be a clear understanding between all parties as to the nature and extent of the intervention. In this case, the written contract required me to set forth the objectives of the intervention and the activities and products of our project and the areas of responsibility for DCW. Even when an intervention does not involve money it is very valuable to have the agreements in writing.

What I failed to do at an early stage (even though by this time I knew better) was to consult with other personnel in DCW, particularly the Reception Center staff whose support and cooperation would be critical. We later encountered some mild resistance which probably could have been avoided if they had been more involved in the initial planning of the project.

The same also was true for the Division of Community Services. Although this early consultation may seem to be a time-consuming and unnecessary effort at the early stages, it will actually be a good investment of time in most interventions.

Later in the project, when we decided to get direct information on the interaction patterns of families, we required cooperation from another division within DCW-the Division of Community Services. The only feasible way to get this information was to ask the Community Service workers throughout the state of Kentucky to administer the home environment battery to the families. It has required a great deal of explanation, encouragement, and continual work on our relationship to obtain and maintain their participation.

A further complication arises from the fact that Jefferson County's (Louisville's county) judicial and screening system for juvenile offenders is independent of DCW. In order to test the families from Jefferson County we have worked out a working agreement with that county's Metropolitan Social Services Department. Since there is a somewhat competitive relationship between this department and DCW, I have been very careful to keep Ben informed of all our arrangements.

Our efforts to obtain measures of the family, which takes us out of the area of juvenile *institutions* and into another system, has been administratively our biggest problem. The real world often does not suffer intersystem efforts gladly. This demands considerable patience and tolerance on the part of the intervener.

Role

In this project the intervener has been defined as an applied researcher *for* the system. I am not just some "academic" type criticizing the system, rather I am a "toiler" helping to work on problems through the collection and manipulation of information. (Anyway, I prefer to think of research in the behavioral sciences as being a method for solving problems rather than some search for absolute "truths" or universal principles.)

Whereas this project does require the cooperation of and accommodation with other systems, the "expertise" and legitimacy of my role has acted to prevent any interference or intrusion into the methods or measures of the project itself. On the conceptual and methodological levels I have a free rein (within budget constraints.)

I personally prefer the researcher-interventionist role to other possible community psychologist roles that may involve more direct service, strict consultation (which is severely limited in terms of power), advocacy (as I have already explained), or social action. I feel that for the community *psychologist,* the applied research emphasis has the advantage of using his legitimate and rather unique training in methodology and measurement, whereas he often has no unique training in the other roles.

Paradoxically, a chief disadvantage of the researcher role lies in a weakness of training in psychology. The emphasis in much of psychology upon the "clean" single-variable, controlled experiment in a contrived environment makes large portions of its research training inappropriate or inapplicable to "dirty" multi-variable problems in natural environments uncontrolled by the researcher. Fortunately, however, from the influence of Barker and his co-workers (Barker, 1957, 1960, 1968; Barker & Gump, 1964; Gump, 1964, 1967, 1969; Barker & Wright, 1949, 1951, 1955), there is increasing work (Caldwell, 1963; Kelly, 1966, 1968, 1971b; Moos, 1969, 1972a, 1972b; Sarason, 1967, 1971; Sells, 1969; Willems & Raush, 1969) that holds promise for "dirty" research in natural environments. Community psychologists particularly need experience in these naturalistic research methods. (I realize this leaves me open to the chant "community psychologists are dirty researchers.")

Resources

An essential resource has already been mentioned—the cooperation of DCW. Other resources have included grant money (around $30,000 a year for the first two years of the project) to pay for a full-time secretary, three half-time research associates (graduate students), about one-fourth of my regular salary, a part-time statistical consultant, supplies, and data analyses. Facilities of the University (the library and computer) have been invaluable resources. While lean, these resources have been adequate for the complexity and scope of this project.

Assessment of the Intervention

What will this intervention accomplish? Its effects might be assessed on two different levels. First, considering the effect of the total over-all project, a comparison could be made of the recidivism rate and runaway rate before and after the project. Second, at the level of assessing the particular effect of using the prediction data for making disposition decisions, the project itself provides data on treatment setting adjustment and postrelease adjustment which can be used in a pre- and postcomparison. Using the prediction data should improve treatment setting adjustment and postrelease adjustment. One difficulty here is that there may be treatment program changes that occur as a result of the project and at about the same time as the introduction of the prediction data. However, improvement as the result of either or both would also reflect a positive effect of the intervention.

As a side effect, the project will allow an examination of the interrelationship among many variables that have heretofore not been studied together, and this may lead to added information for the general field of juvenile delinquency.

NEW COMMUNITY
NETWORK INTERVENTION

As of this writing this project is not an operational intervention, rather it is a preliminary analysis and a plan *for* the intervention. Considering that the intervention would involve the building of a new community in conjunction with a large job and relocation training program, it can safely be described as a large-scale community feature effort. This project also interacted with the preparation of this book. In many instances concepts and research findings put forth in this book were directly applied to the New Community design. Translating these concepts into community operations and mechanisms helped clarify and sometimes changed them.

Overview

This would be a level *six* or network intervention. Its objective in the broadest terms is to design a habitat that provides opportunities for increased psychosocial accord for a racially, culturally, and economically diverse population.

History. This project is unique in many ways, including its beginning: it did not start out as a New Town proposal. The University of Louisville Urban Studies Center under its director, Dr. Joseph Maloney, had been examining ways to provide assistance to Appalachian rural poor who would be migrating to cities. During those explorations (long before I joined the project) was born the idea of building New Communities as a method not only to assist the migration of rural poor but also the urban poor, and to include mobility training, job training, and job placement. In May, 1969, the Urban

Studies Center entered into a contract with the Office of Economic Opportunity to develop preoperational plans for a general system that could be applied to medium-sized cities throughout the country and more specifically for a demonstration New Community in the Louisville urban region. The project thus evolved and became not only a method for lifting people out of poverty but also a potential contribution to a national urban growth policy. These plans (four volumes) were completed (Urban Studies Center, 1971) and delivered in Washington in November, 1971.

Population. For the Louisville demonstration New Community (hereafter referred to as NewCom), the plan was to provide for 5,000 disadvantaged Appalachian families, 5,000 disadvantaged families from Louisville's inner city (mostly black), and 10,000 nondisadvantaged families. The eventual proposed population, then, was to be 20,000 families or about 80,000 people, half of whom had been disadvantaged.

Site. NewCom was to be located within 60 commuting minutes of Louisville. Don Williams, Susan Hoag, and others developed a new, exhaustive, and complex process for analyzing the requirements for an environmental location which simultaneously considers many critical variables: natural environment variables (geology, physiography, hydrology, climate, soils, vegetation, wildlife, visual attributes); linkage variables (transportation, communications, energy and water distribution, waste treatment and disposal); and socioeconomic variables (population characteristics and present location, probable population characteristics and present location, probable population growth directions and distribution, major public/private land holdings, land values). On the basis of this locational process five acceptable areas were found, two of which were deemed preferable.

Space.   Once a site is located, what do 20,000 families require in terms of physical facilities? Carl Sharpe put together the New Community Development Computer Model, which provides for pulling together variables and generating physical performance requirements, which then allows a check on the economic and spatial ranges of the parameters of the variables. For example, space requirements would total 4,870 acres allocated in this way: education 586 acres; public services 1,075 acres; quasi-public nontaxable facilities (e.g., churches, hospitals) 155 acres; private development 262 acres; and housing 2,719 acres.

Money.   What about the capital investment needed? NewCom is designed to operate under the free enterprise system. The bulk of the needed investment would probably come from the sale of obligations that can be guaranteed by full faith and credit of the U. S. Government under the Urban Development and New Community Act of 1970 for up to $50,000,000 for a particular new community. Private money, probably on the order of a million dollars, would be required to start the initial planning process and to carry through until the guaranteed money became available. The Urban Studies Center staff also drafted legislation which was passed by the Kentucky legislature in 1970 which would provide a legal mechanism for setting up a New Community District.

Jobs.   The design spells out in considerable detail a coordinated program for job training, job placement, and mobility training. No family would move into NewCom through this program unless there was a job already available which paid at least $6,000 a year (1969 dollars). Agnes Livingwood, an urban systems analyst with the Urban Studies Center, has calculated that there will be more jobs generated by construction and services within NewCom itself during its first four years than can be filled by people coming through the job and mobility program. Thus the essential ingredient that has been missing in many job training and mobility assistance programs—actual job availability—will be amply provided in the critical early stages.

Scope. The Louisville project is more than another New Town, it is more than another antipoverty program—its scope marks it as a potential major new national weapon against the range of psychological, social, economic, and physical crises that presently plague our urban habitats. This project provides a feasible, integrated, coordinated, *systems* approach to multifaceted, multivariate, monstrous problems.

Method: Preparing the Psychosocial Design

When I joined the project in January, 1971, my responsibility was the "social" section of the over-all NewCom design. There had been some previous work already done which proved helpful. I re-dubbed the section "The Psychosocial Environment" (Murrell, 1971b).

Planning and Choice. As I worked on the project and discussed it with colleagues and friends, I learned that everyone has his own pet theory about how a community should be. And, many people have a volatile emotional reaction to the idea of a *planned* community. Particularly my liberal friends tended to equate planning with coercion. However, they quite rightly did not advocate the logical extension of that premise, i.e., that absence of planning safeguarded freedom of choice.

There is considerable merit in this concern. The wrong kind of planning *can* limit individual choices, and so can nonplanning. We were sensitized to this issue very early and it influnced our process and every decision we made.

Initial Conception. We began the development of the psychosocial design with the central conception of this book;

namely that every individual is constantly confronted by his environment with problems and opportunities. The environment in this case was the New Community which could potentially either facilitate or obstruct these various individual problem solutions. And, potentially what might be facilitative for one individual could be obstructive for another. To be psychosocially responsive in an effective way to its individual inhabitants NewCom would need to allow for a range of alternative problem solutions.

Planning for Individual Differences. As is typical of most behavioral scientists, I suppose, we proceeded from this conception to a review of relevant research. We were determined to begin from the perspective of the individual. We examined the research in three problem-areas that seemed generally relevant to individual-habitat relations: achievement, affiliation, and locus of perceived control. We applied these research findings to the psychosocial institutions of the community, e.g., governance, education, social service, etc. From the research we drew implications as to what effect different policies or programs might have upon individuals who were quite different from one another in that particular problem-area (e.g., how would certain educational policies affect children who had low achievement preferences as well as those children who had high achievement preferences).

We had no desire to make people over, to improve them. We were not social therapists in that sense, but definitely wanted a design that could accommodate diversity of behavior patterns.

Psychosocial Institutions. After reviewing our reviews, consulting our consultants, and planning our plans we got down to the critical work—writing the design itself. In outline, this consisted of listing performance requirements for each of these psychosocial institutions or areas: Governance, Education, Social Services, Leisure-Time, Health and Safety, and Housing.

Areas for Analysis.   For each of these institutions, except housing, we prescribed the following:

1. We stated the objectives the institutions should strive for in terms of the community and its individuals.

2. We stated who in the institution would be responsible to whom in the community for what.

3. We stated the programs the institution should operate.

4. We stated how many and what kind of people would be necessary to carry out the program.

5. In terms of people-activities, we stated the amounts of space that would be needed.

6. We stated the parts that users of that institution could play in its programs.

7. We described mechanisms for coordination among these instititutions.

8. We specified the power relations among these and other institutions or agencies in the community, region, and state.

9. We stated the information that each institution would be required to provide to its governing bodies in order to establish budgets based on performance.

10. We stated possible criteria by which users of the institutions could evaluate its services—this was in a sense a restatement of the institution's objectives in measurement terms.

11. We stated the essential features which should characterize that institution whatever its geographic locale or the nature of the community's population.

Choice-Points in the Psychosocial Design

In the process of pulling this design together into a comprehensive whole, we were constantly being confronted with choice-points in which there were both clear costs and clear benefits to each alternative—it was a question of choosing among trade-offs and trying to combine several alternatives to maximize benefits. There were no "perfect" solutions.

Below I have tried to extricate these choice-points from the many specifications of the design itself and make them explicit because I feel that they reflect dimensions basic to community design. These particular choices are not offered as being either perfect or universal: each has some disadvantage and all communities will have their own special priorities.

Power Distribution: Participation and Accountability.   How widely should power be distributed among the residents? As described earlier, there is research evidence that a comparatively wide distribution of power and decision-making within an organization is psychologically desirable for the individuals and often improves task performance. However, there is also evidence, as reviewed by Porter and Lawler (1965), that the positive effect of wide-spread opportunity to participate in decisions is conditioned by the task and the size of the organization. If participation in decision-making extends too widely it can be so time-consuming and so dissipating of accountability as to seriously reduce task effectiveness. Also, a large proportion of citizens in most of our communities do not seem to *want* such participation, witness for example, the 30% or so who do not even vote in presidential elections. Further, there is evidence that for some individuals having certain kinds of personality characteristics (e.g., preference for an external locus of control) pressure to participate in decision-making would make them anxious and uncomfortable (Watson & Baumal, 1967; Watson, 1967).

Our choice was to provide more opportunities for participation in decisions than is typical in most communities. These opportunities are provided within the governance structure, with comparatively small units, and with clearly delineated accountability. The design *allows for but does not depend upon* high levels of citizen participation.

The governance design gives the best illustration of this choice. The basic elective district (the neighborhood), about 200 families, elects a Neighborhood Representative to sit on a Village Council. He is required to hold a regular monthly meeting in his neighborhood to hear complaints, suggestions, and opinions from residents. There are six Neighborhoods within a Village, giving it between 1,000 and 1,400 families, typically around 4,400 population. Each Village Council selects one of its Councilmen as Spokesman, its representative on the community-wide NewCom Assembly. Also, each Village elects one member to each of six NewCom-wide Monitoring Boards (see below). All residents vote for a NewCom mayor. Not counting the mayor, in a typical Village there would be one resident elected to a governance position for every 100 families. This design had the advantage of giving proportionately more residents a voice in governance than in most communities (in Louisville there are 13 members on the City Board of Aldermen for a population in the city proper of 360,000, or about one representative per 9,000 housing units) and easier access to governance representatives, yet keeps the number a manageable one and within clearly defined accountability.

The governance design is a deliberate use of the representative form of governance, a form which would be familiar to residents and acceptable to the surrounding environment (county and state government). It is patterned after Likert's (1961) linking pin model (see Chapter Four, especially Figure 7) which places a member of each group in another group at the next highest level of the organization.

Sizes: Smallness and Diversity.   What would be the optimum size for NewCom's units—educational units, elective districts, housing arrangements, commercial centers? This was heavily influenced by the governance and educational designs.

There is evidence that smaller rather than larger social groupings have psychological advantages (Barker, 1968; Barker & Gump, 1964; Bechtel, Archapohl, & Binding, 1970). More people can know one another, each individual is needed more in undermanned (smaller) units, and individuals have more opportunity to participate and have a feeling of being more able to influence their community directly. And, smaller sizes allow residents to move about more easily. Smaller sizes are probably also more familiar and comfortable for rural migrants.

On the other hand, large sizes allow a greater range of services, products, and facilities. A high school of 4,000 obviously can support a more varied curriculum and faculty, more specialized equipment and facilities, than a high school of 400. A Village of 10,000 could support a greater variety of stores, and consequently of products, than a Village of 5,000.

We opted for smaller rather than larger sizes in the "living" units: elective districts of 200 families, autonomous educational districts of about 1,200 families, housing concentrations from the cluster (25 dwelling units) through the Neighborhood (about 200 dwelling units) to the Village (about 1,200 dwelling units). To balance the disadvantage of "diversity-loss" of small sizes, we recommend that each Village contain a specialty which would then be used by other Villages. We recommend that each Village educational unit cooperate with other Villages so that at least at upper-age levels each could share its specialty (one Village having a computer console, another having laboratory facilities, another shop facilities, etc.). This coordination could be facilitated by the Education Monitoring Board. We have also recommended that Village commercial centers provide specialty areas in addition to basic services (e.g., one Village specializing in clothing stores, another in appliance stores, etc.). A resident then could have considerable commercial choice across NewCom, in addition to using nearby Louisville.

Population Mix: Integration and Social Comfort. This project was designed to allow people to pull themselves out of poverty. On a value basis it was quite clearly opposed to racial or economic segregation. This issue was not a choice-point.

The choice was how to effect integration while at the same time maintaining a modest level of social comfort among face-to-face neighbors.

There is considerable evidence that positive social relations are enhanced by similarity among the parties—similarity in race, religion, ethnicity, occupation, values, and age (Broxton, 1962; Byrne & Wong, 1962; Festinger, 1950; French, 1951; Lazarsfeld & Merton, 1954; Newcomb, 1956, 1958; Precker, 1952; Smith, 1957; Thibaut & Kelly, 1959). There is also evidence that status congruent groups (members are roughly equivalent in status) are generally more effective than status incongruent groups (Exline & Ziller, 1959; Triandis, 1966; Trow & Herschdorfer, 1965).

There is also evidence that social relations are enhanced by cooperative, democratic, equal-status conditions (Berkowitz, 1953; Gottheil, 1955; Phillips & D'Amico, 1956; Rehage, 1951; Solomon, 1960; Stendler, Damrin & Haines, 1951; White & Lippitt, 1960). Studies of residential contact between different ethnic groups in noncompetitive, equal-status situations have generally resulted in favorable changes in attitudes (Deutsch & Collins, 1958; Irish, 1952; Wilner, Wakely & Cook, 1952). Gans (1970) suggests from his observations in new suburbs that values regarding child-rearing methods, leisure-time activities, cultural tastes, and temperament are most important in determining the degree of compatibility among residents.

The implications of this research for racial integration in New Com is that similarity in income, salient values, and life-cycle stage under a cooperative democratic atmosphere offers the optimal condition for positive social relations among residents.

Our choice was to *homogenize* housing costs (guiding income similarity) and housing types (guiding life-cycle stage similarity) at the *face-to-face* housing level, the cluster (about 25 dwelling units); but to distribute these clusters in such a way that Neighborhoods and Villages would be heterogeneous in these respects. Thus, governance and educational districts would not have concentrations of any one income or age group. To further enhance compatibility within the cluster we have suggested a voluntary Compatibility Service via which a prospective buyer of a house in a particular cluster can fill out a values questionnaire which would then be compared against the composite pattern of the values of occupants of that cluster. This would only inform the prospective buyer about the closeness of his values to those in the cluster; it would not in any way regulate his choice.

Legally, there is no way to regulate who buys a house where. NewCom's only influence is in the initial distribution of housing costs and types. There will be, however, strong recommendations to buyers that they not congregate by race or place-of-origin, and hopefully a community-wide norm will be established to that effect.

Organization of Services: Coordination and Decentralization. To what degree should services be organized in small autonomous units close to their users? Decentralization allows for easier access by users, better accountability, and less time and effort fighting through bureaucratic structures. However, coordination and centralization would allow for more and perhaps better utilization of resources, and more comprehensive responses to NewCom-wide problems.

Our choice has been to locate administrative autonomy, accountability, and financial support for Education, Social Services, and Leisure-Time at the Village level. Health and Safety, which includes fire and police protection, would be NewCom-wide. We have suggested mechanisms to facilitate coordinations: e.g., staffs of Social Service, Leisure-Time, Village Health, and Religion would be officed in close physical proximity and would share secretarial support staff; a NewCom-wide Human Services Resource Unit would provide support services (computer facilities and personnel, research staff, consultant funds and positions, etc.) to Social Services,

Education, Health and Safety, Leisure-Time, the NewCom
mayor, and the Monitoring Boards, but would have no policy-
making power; there would be a number of joint appointments
across institutions (e.g., a Home-School coordinator would have
a joint appointment in Education and Social Services); after
NewCom has grown to around 40,000 or 50,000 population a
NewCom Social Services Committee is recommended to
coordinate and help evaluate psychosocial problems and
programs for all of NewCom.

Change: Adaptiveness and Stability.   For the community to
be continuously responsive to its individual residents, it must
be able to change. It must change as NewCom grows, as its
population alters in composition, and as the surrounding
regional and national societies change. However, change efforts
are often resisted, especially if they are coercive or accusatory.
Moreover, sudden, episodic, and unplanned-for changes disrupt
stability and routine which are important contributors to task
effectiveness. To be viable, the system must possess dynamic
stability (Berrien, 1968).

Our choice has been to try to bureaucratize corrective
mechanisms so that change is constant, gradual, routine, and
expected. We also wanted changes to be influenced by consumers of services, not exclusively by delivery personnel
or governing bodies. By giving users more direct power over
their institutions we hoped the latter would be more aware
of and more motivated to be adaptive to changes in the population's needs and preferences. Two of these corrective-feedback
mechanisms   are   the   habitability   survey   and   the
Monitoring Boards.

Habitability Survey.   We have recommended that every two
years the users of an instititution's services be surveyed as to
their level of satisfaction with its services and their evaluation
of its strong and weak points. Criterion levels of satisfaction by

users would be pre-set by the Monitoring Board of each in-stititution. If user levels of satisfaction turned out to be below criterion, the head administrator would automatically be fired. For example, if the level of satisfaction by parents and children in "Cooper" Village's educational system were below the pre-set criterion, then Cooper's superintendent would be fired. Such administrators would have certain rights of appeal, and, of course, there would have to be stipulations regarding the representativeness of the respondent sample, the minimum percentage that would have to respond before the results would be official, and protection of anonymity for respondents.

Monitoring Boards. The Monitoring Board is also a built-in corrective feedback mechanism. It is an elected special governance arm that itself has no policy-making or direct budgetary power with regard to its respective institution; its explicit purposes are to study and evaluate the performance of services and to facilitate information flow between users and service personnel. We have recommended a Monitoring Board for each of these areas: Education, Social Services, Leisure-Time, Health and Safety, Sanitation-Utilities, and Tran-sportation. Others, of course, could be added. Each Board collects data on its institution's services, it submits reports and budget recommendations to the appropriate governance bodies, and each Board has one vote in the NewCom Assembly. In systems terms, the Monitoring Board acts upon the feedback loop of an institution and has power to influence how its outputs are transformed into its inputs; it does not interfere in the throughput operations.

NewCom as a System

The Louisville NewCom Project is unique in that it proposes a New Town as a *method* for working on social problems. The Psychosocial Design's chief claim to uniqueness is that it attempts to pull together an integrated system of psychosocial concerns. This should have obvious appeal to community mental health people who have been obstructed by interagency jealousies and noncooperation. It has been typical of other New Town planning (e.g., Lemkau, 1969) to assemble specialists from various areas, e.g., recreation, religion, mental health, etc., and then have them talk or write papers which would then presumably be used by architects and developers. However, these different inputs have not been integrated, not related to one another. This, it seems to me, has led to the same fragmentation and planning-by-isolated-part that so characterizes our present communities.

Our psychosocial design *determined* the physical housing arrangements and sizes of areas on the basis of its governance, educational, and population-mix requirements. It attempted to tie various human services together in specified relationships that should prevent both overlap and underprovision of services. It tried to allow for attacks upon social problems by various institutions *in concert*. As may be obvious, general systems theory was a very helpful conceptual tool in organizing and writing this design.

Role

Here I would characterize my role as that of an applied behavioral scientist—using information from a variety of sources and fields, extrapolating and interpreting the implications for NewCom, making guesses that were hopefully educated ones, and trying to organize this information into a feasible psychosocial "blueprint." It was very helpful to have the basic conceptual framework of this book in mind; it gave me a way to begin, to organize, to interweave components. Having a clear conceptual framework is essential for a project of this size.

Part of my role also required interdisciplinary collaboration.

The physical planners asked hard questions, e.g., "what should be the socioeconomic status mix in Neighborhoods and Villages?" (This, of course, determined allocation of housing of different costs.) Or, "what distribution of family size and age do you expect in NewCom?" Also, the economists imposed constraints which required a working through of compromises and choosing among priorities.

Resources

The Urban Studies Center received $262,000 from OEO for the preoperational planning of NewCom. Over the span of some two years many people worked on many different facets of the project, the most extensive of which was the environmental location study.

For my part, I had two research assistants, money for part of my University salary, money for consultants, and the secretarial support of the Urban Studies Center. My scarcest commodity was time—we had to meet the OEO deadline in November, 1971.

Assessment of the Intervention

The Habitability Survey is a built-in, on-going method of regularly assessing the success of NewCom. It will reflect areas of greater or lesser effectiveness. It, along with other mechanisms such as the Monitoring Board, not only evaluates but also changes the habitat. Since NewCom will not come to a defined end, assessing its effects cannot be an absolute or fixed appraisal, but rather must occur periodically over time. Different aspects of NewCom may be more effective at different times; for example, we have proposed that our governance system be terminated at the end of five years and the community be required to devise another one since our plan is geared to new arrivals and the beginning of NewCom. A more innovative governance structure might be better and possible at a later stage in NewCom's development.

At this time, it is my judgment that we do not know how to assess the effectiveness of communities, partly because we would be unable to arrive at consensus criteria. Alberts' work (1970), however, provides a start in this direction by recognizing the need for criteria both for the individual and the community-at-large.

As of this writing, the actual construction of a Louisville NewCom is undetermined. However, the design is already having inputs into other new town developments and is receiving a fair hearing in government councils in Washington. For example, several of us on the New Com project have been asked to advise the Woodlands new town project now under development near Houston. At least from the initial response to the design, it appears to have considerable intervention potential even if NewCom itself is never actually built.

EVALUATION OF INTERVENTIONS

There has been only a limited amount of work on the actual evaluation of interventions. Fairweather (1967, 1969) following an experimental model basically compares the experimental social system with the "old" system that it is trying to improve upon. Sarason (1966, 1967, 1971) provides many helpful observations and insights regarding the process of interventions. Alberts (1970) has faced the issue of "to whom is the intervention for" head-on, and he has provided operational definitions for evaluating the performance of social service programs. Forrester (1969) has faced the large complex social system of the urban habitat. By the use of simulation models he has attempted to assess, post-hoc, the effects of such large-scale interventions as the Urban Renewal Program upon the industry, employment, and housing of cities.

Kelly (1971a) has most directly addressed the task of evaluating interventions and has put forth the thesis that the uniqueness of community psychology is in the verification of interventions that work in a variety of settings. Kelly describes interventions at three levels: mental health consultation, organizational change, and community development. He applies the work of Campbell and Stanley (1966) to suggest ways of managing some of the methodological problems. The importance of obtaining preintervention measures and of having similar systems not receiving the intervention available for comparison is particularly stressed. This paper by Kelly should be required reading for all community psychologists.

INTERVENTION GUIDES

The following are considered imperative for effective interventions and for keeping the intervener out of trouble. Hopefully this list will serve to orient and remind the intervener.

I. Know Thy System

A. Do not attempt an intervention before you have enough information about the system upon which to evaluate the intervention.

B. Know the intersystem network of the system, particularly its power relationships with its suprasystem and implicated systems.

C. Expect and look out for covert alliances and conflicts of interests within the system which may attempt to ensnare and misuse the intervention.

II. Know Thy Role

A. Keep your input sources informed, protect your power lines.

B. Be clear as to whose agent you are (know to which echelon in the system you are responsible) and make sure that the rest of the system identifies you in the same way. Do not try to misrepresent yourself.

C. Be certain that you and the system agree as to your legitimate role functions. A written agreement in advance is desirable.

III. Know Thy Intervention

A. State the specific objectives of the intervention in writing before you begin it. Have clear written agreements with the system regarding these objectives.

B. In planning, strive to make interventions nonzero-sum "games." Each individual should have at least no irretrievable loss as a result of the intervention.

C. Strive to design the intervention so that it will *remain* in the system's structure after you and your intervention project are gone.

D. As part of your intervention design, build in ways for the intervention procedures to be changed over time on the basis of feedback mechanisms—build in methods for continually assessing the effects of the intervention.

E. Strive for a collaborative process with the system. Involve critical implementation personnel as early as possible in the planning of the intervention.

F. Strive to anticipate effects of the intervention on other systems (no system is independent).

G. The more complex (the higher the level) the intervention, the greater must be the resources of the intervener.

REFERENCES

Adelson, D. Toward a conception of community psychology: The implications of cultural pluralism. In D. Adelson (Ed.), *Man as the measure: The crossroads.* New York: Behavioral Publications, 1972. Pp. 1-16.

Aiken, M. The distribution of community power: Structural bases and social consequences. In M. Aiken & P.E. Mott (Eds.), *The structure of community power.* New York: Random House, 1970. Pp. 487-525.

Alberts, D.S.*A plan for measuring the performance of social programs.* New York: Praeger, 1970.

Allport, F.H.*Institutional behavior.* Chapel Hill, N.C.: Univ. of North Carolina Press, 1933.

Allport, G. The open system in personality theory. *Journal of Abnormal Psychology,* 1960, *61,* 301-311.

Altrocchi, J., Spielberger, C., & Eisdorfer, C. Mental health consultation with groups. In P. Cook (Ed.), *Community psychology and community mental health.* San Francisco: Holden-Day, 1970. Pp. 119-128.

Amidon, E., & Flanders, N. The effects of direct and indirect teacher influence on dependence-prone students learning geometry.*Journal of Educational Psychology,* 1961, *52,* 286-291.

Argyris, C. *Personality and organization.* New York: Harper, 1957.

Artiss, K.L. (Ed.), *The symptom as communication in schizophrenia.* New York: Grune & Stratton, 1959.

Astin, A. An empirical characterization of higher educational institutions. *Journal of Educational Psychology,* 1962, *53,* 224-235.

Bard, M. The role of law enforcement in the helping system. *Community Mental Health Journal,* 1971, *7,* 151-160.

Barker, R.G., Structure of the stream of behavior. In: *Proceedings of the 15th international congress of psychology, 1957.* Pp. 155-156.

Barker, R.G. Ecology and motivation. In M.R. Jones (Ed.), *Nebraska Symposium on motivation.* Lincoln, Nebr.: Univ. of Nebraska Press, 1960. Pp. 1-49.

Barker, R.G. (Ed.), *The stream of behavior.* New York: Appleton-Century-Crofts, 1963.

Barker, R.G. *Ecological psychology.* Stanford, Calif.: Stanford Univ. Press, 1968.

Barker, R.G., & Gump, P.V. *Big school, small school.* Stanford, Calif.: Stanford Univ. Press, 1964.

Barker, R.G., & Wright, H.F. Psychological ecology and the problem of psychosocial development. *Child Development,* 1949, *20,*131-143.

Barker, R.G., & Wright, H.F. *One boy's day.* New York: Harper & Row, 1951.

Barker, R.G., & Wright, H.F. *Midwest and its children.* New York: Harper & Row, 1955.

Bateson, G., Jackson, D., Haley, J., & Weakland, J. Toward a theory of schizophrenia. *Behavioral Science,* 1956, *1,* 251-264.

Bay, C. A social theory of higher education. In N. Sanford (Ed.), *The American college.* New York: Wiley, 1964. Pp. 972-1005.

Beach, L. Sociability and academic achievement in various types of learning situations. *Journal of Educational Psychology,* 1960, *51,* 208-212.

Bechtel, R., Archepohl, C., & Binding, F. East side, west side and midwest: A behavioral comparison of three environments. *Man-Environment Systems,* 1970, *1,* 32

Becker, W.C. Consequences or different kinds of parental discipline. In M. Hoffman & L.W. Hoffman (Eds.), *Review of child development research: Volume one.* New York: Russell Sage Foundation, 1964. Pp. 169-208.

Bennett, C., Anderson, L., Cooper, S., Hassol, L., Klein, D., & Rosenblum, G. (Eds.), *Community psychology.* Boston: Boston University Press, 1966.

Bennis, W. Post-bureaucratic leadership. *Trans-action,* 1969, *6,* 44-51, 61.

Berkowitz, L. Sharing leadership in small, decision-making groups. *Journal of Abnormal and Social Psychology,* 1953,*48,* 231-238.

Berrien, F.K. *General and social systems.* New Brunswick, N.J.: Rutgers University Press, 1968.

Bertalanffy, L. v General system theory. *General Systems,*1956,*1,* 1-10.

Bertalanffy, L. v. General system theory—a critical review. *General Systems,* 1962, *7,* 1-20.

Bexton, W., Heron, W., & Scott, T. Effects of decreased variation in the sensory environment. *Canadian Journal of Psychology,* 1954, *8* 70-76.

Blake, R.R., Moutin, J.S.., Barnes, J.S., & Greiner, L.E. Breakthrough in organizational development. *Harvard Business Review,*

1964, *42*, 133-155.

Bloom, B. Strategies for the prevention of mental disorders. In G. Rosenblum (Ed.), *Issues in community psychology and preventive mental health.* New York: Behavioral Publications, 1971. Pp. 1-20.

Bouma, D.H. Analysis of the social power position of a real estate board. In M. Aiken & P.E. Mott (Eds.), *The structure of community power.* New York: Random House, 1970. Pp. 367-377.

Braginsky, B.M., Grosse, M., & Ring, K. Controlling outcomes through impression-management: An experimental study of the manipulative tactics of mental patients. *Journal of Consulting Psychology,* 1966, *30,* 295-300.

Braginsky, B.M., & Braginsky, D.D. Schizophrenic patients in the psychiatric interview: An experimental study of their effectiveness at manipulation. *Journal of Consulting Psychology,* 1967, *31,* 543-547.

Braginsky, B.M., Holzberg, J., Finison, L., & Ring, K. Correlates of the mental patient's acquisition of hospital information. *Journal of Personality,* 1967, *35,* 323-342.

Braginsky, B.M., Holzberg, J., Ridley, D., & Braginsky, D.D. Patient styles of adaptation to a mental hospital. *Journal of Personality,* 1968, *36,* 283-298.

Bronfenbrenner, U., Devereaux, E., Jr., Suci, G., & Rodgers, R. Adults and peers as sources of conformity and autonomy. Unpublished study. Ithaca, N.Y.: Cornell Univ., Dept. Child Development and Family Relations, 1965.

Broxton, J. A method of predicting roommate compatibility for college freshmen. *Journal of the National Association of Women Deans and Counselors,* 1962, *21,* 602-605.

Buckley, W. *Sociology and modern systems theory.* Englewood Cliffs, N.J.: Prentice-Hall, 1967.

Buckley, W. Society as a complex adaptive system. In W. Buckley (Ed.), *Modern systems research for the behavioral scientist.* Chicago: Aldine, 1968. Pp. 490-513.

Byrne, D., & Wong, T.J. Racial prejudice, interpersonal attraction, and assumed dissimilarity of attitudes. *Journal of Abnormal and Social Psychology,* 1962, *65,* 246-253.

Caldwell, B.M. A new approach to behavioral ecology. In J.P. Hill (Ed.), *Minnesota Symposia on Child Psychology,* 1968, *2,* 74-109.

Campbell, D.T., & Stanley, J.C. *Experimental and quasi-experimental designs for research.* Chicago: Rand McNally, 1966.

Campbell, J.P. Personnel training and development. *Annual Review of Psychology,* 1971, *22,* 565-602.

Campbell, J.P., & Dunnette, M.D. Effectiveness of T-group experiences in managerial training and development. *Psychological Bulletin,* 1968, *70,* 73-104.

Caplan, G., & Grunebaum, H. Perspectives on primary prevention: A review. In P. Cook (Ed.), *Community psychology and community mental health.* San Francisco: Holden-Day, 1970. Pp. 66-90.

Carlson, S. *Executive Behavior, A study of the work load and the working methods of managing directors.* Stockholm: Stromberg, 1951.

Carson, R.C. *Interaction concepts of personality.* Chicago: Aldine, 1969.

Carter, J., Jr. (Ed.), *Research contributions from psychology to community mental health.* New York: Behavioral Publications, 1968.

Cloward, R., & Ohlin, L. *Delinquency and opportunity: A theory of delinquent gangs.* Glencoe, Ill.: Free Press, 1960.

Coleman, J., et al. *Equality of educational opportunity.* Washington: U.S. Govt. Printing Office, No. FS 5.238:38001, 1966.

Cook, P.E. (Ed.), *Community psychology and community mental health.* San Francisco: Holden-Day, 1970.

Cowen, E.L., Gardner, E.A., & Zax, M. (Eds.), *Emergent approaches to mental health problems.* New York: Appleton-Century-Crofts, 1967.

Cowen, E., Izzo, L., Miles, H., Telschow, E., Trost, M., & Zax, M. A preventive mental health program in the school setting: Description and evaluation. *Journal of Psychology.* 1963, *30,* 381-387.

Cowen, E.L., & Zax, M. The mental health fields today: Issues and problems. In E. Cowen, E. Gardner, & M. Zax (Eds.), *Emergent approaches to mental health problems.* New York: Appleton-Century-Crofts, 1967. Pp. 3-29.

Cowen, E.L., Zax, M., Izzo, L., & Trost, M.A. Prevention of emotional disorders in the school setting: A further investigation. *Journal of Consulting Psychology,* 1966, *30,* 381-387.

Cowen, E.L., & Zax, M. Early detection and prevention of emotional disorder: Conceptualizations and programming. In J. Carter, Jr.

(Ed.), *Research contributions from psychology to community mental health.* New York: Behavioral Publications, 1968. Pp. 46-59.

Crandall, V., Katkovsky, W., & Preston, A. A conceptual formulation of some research in children's achievement development. *Child Development*, 1960, *31*, 787-797.

Cyert, R.M., & MacCrimmon, K.R. Organizations. In G. Lindzey & E. Aronson (Eds.), *Handbook of social psychology.* Vol. I. (2nd ed.) Boston: Addison-Wesley, 1968.

Deutsch, M., & Collins, M. The effect of public policy in housing projects upon interracial attitudes. In E. Maccoby, T.M. Newcomb, & E.L. Hartley (Eds.), *Readings in social psychology.* (3rd ed.) New York: Holt, 1958. Pp. 612-623.

Edwards, D.W. The development of a questionnaire method of measuring exploration preferences. In M.J. Feldman (Ed.), *Studies in psychotherapy and behavior change.* Buffalo: State Univ. of New York at Buffalo, 1971. Pp. 99-107.

Emerson, R.M. Power-dependence relations. *American Sociological Review,* 1962, *27,* 31-35.

Endler, N.S., & Hunt, J. McV. Sources of behavioral variance as measured by the S-R Inventory of Anxiousness. *Psychological Bulletin,* 1966, *65,* 336-346.

Evan, W.M. The organization-set: Toward a theory of interorganizational relations. In J.D. Thompson (Ed.), *Approaches to organizational design.* Pittsburgh: University of Pittsburgh Press, 1966. Pp. 175-191.

Exline, R.V., & Ziller, R.C. Status congruency and interpersonal conflict in decision-making groups. *Human Relations,* 1959, *12,* 147-162.

Fairweather, G.W. *Methods of experimental social innovation.* New York: Wiley, 1967.

Fairweather, G.W., Sanders, D., Maynard, H., Cressler, D., & Bleck, D. *Community life for the mentally ill.* Chicago: Aldine, 1969.

Featherstone, J. Anti-city, a crisis of authority. *The New Republic,* 1969, *161,* 20-23.

Ferriera, A.J., & Winter, W. D. Family interaction and decision-making. *Archives of General Psychiatry,* 1965, *13,* 214-223.

Ferriera, A.J., & Winter, W. D. Decision-making in normal and abnormal two-child families. *Family Process,* 1968, *7,* 17-36.

Festinger. L. Laboratory experiments: The role of group

belongingness. In J. G. Miller (Ed.), *Experiments in social process.* New York: McGraw-Hill, 1950. Pp. 31-46

Foa, U. Interpersonal and economic resources. *Science.* 1971, *171,* 345-351.

Fontana, A.F., & Klein, E. B. Self-presentation and the schizophrenic "deficit." *Journal of Consulting and Clinical Psychology,* 1968, *32,* 250-256.

Forehand, G.A., & von Haller Gilmer, B. Environmental variation in studies of organizational behavior. *Psychological Bulletin,* 1964, *62,* 361-382.

Forrester, J. W. *Urban dynamics.* Cambridge, Mass.: The M. I. T. Press, 1969.

Freeman, L.C., Fararo, T., Bloomberg, W., Jr., & Sunshine, M. Locating leaders in local communities: A comparison of some alternative approaches. In M. Aiken & P. E. Mott (Eds.), *The structure of community power.* New York: Random House, 1970. Pp. 340-347.

French, R. L. Sociometric status and individual adjustment among Naval recruits. *Journal of Abnormal and Social Psychology,* 1951, *46,* 64-72.

Frick, F. C. Information theory, In S. Koch (Ed.), *Psychology: A study of a science.* Vol. 2. New York: McGraw-Hill, 1959. Pp. 611-615.

Gans, H. J. Planning and social life: Friendship and neighbor relations in suburban communities. In H. M. Proshansky, W. H. Ittelson, & L. G. Rivlin (Eds.), *Environmental psychology.* New York: Holt, Rinehart, 1970. Pp. 501-509.

Glidewell, J., Kantor, M., Smith, L., & Stringer, L. Socialization and social structure in the classroom. In L. Hoffman & M. Hoffman (Eds.), *Review of Child Development Research.* Vol. 2. New York: Russell Sage, 1966. Pp. 221-256.

Glidewell, J. New psychosocial competence, social change and tension management. In J. Carter, Jr. (Ed.), *Research contributions from psychology to community mental health.* New York: Behavioral Publications, 1968. Pp. 100-110.

Glidewell, J. Priorities for psychologists in community mental health. In G. Rosenblum (Ed.), *Issues in community psychology and preventive mental health.* New York: Behavioral Publications, 1971. Pp. 141-153. (a)

Glidewell, J. System linkage and distress at school. In M.J. Feldman (Ed.), *Studies in psychotherapy and behavior change.* Buffalo, N.Y.: State University of New York at Buffalo, 1971. Pp. 27-44. (b)

Golann, S., & Eisdorfer, C. (Eds.) *Handbook of community psychology and mental health.* New York: Appleton-Century-Crofts, 1972.

Gordon, I. Stimulation via parent education. *Children,* 1969, *16,* 57-59.

Gottheil, E. Changes in social perceptions contingent on competing or cooperating. *Sociometry,* 1955, *18,* 132-137.

Greiner, L. E. Antecedents of planned organizational change. *Journal of Applied Behavioral Science.* 1967, *3,* 51-86.

Grimes, J., & Allinsmith, W. Compulsivity, anxiety, and school achievement. *Merrill-Palmer Quarterly,* 1961, *7,* 247-271.

Gross, N., Mason, W., & McEachern, A.W., *Explorations in role analysis: Studies of the school superintendency role.* New York: Wiley, 1958.

Gump, P. V. Environmental guidance of the classroom behavioral system. In B. J. Biddle & W. J. Ellena (Eds.), *Contemporary research on teacher effectiveness.* New York: Holt, Rinehart & Winston, 1964. Pp. 165-195.

Gump, P. V. Persons, settings, and larger contexts. In B. Indik & K. Berrien (Eds.), *People, groups, and organizations: An effective integration.* New York: Teachers College, Columbia Univ. Press, 1967.

Gump, P. V. Intra-setting analysis: The third grade classroom as a special but instructive case. In E. P. Willems & H. L. Raush (Eds.), *Naturalistic viewpoints in psychological research.* New York: Holt, Rinehart & Winston, 1969. Pp. 200-220.

Haberstroh, C. J. Organizational design and systems analysis. In J. March (Ed.), *Handbook of organizations.* Chicago: Rand-McNally, 1965.

Haley, J. *Strategies of psychotherapy.* New York: Grune & Stratton, 1963.

Hall, A., & Fagen, R. Definition of a system. *General Systems,* 1956 *1,* 18-28.

Halpin, A., & Croft, D. *The organizational climate of schools.* Chicago: Midwest Administration Center, Univ. of Chicago, 1963.

Hardin, G. The cybernetics of competition: A biologist's view of society. In W. Buckley (Ed.), *Modern systems research for the behavioral scientist.* Chicago: Aldine, 1968. Pp. 449-459.

Hemphill, J., & Westie, C. The measurement of group dimensions. *Journal of Psychology,* 1950, *29,* 325-342.

Himmelweit, H.T., & Swift, B. A model for the understanding of school as a socializing agent. In P. Mussen, J. Langer, & M. Covington (Eds.), *Trends and issues in developmental psychology.* New York: Holt, Rinehart, & Winston, 1969. Pp. 154-181.

Holland, J. *The psychology of vocational choice.* Waltham, Mass.: Blaisdell Publishing Co., 1966.

Homans, G. C. *The human group* New York: Harcourt, Brace & World, 1950.

Hulin, C., & Blood, M. Job enlargement, individual differences, and worker responses. *Psychological Bulletin,* 1968, *69,* 41-55.

Hunt, J. McV. Toward the prevention of incompetence. In J. Carter, Jr. (Ed.), *Research contributions from psychology to community mental health.* New York: Behavioral Publications, 1968. Pp. 19-45

Hunt, R. G. Role and role conflict. In E. P. Hollander & R. G. Hunt (Eds.), *Current perspectives in social psychology.* (2nd ed.) New York: Oxford, 1967.

Irish, D. P. Reactions of Caucasian residents to Japanese-American neighbors. *Journal of Social Issues,* 1952, *8,* 10-17.

Iscoe, I., Pierce-Jones, J., Friedman, S., & McGehearty, L. Some strategies in mental health consultation: A brief description of a project and some preliminary results. In E. Cowen, E. Gardner, & M. Zax (Eds.), *Emergent approaches to mental health problems.* New York: Appleton-Century-Crofts, 1967. Pp. 307-330.

Iscoe, I., & Spielberger, C.   The emerging field of community psychology. In I. Iscoe & C. Spielberger (Eds.), *Community psychology: Perspectives in training and research.* New York: Appleton-Century-Crofts, 1970.

Joint Commission on Mental Illness and Health. *Action for mental health.* New York: Basic Books, 1961.

Kagan, J., & Moss, H. Parental correlates of a child's IQ and height: Across-validation of the Berkeley Growth Study results. *Child Development,* 1959, *30,* 325-332.

Kahn, A. J. *Theory and practice of social planning.* New York: Russell Sage Foundation, 1969.

Kahn, R. L. Implications of organizational research for community mental health. In J. Carter, Jr. (Ed.), *Research contributions from psychology to community mental health.* New York: Behavioral Publications, 1968. Pp. 60-74.

Katz, D. The motivational basis of organizational behavior. *Behavioral Science,* 1964, *9,* 131-146.

Katz, D., & Kahn, R. L. *The social psychology of organizations.* New York: Wiley, 1966.

Katz, D., Maccoby, N., & Morse, N. Productivity, supervision and morale in an office situation. Ann Arbor, Mich.: Institute for Social Research, 1950.

Katz, J., & Sanford, N. The curriculum in the prespective of the theory of personality development. In N. Sanford (Ed.), *The American college.* New York: Wiley, 1962. Pp. 418-444.

Kellam, S., & Schiff, S. The Woodlawn Mental Health Center: A community mental health center model. *Social Service Review,* 1966, *40,* 255-263.

Kelly, J. G. Ecological constraints on mental health services. *American Psychologist.* 1966, *21,* 535-539.

Kelly, J. G. Toward an ecological conception of preventive interventions. In J. Carter, Jr. (Ed.), *Research contributions from psychology to community mental health.* New York: Behavioral Publications, 1968. Pp. 75-99.

Kelly, J. G. The quest for valid preventive interventions. In G. Rosenblum (Ed.), *Issues in community psychology and preventive mental health.* New York: Behavioral Publications, 1971. Pp. 109-139. (a)

Kelly, J.G. The coping process in varied high school environments. In M.J. Feldman (Ed.) *Studies in psychotherapy and behavior change.* Buffalo: State Univ. of New York at Buffalo, 1971. Pp. 95-99. (b)

Klein, D. The prevention of mental illness. *Mental Hygiene,* 1961, *45,* 101-109.

Klein, D. C. *Community dynamics and mental health.* New York: John Wiley, 1968.

Kornhauser, A. W. *Mental health of the industrial worker: A Detroit study.* New York: John Wiley, 1965.

Langer, T., & Michael, S. *Life stress and mental health.* London: Free Press of Glencoe, 1963.

Lawrence, P., & Lorsch, J. *Developing organizations: Diagnosis and action.* Reading, Mass.: Addison-Wesley, 1969.

Lazarsfeld, P.F., & Merton, R. K. Friendship as social process: A substantive and methodological analysis. In M. Berger, T. Abel, & C. H. Page (Eds.), *Freedom and control in modern society.* New York: Van Nostrand, 1954. Pp. 18-66.

Leary, T. *Interpersonal diagnosis of personality.* New York: Ronald Press, 1957.

Leavitt, H. J., & Bass, B. M. Organizational psychology. *Annual Review of Psychology,* 1964, *15,* 371-398.

Lehmann, S. Community and psychology and community psychology. *American Psychologist,* 1971, *26,* 554-560.

Lemkau, P.V. The planning project for Columbia. In M. Shore & F. Mannino (Eds.), *Mental health and the community: Problems, programs, and strategies.* New York: Behavioral Publications, 1969. Pp. 193-204.

Lewin, K. *Field theory in social science.* New York: Harper & Row, 1951.

Lichtman, C.M., & Hunt, R. G. Personality and organization theory: A review of some conceptual literature. *Psychological Bulletin,* 1971, *76,* 271-294.

Likert, R. *New patterns of management.* New York: McGraw-Hill, 1961.

Likert, R. *The human organization.* New York: McGraw-Hill, 1967.

Likert, R., & Willits, J. *Morale and agency management.* Hartford, Conn.: Life Insurance Agency Management Assn., 1940, 4 vols.

Lipton, H. The challenges of community psychology. *American Psychological Association Division of Community Psychology Newsletter,* 1968, *2* (2), 4-5.

Litwak, E., & Hylton, L.F., Interorganizational analysis: A hypothesis on coordinating agencies. *Administrative Science Quarterly,* 1962, *6,* 395-420.

Litwin, G., & Stringer, R., Jr. *Motivation and organizational climate.* Boston: Div. of Research, Harvard Business School, 1968.

McClintock, S.K., & Rice, R. The development of a thematic measure of preferences for exploration. In M. J. Feldman (Ed.), *Studies in psychotherapy and behavior change.* Buffalo: State Univ. of New York at Buffalo, 1971. Pp. 107-113.

McGee, D. P. A study of black alienation and academic achievements in black adolescents. In M. J. Feldman (Eds), *Studies in psychotherapy and behavior change*. Buffalo: State Univ. of New York at Buffalo, 1971. Pp. 147-166.

MacGregor, D. Adventure in thought and action. In *Proceedings of the fifth anniversary convocation of the school of industrial management*. Cambridge, Mass.: M. I. T. Press, 1957.

McKeachie, W. Motivation, teaching methods, and college learning. In M. R. Jones (Ed.), *Nebraska symposium on motivation*. Lincoln: Univ. of Nebraska Press, 1961. Pp. 111-142.

Marris, P., & Rein, M. *Dilemmas of social reform*. New York: Atherton, 1967.

Maruyama, M. The second cybernetics: Deviation-amplifying mutual causal processes. In W. Buckley (Ed.), *Modern systems research for the behavioral scientist*. Chicago: Aldine, 1968. Pp. 304-313.

Mayo, E. *The human problems of industrial civilization*. New York: MacMillan, 1933.

Miller, E.J., & Rice, A. K. *Systems of organization: The control of task and sentient boundaries*. London: Tavistock, 1967.

Miller, G.A., Galanter, E., & Pribram, K. *Plans and the structure of behavior*. New York: Holt, 1960.

Mischel, W. *Personality and assessment*. New York: John Wiley, 1968.

Moos, R. Situational analysis of a therapeutic community milieu. *Journal of Abnormal Psychology*, 1968, *73*, 49-61. (a)

Moos, R. The assessment of the social climates of correctional institutions. *Journal of Research in Crime and Delinquency*, 1968, *5*, 174-188. (b)

Moos, R. Sources of variance in responses to questionnaires and in behavior. *Journal of Abnormal Psychology*, 1969, *74*, 405-412.

Moos, R. Assessment of the psychosocial environments of community-oriented psychiatric treatment programs. *Journal of Abnormal Psychology*, 1972, *79*, 9-18. (a)

Moos, R. British psychiatric ward treatment environments. *British Journal of Psychiatry*, In press, 1972. (b)

Moos, R. Systems for the assessment and classification of human environments: An overview. Stanford, Calif.: Social Ecology Laboratory, Dept. of Pyschiatry, Stanford Univ. 1972 (c) Mimeographed.

Moos, R., & Houts, P. The assessment of social atmospheres in psychiatric wards. *Journal of Abnormal Psychology,* 1968, *73,* 595-604.

Moos, R., & Otto, J. The Community-Oriented Programs Environment Scale: A methodology for the facilitation and evaluation of social change. *Community Mental Health Journal,* 1972, *8,* 28-37.

Morse, N., & Reimer, E. The experimental change of a major organizational variable. *Journal of Abnormal and Social Psychology,* 1956, *52,* 120-129.

Murray, H. A. *Explorations in personality.* New York: Oxford University Press, 1938.

Murrell, S. Community involvement in mental health programs: The Wyandotte County Mental Health and Guidance Center. *Community Mental Health Journal,* 1969, *5,* 82-87.

Murrell, S. An open system model for psychotherapy evaluation. *Community Mental Health Journal,* 1971, *7,* 209-217. (a)

Murrell, S. (Ed.) *The psychosocial environment for the new communities family mobility system.* Vol. 2 of OEO Grant 8002 Report. Louisville: Urban Studies Center, 1971. (b)

Murrell, S. Family interaction variables and adjustment of nonclinic boys. *Child Development,* 1971, *42,* 1485-1494. (c)

Newbrough, J. R. Community mental health: A movement in search of a theory. In *Community menaal health: Individual adjustment or social planning?* Bethesda, Md.: NIMH, 1964. Pp. 1-18.

Newbrough, J. R. Community psychology: A new specialty in psychology? In D. Adelson & B. Kalis (Eds.), *Community psychology and mental health.* Scranton, Pa.: Chandler, 1970. Pp. 36-51.

Newcomb, T. M. The prediction of interpersonal attraction. *American Psychologist,* 1956, *11,* 575-586.

Newcomb, T.M. The cognition of persons as cognizers. In R. Tagiuri & L. Petrullo (Eds.), *Person perception and interpersonal behavior.* Stanford, Calif.: Stanford Univ. Press, 1958. Pp. 179-190.

Newcomb, T.M. Varieties of interpersonal attraction. In D. Cartwright & A. Zandler (Eds.), *Group dynamics.* Evanston, Ill.: Row, Peterson, 1960. Pp. 104-119.

Newman, B.M., & Gordon, T. A. Socialization experiences for the development of exploration perferences. In J. Feldman (Ed.),

Studies in psychotherapy and behavior change. Buffalo: State Univ. of New York at Buffalo, 1971. Pp. 124-134.

Osmond, H. The relationship between architect and psychiatrist. In C. Goshen (Ed.) *Psychiatric architecture.* Washington, D. C.: American Psychiatric Assn., 1959.

Pace, R. *College and university environment scales.* Princeton, N.J.: Educational Testing Service, 1969.

Parsons, T. *The social system.* Glencoe, Illinois: The Free Press, 1951.

Patton, J. A study of the effects of student acceptance of responsibility and motivation on course behavior. Unpublished doctoral dissertation, Univ. of Michigan, 1965.

Pelz, D. C. The influence of the supervisor within his department as a conditioner of the way supervisory practices affect employee attitudes. Unpublished doctoral dissertation, Univ. of Michigan, 1951.

Pelz, D.C. Influence: A key to effective leadership in the first-line supervisor. *Personnel,* November 1952, 3-11.

Pervin, L. Performance and satisfaction as a function of individual-environmental fit. *Psychological Bulletin,* 1968, *69,* 56-68.

Peterson, R., et al. *Institutional functioning inventory.* Princeton, N. J. : Educational Testing Service, 1970.

Phillips, B.N., & D'Amico, L. A. Effects of cooperation and competition on the cohesiveness of small face-to-face groups. *Journal of Educational Psychology,* 1956, *47,* 65-70.

Pierce, W.D., Trickett, E.J., & Moos, R. Changing ward atmosphere through staff discussion of the perceived ward environment. *Archives of General Psychiatry,* 1972, *26,* 35-41.

Porter, L.W., & Lawler, E.E., III. Properties of organizational structure in relation to job attitudes and job behavior. *Psychological Bulletin,* 1965, *64,* 23-51.

Precker, J. A. Similarity of valuings as a factor in selection of peers and near authority figures. *Journal of Abnormal and Social Psychology,* 1952, *47,* 406-414.

Quay, H.C., & Parsons, L.B. *The differential behavioral classification of the juvenile offender.* (2nd ed.) U. S. Dept. of Justice, 1971.

Rae-Grant, Q., & Stringer, L. A. Mental health programs in the schools. In M. Shore & F. Mannino (Eds.), *Mental health and the community: Problems, programs and strategies.* New York: Behavioral Publications, 1969. Pp. 83-99.

Raush, H., Dittman, A., & Taylor, T. Person, setting, and change in social interaction. *Human Relations,* 1959, *12,* 361-378.

Raush, H.L., Farbman, I., & Llewellyn, L. G. Person, setting, and change in social interaction: II. A normal control study. *Human Relations,* 1960, *13,* 305-332.

Rehage, K. J. A comparison of pupil-teacher planning and teacher-directed procedures in eighth grade social studies classes. *Journal of Educational Research,* 1951, *45,* 111-115.

Reiff, R. The ideological and technological implications of clinical psychology. In C. Bennett, L. Anderson, S. Cooper, L. Hassol, D. Klein, & G. Rosenblum (Eds.), *Community psychology.* Boston: Boston University Press, 1966. Pp. 51-64.

Reiff, R. Mental health manpower and institutional change. In E. Cowen, E. Gardner, & M. Zax (Eds.), *Emergent approaches to mental health problems.* New York: Appleton-Century-Crofts, 1967. Pp. 74-88.

Reiff, R. Social intervention and the problem of psychological analysis. *American Psychologist,* 1968, *23,* 524-531.

Roethlisberger, F., & Dickson, W. *Management and the worker.* Cambridge, Mass.: Harvard Univ. Press, 1939.

Roistacher, R. C. Peer nominations of exploratory behavior. In M. J. Feldman (Ed.), *Studies in psychotherapy and behavior change.* Buffalo: State Univ. of New York at Buffalo, 1971. Pp. 113-124.

Rokeach, M. Long-range experimental modification of values, attitudes, and behavior. *American Psychologist,* 1971, *26,* 453-459.

Rommetveit, R. *Social norms and roles.* Minneapolis, Minn.: University of Minnesota Press, 1955.

Rotter, J. B. Generalized expectancies for internal versus external control of reinforcement. *Psychological Monographs: General and Applied,* 1966, *80,* 1-28.

Sampson, E. The study of ordinal position: Antecedents and outcomes. In B. Maher (Ed.), *Progress in experimental personality research.* New York: Academic Press, 1965. Pp. 175-228.

Sarason, S.B., Levine, M., Goldenberg, I.I., Cherlin, D. L., & Bennett, E. *Psychology in community settings.* New York: John Wiley, 1966.

Sarason, S. B. Towards a psychology of change and innovation. *American Psychologist,* 1967, *22,* 227-223.

Sarason, S. B. *The culture of the school and the problem of change.* Boston: Allyn and Bacon, 1971.

Sarbin, T. R. A role-theory perspective for community psychology: The structure of social identity. In D. Adelson & B. L. Kalis (Eds.), *Community psychology and mental health.* Scranton, Pa.: Chandler, 1970. Pp. 89-113.

Schein, E. *Organizational psychology.* Englewood Cliffs, N. J.: Prentice-Hall, 1965.

Schmuck, R.A., & Van Egmond, E. Sex differences in the relationship of interpersonal perceptions to academic performance. *Psychology in the Schools,* 1965, *2,* 32-40.

Schneider, B., & Bartlett, C. J. Individual differences and organizational climate: 1. The research plan and questionnaire development. *Personnel Psychology,* 1968, *21,* 323-333.

Schoggen, P. Environmental forces in the every day lives of children. In R. G. Barker (Ed.), *The stream of behavior.* New York: Appleton-Century-Crofts, 1963. Pp. 42-69.

Scribner, S. What is community psychology made of ? *American Psychological Association Division of Community Psychology Newsletter,* 1968, *2* (1), 4-6.

Sears, R. A theoretical framework for personality and social behavior. *American Psychologist,* 1951, *6,* 476-483.

Seashore, S. *Group cohesiveness in the industrial work group.* Ann Arbor, Mich.: Institute for Social Research, 1954.

Sechrest, L., & Wallace, J. *Psychology and human problems.* Columbus, Ohio: Merrill Books, 1967.

Secord, P.F., & Backman, C. W. Personality theory and the problem of stability and change in individual behavior: An interpersonal approach. *Psychological Review,* 1961, *68,* 22-28.

Secord, P.F., & Backman, C.W. An interpersonal approach to personality. In B. A. Maher (Ed.), *Progress in experimental personality research.* New York: Academic Press, 1965. Pp. 91-125.

Seiler, J. *Systems analysis of organizational behavior.* Homewood, Ill.: Dorsey Press, 1967.

Sells, S. B. Ecology and the science of psychology. In E. P. Willems & H. L. Raush (Eds.), *Naturalistic viewpoints in psychological research.* New York: Holt, Rinehart & Winston, 1969. Pp. 15-30.

Shaw, M. Communication networks. In L. Berkowitz (Ed.), *Advances in experimental social psychology.* New York: Academic Press, 1964. Pp. 111-147.

Shore, M.F., & Mannino, F.V., (Eds.), *Mental health and the community: Problems, programs and strategies.* New York: Behavioral Publications, 1969.

Skinner, B. F. Beyond freedom and dignity. *Psychology Today,* 1971, *5,* 37-80.

Smith, A. J. Similarity of values and its relation to acceptance and the projection of similarity. *Journal of Psychology,* 1957, *43,* 251-260.

Solomon, L. The influence of some types of power relationships and game strategies upon the development of interpersonal trust. *Journal of Abnormal and Social Psychology,* 1960,*61,* 223-230.

Solomon, P., Kubzansky, P., Leiderman, P., Mendelson, J., Trumball, R., & Wexler, D. (Eds.), *Sensory deprivation.* Cambridge, Mass.: Harvard Univ. Press, 1961.

Sontag, K., & Kagan, J. The emergence of intellectual achievement motives. *American Journal of Orthopsychiatry,* 1963, *33,* 532-535.

Spielberger, C. A mental health consultation program in a small community with limited professional mental health resources. In E. Cowen, E. Gardner, & M. Zax (Eds.), *Emergent approaches to mental health problems.* New York: Appleton-Century-Crofts, 1967. Pp. 214-236.

Stein, K.B., Sarbin, T.R., & Kulik, J.A. Further validation of antisocial personality types. *Journal of Consulting and Clinical Psychology,* 1971, *36,* 177-182.

Stendler, C., Damrin, D., & Haines, A. Studies in cooperation and competition: I. The effects of working for group and individual rewards on the social climate of children's groups. *Journal of Genetic Psychology,* 1951, *79,* 173-197.

Stogdill, R. Dimensions of organization theory, In J. D. Thompson (Ed.), *Approaches to organizational design.* Pittsburgh: Univ. of Pittsburgh Press, 1966. Pp. 1-56.

Strauss, G. Some notes on power equalization. In H. Leavitt (Ed.), *The social science of organizations.* Englewood Cliffs, N. J.: Prentice-Hall, 1963.

Straus, M. Conjugal power structure and adolescent personality.

Marriage and the Family, 1962, *24*, 19-25.

Tharp, R.G., Cutts, R.I., & Burkholder, R. The community mental health center and the schools: A model for collaboration through demonstration. *Community Mental Health Journal*, 1970, *6*, 126-135.

Thibaut, J.W., & Kelley, H. H. *The social psychology of groups. New York: John Wiley, 1959.*

Thompson J.D., (Ed.), *Approaches to organizational desi n.* Pittsburgh: Univ. of Pittsburgh Press, 1966.

Todd, D. M. Peer structure and help-giving for adolescent boys: A case study of social processes in a high school. In M. J. Feldman (Ed.), *Studies in psychotherapy and behavior change.* Buffalo: State Univ. of New York at Buffalo, 1971. Pp. 142-146.

Triandis, H. C. Notes on the design of organizations. In J. D. Thompson (Ed.), *Approaches to organizational design.* Pittsburgh: Univ. of Pittsburgh Press, 1966. Pp. 57-102.

Trist, E. L., & Bamforth, K. W. Some social and psychological consequences of the long-wall method of coal-getting. *Human Relations*, 1951, *4*, 3-38.

Trow, D., & Herschdorfer, G. *An experiment on the status incongruence phenomenon.* Binghamton, N.Y., State University of New York, Technical Report 3, Contract Nonr-3679(00), 1965.

Urban Studies Center, University of Louisville. *The new communities family mobility system.* Louisville, Ky.: University of Louisville, Urban Studies Center, 1971.

Useem, J. The sociology of power. Unpublished paper read at annual meeting of American Sociological Association, 1950.

Vroom, V. *Some personality determinants of the effects of participation.* Englewood Cliffs, N. J.: Prentice-Hall, 1960.

Vroom, V. H. *Motivation in management.* American Foundation for Management Research, Ann Arbor, Mich., 1965.

Walton, J. Substance and artifact: The current status of research on community power structure.*American Journal of Sociology*, 1966, *71*, 430-438.

Walton, J. A systematic survey of community power research. In M. Aiken & P. E. Mott (Eds.), *The structure of community power.* New York: Random House, 1970. Pp. 443-464.

Watson, D. Relationship between locus of control and anxiety.*Journal of Personality and Social Psychology,* 1967, *6,* 91-92.

Watson, D., & Baumal, E. Effects of locus of control and expectation of future control upon present performance. *Journal of Personality and Social Psychology,* 1967, *6,* 212-215.

Weiss, E. L. Relation of personnel statistics to organizational structure. *Personnel Psychology,* 1957, *10,* 27-42.

Weissman, H. Priorities in social services for the slum neighborhood. In M. Shore and F. Mannino (Eds.), *Mental health and the community: Problems, programs, and strategies.* New York: Behavioral Publications, 1969. Pp. 149-160.

White, R., & Lippitt, R. Leader behavior and member reaction in three "social climates." In D. Cartwright and A. Zander (Eds.), *Group dynamics: Research and theory.* (2nd ed.) Evanston, Ill.: Row, Peterson, 1960. Pp. 527-553.

Whyte, W. F. *Money and motivation: An analysis of incentives in industry.* New York: Harper, 1955.

Willems, E.P., & Raush, H.L., (Eds.), *Naturalistic viewpoints in psychological research.* New York: Holt, Rinehart & Winston, 1969.

Wilner, D.M., Wakely, R.P., & Cook, S. W. Residential proximity and intergroup relations in public housing projects. *Journal of Social Issues,* 1952 *8,* 45-69.

Winterbottom, M. The relation of need for achievement to learning experience in independence and mastery. In J. W. Atkinson (Ed.), *Motives in fantasy, action and society.* Princeton: Van Nostrand, 1958. Pp. 453-478.

Wolf, R. The measurement of environments. In A. Anastasi (Ed.), *Testing problems in perspective.* Washington, D.C.: American Council on Education, 1966. Pp. 491-503.

Woodward, J. *Management and technology.* London: Her Majesty's Stationery Office, 1958.

Worthy, J. C. Organizational structure and employee morale. *American Sociological Review,* 1950, *15,* 169-179.

Zurcher, L. Implementing a community action agency. In M. Shore & F. Mannino (Eds.), *Mental health and the community: Problems, programs, and strategies.* New York: Behavioral Publications, 1969. Pp. 7-20.

Appendix

COMMUNITY-ORIENTED PROGRAMS ENVIRONMENT SCALE(COPES)*

Form C [Real Program]

Program _____ Name _____

Sex: Male _____ Female _____

Age: _____

Are you a: Member _____ or on the Staff _____. How long have you been (or worked) in this program?___years___ months ___weeks. In your lifetime, how much time have you spent (or worked) in mental hospitals?___years___months___weeks. If you are a staff member, what is your job title? (No abbreviations, please)

_____

* For Halfway Houses, Sheltered Workshops, Day Programs, and Rehabilitation Centers. Copyright: Rudolf H. Moos, 1970, 1971

INSTRUCTIONS

There are 102 statements in this booklet. They are statements about programs. You are to decide which statements are true of your program and which are not.

True—Circle the T if you think the statement is True or mostly True of your program.

False—Circle the F if you think the statement is False or mostly False of your program.

Please be sure to answer every item.

T F 1. Members can leave the program whenever they want to.

T F 2. Staff always compliment a member who does something well.

T F 3. There is relatively little emphasis on making specific plans for leaving this program.

T F 4. Staff don't order the members around.

T F 5. It's hard to get a group together for card games or other activities.

T F 6. Members here follow a regular schedule every day.

T F 7. Members talk relatively little about their past.

T F 8. Members are strongly encouraged to express themselves freely here.

T F 9. Members put a lot of energy into what they do around here.

T F 10. Members sometimes play practical jokes on each other.

T F 11. This is a lively place.

T F 12. Members never know when staff will ask to see them.

T F 13. Members can wear whatever they want.

T F 14. Members tend to hide their feelings from one another.

T F 15. The healthier members here help take care of the less healthy ones.

T F 16. This program emphasizes training for new kinds of jobs.

T F 17. Once a schedule is arranged for a member, the member must follow it.

T F 18. Staff encourage members to express their anger openly here.

T F 19. Some members look messy.

T F 20. Members tell each other about their intimate personal problems.

T F 21. It is important to carefully follow the program rules here.

T F 22. A lot of members just seem to be passing time here.

T F 23. It's hard to get people to argue around here.

T F 24. The members always know when the staff will be around.

T F 25. There is no membership government in this program.

T F 26. Members spontaneously set up their own activities here.

T F 27. Staff have relatively little time to encourage members.

T F 28. Most members are more concerned with the past than with the future.

T F 29. The staff very rarely punish members by taking away their privileges.

T F 30. This program has very few social activities.

T F 31. Members' activities are carefully planned.

T F 32. Members hardly ever discuss their sexual lives.

T F 33. The members are proud of this program.

T F 34. Members often gripe.

T F 35. Things are sometimes very disorganized around here.

T F 36. The staff almost always act on members' suggestions.

T F 37. When members disagree with each other, they keep it to themselves.

T F 38. The staff know what the members want.

T F 39. Members here are expected to demonstrate continued concrete progress toward their goals.

T F 40. Everyone knows who's in charge here.

T F 41. Personal problems are openly talked about.

T F 42. Very few things around here ever get people excited.

T F 43. Staff here never start arguments.

T F 44. If a member breaks a rule, he knows what the consequences will be.

T F 45. Very few members have any responsibility for the program here.

T F 46. Members say anything they want to the staff.

T F 47. Members seldom help each other.

T F 48. There is relatively little emphasis on teaching members solutions to practical problems.

T F 49. Members can call staff by their first names.

T F 50. This is a very well organized program.

T F 51. Members are rarely asked personal questions by the staff.

T F 52. Discussions are very interesting here.

T F 53. Members often criticize or joke about the staff.

T F 54. People are always changing their minds here.

T F 55. Members can leave here anytime without saying where they are going.

T F 56. It is hard to tell how members are feeling here.

T F 57. Staff are vary interested in following up members once they leave the program.

T F 58. Members are expected to make detailed specific plans for the future.

T F 59. Members who break the rules are punished for it.

T F 60. Members often do things together on the weekends.

T F 61. Staff are mainly interested in learning about members' feelings.

T F 62. Very few members ever volunteer around here.

T F 63. Members here rarely argue.

T F 64. If a member's program is changed, staff always tell him why.

T F 65. Staff rarely give in to pressure from members.

T F 66. Members can generally do whatever they feel like here.

T F 67. Staff sometimes don't show up for their appointments with members.

T F 68. There is relatively little discussion about exactly what members will be doing after they leave the program.

T F 69. Members may interrupt staff when they are talking.

T F 70. There is relatively little sharing among the members.

T F 71. The staff make sure that this place is always neat.

T F 72. The members rarely talk with each other about their personal problems.

T F 73. Members are pretty busy all of the time.

T F 74. Staff here think it is a healthy thing to argue.

T F 75. Members never quite know when they will be considered ready to leave this program.

T F 76. Members are expected to take leadership here.

T F 77. Members tend to hide their feelings from the staff.

T F 78. Members are given a great deal of individual attention here.

T F 79. Members are taught specific new skills in this program.

T F 80. Members will be transferred or discharged from this program if they don't obey the rules.

T F 81. The staff go out of their way to help new members get acquainted here.

T F 82. The dayroom or livingroom is often untidy.

T F 83. Members are expected to share their personal problems with each other.

T F 84. Members here rarely become angry.

T F 85. Members are strongly encouraged to express their feelings.

T F 86. Staff care more about how members feel than about their practical problems.

T F 87. Members are rarely kept waiting when they have appointments with staff.

T F 88. The staff strongly encourage members to be neat and

orderly here.

T F 89. Members are rarely encouraged to discuss their personal problems here.

T F 90. Staff sometimes argue openly with each other.

T F 91. There are often changes in the rules here.

T F 92. Staff rarely give members a detailed explanation of what the program is about.

T F 93. Members here are very strongly encouraged to be independent.

T F 94. Members are careful about what they say when staff are around.

T F 95. Members must make detailed plans before leaving the program.

T F 96. The staff make and enforce all the rules here.

T F 97. This place usually looks a little messy.

T F 98. Staff strongly encourage members to talk about their past.

T F 99. There is very little group spirit in this program.

T F 100. If a member fights with another member, he will get into real trouble with the staff.

T F 101. The program rules are clearly understood by the members.

T F 102. The staff tend to discourage criticism from members.

SUBJECT INDEX

NAME INDEX

Adelson, D., 6, 13
Aiken, M., 153
Alberts, D., 251
Allinsmith, W., 187
Allport, F., 65
Allport, G., 51
Altrocchi, J., 5
Amidon, E., 188
Archapohl, C., 243
Argyris, C., 56, 101, 104
Artiss, K., 49
Astin, A., 146

Backman, C., 26, 34-41, 42, 49, 51, 80
Bamforth, K., 109, 187
Bandura, A., 70
Bard, M., 185
Barker, R., 11, 20, 129-132, 145, 234, 243
Barnard, C., 150
Barnes, J., 110
Bartlett, C., 111
Bass, B., 101
Bateson, G., 28
Baumal, E., 242
Bay, C., 188
Beach, L., 188
Bechtel, R., 243
Becker, W., 43-44
Bennett, C., 6, 15

Bennis, W., 101, 102
Berkowitz, L., 245
Berrien, F., 9, 66, 93, 96, 110, 114, 154, 155, 156, 247
Bertalanffy, L., 91, 92
Bexton, W., 121
Binding, F., 243
Blake, R., 110
Blood, M., 56, 102, 104
Bloom, B., 184
Bloomberg, W., 153
Bontrager, H., 209
Bouma, D., 159-162, 220
Braginsky, B., 48, 49
Braginsky, D., 48, 49
Bronfenbrenner, U., 77
Broxton, J., 245
Buckley, W., 90, 189
Burkholder, R., 145, 185
Bush, R., 203
Byrne, D., 245

Caldwell, B., 234
Campbell, D., 252
Campbell, J., 102
Caplan, G., 184, 185, 190
Carlson, S., 109
Carson, R., 26, 35, 41-50, 51, 61, 72, 73
Carter, J., 192
Cloward, R., 7

283